CONFIDANTE OF
'TYRANTS'

THE INSIDE STORY OF
THE AMERICAN WOMAN
TRUSTED BY THE US's
BIGGEST ENEMIES

This book is dedicated to the memory of my sweet friend Evio di Marzo, killed in Caracas, Venezuela, on 28 May 2018. May his kind, generous and creative spirit guide us on the path to justice.

About the author

Eva Golinger is an attorney specializing in international human rights and immigration law based in New York. She is a graduate of Sarah Lawrence College and holds a J.D. from CUNY Law School. She is winner of the International Journalism Award in Mexico and multiple book awards in Venezuela. She is author of six non-fiction books including *The Chávez Code*, which was based on extensive research using the Freedom of Information Act (FOIA) to declassify CIA and other US government documents on Washington's role in the 2002 coup d'état against Hugo Chávez. Her work has been covered by *The New York Times*, *The Washington Post*, *Newsday*, *The Chicago Tribune*, Reuters, AP, NPR, CNN, BBC, *The International Herald Tribune*, *The Wall Street Journal*, *The Los Angeles Times* and other major media around the world. She lived in Venezuela for many years and counseled several Presidents, Foreign Ministers and senior officials in Latin America and was an Advisor to former Venezuelan President Hugo Chávez for nearly a decade. Follow her on Twitter @evagolinger.

CONFIDANTE OF 'TYRANTS'

THE INSIDE STORY OF THE AMERICAN WOMAN TRUSTED BY THE US's BIGGEST ENEMIES

Eva Golinger

New Internationalist

Confidante of 'Tyrants'
The inside story of the American woman trusted by
the US's biggest enemies

First published in 2018 by
New Internationalist
The Old Music Hall
106-108 Cowley Road
Oxford OX4 1JE
newint.org

Editor: Chris Brazier
Design: Juha Sorsa

Printed by TJ International Limited, Cornwall, UK, who hold
environmental accreditation ISO 14001.

Mixed Sources
Product group from well-managed
forests and other controlled sources
www.fsc.org Cert no. SGS-COC-2482
© 1996 Forest Stewardship Council
FSC

Library of Congress Cataloging-in-Publication Data
A catalog record for this book is available from the Library of Congress.
British Library Cataloguing-in-Publication Data
A catalogue record for this book is available from the British Library.

ISBN 978-1-78026-467-7
ISBN ebook 978-1-78026-468-4

Contents

Foreword
by Marjorie Cohn

The United States has a shameful history of interfering in the internal affairs of nearly every country in Latin America. Initially pursuing Manifest Destiny and later the fight against communism, the US has meddled with, manipulated and overthrown sovereign governments.

In many instances, the CIA funded and aided the local opposition, helping to engineer coups and install regimes friendly to US investment. At the notorious 'School of the Americas' in Panama, US experts taught Latin American dictators and military leaders torture techniques to help them control their populations.

Forcible regime change violates the Charter of the Organization of American States, which says: 'Every State has the right to choose, without external interference, its political, economic, and social system and to organize itself in the way best suited to it, and has the duty to abstain from intervening in the affairs of another State.'

Yet, building on Barack Obama's punishing sanctions against Venezuela, the Trump administration is threatening military invasion and regime change. Venezuela has the world's largest oil reserves and the United States is the principal consumer of its black gold. This would not be the first time the US attempted to facilitate a coup in Venezuela. In 2002, the George W Bush administration aided and abetted a coup attempt. Successive US regimes have considered socialist Venezuela a threat to global capitalism.

As Símon Bolívar, Venezuela's second president, said in the 19th century, the United States continues to 'plague [the] America[s] with misery in the name of liberty'.

Since Hugo Chávez was elected president in 1998, the US government has tried covertly and overtly to undermine his 'Bolivarian Revolution', channeling millions of dollars to opposition groups working for regime change. Chávez was beloved in Venezuela and throughout Latin America. He used Venezuela's vast oil resources to eradicate poverty and illiteracy, and to provide free and universal healthcare and education.

When Chávez died in 2013, his chosen successor, Nicolas Maduro, was elected president. Although Maduro vowed to continue Chávez's Bolivarian Revolution, mismanagement, corruption and autocratic leadership, combined with illegal US financial sanctions, contributed to economic hardship for the Venezuelan people. Oil prices fell in 2016, causing Venezuela's economy to collapse with hyperinflation two years later.

It was against this backdrop that Maduro was re-elected to a six-year term in 2018. Voter turnout was 46 per cent, the lowest since Chávez's first election in 1998 (turnout in the 2016 US presidential election was 58 per cent). The opposition's boycott of the election and the US government's support of the boycott and pre-emptive refusal to recognize the results led to Maduro's victory over opponent Henri Falcon.

Eva Golinger was a close confidante of Chávez. She came to his attention after her investigative efforts confirmed the CIA's direct involvement in the foiled 2002 coup. Dubbed the 'Girlfriend of Venezuela', Golinger traveled with Chavez on what he called his 'Axis of Evil' tour, rubbing elbows with Fidel Castro and other world leaders whom the US despised. Golinger's riveting memoir provides a rare window into the Bolivarian Revolution, warts and all.

Marjorie Cohn is Professor Emerita, Thomas Jefferson School of Law, and was formerly President of the National Lawyers Guild.

1

Over the brink

The phone rang just as I was folding up my winter jacket and shoving it into my already bulging suitcase. 'Comrade,' said the deep voice on the other end of the line. I tensed up, knowing that what was coming next, whatever it was, meant I would most likely have to delay my flight to New York that afternoon.

'*Hola*,' I answered, adding a half-hearted 'at your service'. It was Nicolas Maduro, then Venezuela's towering Foreign Minister – and by towering I mean really tall. He was six foot three inches, more than a foot taller than me, with a big black bushy mustache and smiling eyes, his cheek scarred by police brutality during an anti-government protest in the late 1970s.

'The President has a very special request for you. He asked me to call you personally.' We had only been back in Caracas for about a month after an intense two-week trip abroad which Venezuelan President Hugo Chávez had termed the 'Axis of Evil Tour'. Visiting hotspots like Libya, Syria, Iran, Belarus, Ukraine, Russia and Cuba was a strangely common situation for me these days, ever since I had become a close friend and confidante of Chávez.

Yes, Chávez. A figure larger than life, loved and hated by millions, who had proclaimed me the 'Girlfriend of Venezuela' and one of the bravest women he'd ever known. 'Look at her face,' he said about me once on live television. 'She looks so tender, like an angel, but when she opens her mouth she's on fire, more valiant than anyone'.

Back in 2003 when I was a newly minted lawyer living in New York City, I started what I thought was a shot-in-the-dark investigation into a possible CIA role in the failed 2002 coup d'état against Chávez. I figured I would write a few articles, maybe even a book if I found something really compelling, but I never thought that my whole life would change and I would be propelled into a world of espionage, intrigue and global power. Nor could I have foreseen that my investigations would become a point of reference for Fidel Castro as well as Chávez, and would make me a thorn in the side of the Pentagon, which once referred to me as a 'troublemaker' – not the only time in my life that I have been called that.

Yet now I was wandering the halls of presidential palaces, rubbing elbows with controversial world leaders and being declared an enemy of my own country. I came to know and even befriend some of these men, whom so many in the world saw as tyrants. However extraordinary they were as individuals, I saw them unveiled as people with flaws and even some surprising elements of humility, trying their best to do their jobs and serve their countries. I also saw abuse of power, corruption and bending the rule of law in the name of the 'greater good', something which so often resulted from politics based on cult of personality, polarization and 'you're either with me or against me' extremist ideologies. I witnessed how easily a population can be seduced by charismatic leaders who pledge to improve lives and radically transform the system, and how quickly it can all unravel, to the detriment of democratic institutions. Over the past couple of years, watching a similar scenario play out in real time in the United States with Donald Trump as President has given me a nightmarish sense of *déjà vu*. I honestly believe that Trump's personal behavior has been more reprehensible than anything I witnessed during over a decade as a confidante of Chávez and a friend of Fidel Castro, years in which I also spent time with the likes of Qadafi, Putin, Assad, Ahmadinejad and other highly controversial world leaders. Donald Trump seems to be petty, narcissistic and frighteningly immature for a man of his wealth and power; he also appears to be repugnantly vengeful. Worst of all, Trump commands the largest nuclear arsenal in the world, and he's already admitted – on Twitter, his favorite medium – that he's keen to use it.

Every time I see Trump's impulsive, erratic tweets lashing out at the media, screaming all in caps that his critics and detractors should be silenced, ridiculed or destroyed, I want to yell as loud as I can at everyone: 'stop it now, before it's too late!' I have seen how raw power unchecked can quickly pulverize a democracy and plunder a robust economy, leaving the people demoralized and desperate. I have learned from experience that enabling a president to accumulate too much power – no matter how noble his mission and sincere his intentions – while demolishing any semblance of an independent press or viable opposition, is most likely a recipe for disaster, and a possible path to dictatorship or another hybrid form of authoritarianism. Even worse, once that leader is out of the picture, through death or alternating power – if that possibility still exists – the system can violently implode.

'The Comandante wants you to give a speech in a solemn state event on Thursday in defense of our national sovereignty and against foreign interference,' said the voice on the other end of the phone, the man who just a few years later was to lead one of the most dysfunctional governments in Venezuela's contemporary history.

I sighed deeply, resigning myself to my fate. 'Of course,' I said, 'I'd be honored.'

Maduro told me to prepare something good since it was going to be a major event with all branches of government present. 'You'll get 30 minutes to talk,' he assured me, 'so give it your best.' I would be the keynote speaker.

I broke the news to my father, who had just undergone hip surgery and was waiting for me to help take care of him during his recovery. I told him my trip home would be delayed a few days because of an event with the President. Both my parents, divorced long ago, were used to my unusual life, though they never fully understood what I was actually doing and why I had chosen this path. They did, however, always support my choices – something I was deeply grateful for, especially considering I had made some really risky and unconventional decisions. On this occasion my dad was understanding – after all, he knew I couldn't say no to Chávez. No more than a week, I assured him, then I'll be there with you.

Gearing up for the speech

By the time Thursday came, I hadn't been told much more about the event except that it would be held in the Legislative Palace in the center of historic downtown Caracas. Maduro's assistant had called me a few times just to make sure I was getting prepared but, as usual with presidential events, nothing was fully defined until the last minute and those who knew anything were tight-lipped, both for security reasons and because they knew everything could change at any moment. That's how it was with Chávez. He was famously unpunctual, impulsive and somewhat of a control freak. Everything revolved around his whims and few dared to challenge him without risking their own power and access to his inner circle. I was among those few. I often spoke to him with a blunt frankness he found abrasive and unsettling, but he liked me. And he trusted me and believed in what I had to say.

I put on a crimson red dress with a low-cut cleavage I'd been saving for a special occasion, matched it with a cropped black cardigan, and tucked my speech into my small, red leather backpack. I no longer had bodyguards, having bade them farewell after feeling suffocated as a young single woman yearning for normal social interactions and tired of being isolated from the tangible real life beyond my heavy steel-bolted doors and armed protectors. I opted not to take my gun, a sleek, black nine-millimeter beretta. While the thought of it tucked away in my house made me feel safer, the idea of carrying it around terrified me. I always felt as though having the gun in public would attract violence. Maybe it was just my paranoid imagination, but the gun stayed behind. I walked out of my building, past the security guards at the front gate and down the street two blocks to the Metro.

People driving by would occasionally recognize me, but at least they weren't spitting out the window at me in hatred anymore. Instead they were yelling, '*Hola* Eva!', or '*Te Amo!*' (I love you!). Those were peak times for Chávez and his movement in Venezuela. The economy was booming, oil prices were at an all-time high and his popularity was well over the 60-per-cent mark. The opposition was depleted and in retreat, having suffered several direct political defeats during the previous years, and had realized they were unable to match Chávez's power and charisma.

I took the Metro to the Capitolio stop in downtown Caracas, a few blocks from the National Assembly. I was several hours early, as Maduro had instructed me to be. Because of presidential security checks, all guests were told to arrive two to three hours early at Chávez's events, even though he generally was two to three hours late. I always came prepared at minimum with a bottle of water and a dark chocolate bar in my bag to get me through the long wait. I'd become accustomed to this during my years in the country – unpunctuality was an embedded cultural code accepted as a matter of fact by Venezuelans and received with hair-pulling frustration by everyone else.

When I arrived at the front gate of the Legislative Palace the Presidential Guard had already taken it over. Their bright forest-green uniforms topped with red berets were easily recognizable wherever they went. And where they were, you knew Chávez would be, or at least that was the plan. I approached a guard who looked not a day over 18 and told him I was there for the event. He had no idea who I was and said I couldn't go in. I told him I was the main speaker, invited by Chávez. He looked at me like I was just another crazy lady trying to get close to the President and weasel my way inside. He stood his ground.

I sighed to myself in frustration, thinking how tired I was of this. All these years by Chávez's side and each time it was like starting anew. I didn't expect them all to know me, but you would have thought they'd at least have a list of the participants that would include the main speaker at the event.

Finally, after telling him my name over and again and insisting he call his superiors, even threatening that he would be in big trouble if he didn't listen to me, I was let in. I knew that whichever colonel or general was in charge of presidential security that day would have had to intervene and authorize my entry. The last thing they wanted was to make Chávez angry and they all lived in fear that I would tell him what had happened.

The protocol officer who accompanied me to the salon where the event would be held also apologized profusely but I shrugged it off and told him everything was fine. I was really just fed up with all the chaos and inefficiency, with the rigidity that contrasted bizarrely with the utter lack of organization or cohesiveness. I was honored to be participating in this major event, but I already had one foot out the door. I wanted to go home, back to New York. I missed my parents, my city and the comfort of my culture. I was exhausted from being a triple outsider: a foreigner, a woman and a nonconformist. I was tired of chasing Chávez around everywhere and constantly struggling for every little detail.

'Señora': the protocol officer gestured for me to enter a room I'd never been in before. It was grandiose and elegant. The walls were covered in life-size portraits of historical male figures: founding fathers, warriors, generals and liberators. It was the Elliptical Salon, a room practically untouched and hidden from view except for high-level state events. The walls breathed history, with brilliantly painted battle scenes from Venezuela's independence war, defining moments in the country's fight for sovereignty. In the center of the room was a large walnut table with a glass covering. I approached it practically on tiptoe since the soaring ceilings coated with oil-painted portraits echoed my every move.

Under the glass was Venezuela's original Constitution and Declaration of Independence. Script on parchment, with the signature of Simon Bolivar, the nation's founding father. I was the first in the room and held my breath as I savored the moment alone. I was standing in a time machine encapsulating the history of Venezuela, my adopted nation. I felt a shiver throughout my body and a tingle in my veins, as though my far-removed Venezuelan bloodlines were calling out to me. I was there to claim them, to raise my voice in defense of their sovereign rights, their dignity, their right to exist in the face of foreign threats. Threats, ironically, from my birth country. Would I ever be able to reconcile the contradictions within me?

Enter Chávez

The towering and ornately carved wooden doors swung open and the guests began arriving, taking their seats as they ooed and ahed at the breathtaking beauty of the room. A few came over to greet me, shaking my hand and offering their admiration. There were ministers (cabinet members), ambassadors, governors, mayors and members of the legislature, the National Assembly. It was an unusually formal, staunch protocol event – the kind Chávez generally abhorred and rebelled against. Yet here we were, and here I was in the center of it all.

The heads of each of Venezuela's five branches of government began arriving, and Nicolas Maduro rushed in, waving and shaking hands as he made his way towards me. 'Look,' he said anxiously, 'you need to shorten your speech.'

My heart stopped. Seriously? You're telling me this now? I asked him how much. After all, he had told me 30 minutes and I had prepared it to a tee. 'Fifteen minutes maximum.' I looked at him with wide eyes that relayed my intense frustration, surprise and anxiety without speaking. Okay, I said, as I began crossing out entire paragraphs of my written text. 'Thanks, Comrade,' he said, and assured me I'd do fine. Yeah, I thought to myself, you're not the one who has to cut out literally half a speech in the next two minutes before Chávez arrives and still make it sound coherent.

Two minutes later Maduro's assistant, Gustavo, approached me. 'How are you doing, Comrade?' He wanted to make sure I was ready. Chávez had arrived. I nodded and said I was as ready as I could be at that stage. I knew that if I had to cut my speech short, it meant that something had come up and Chávez probably wasn't in a great mood. But, just as my mind began spinning with every possible thing that could go wrong, he entered the salon, wearing a tailored black suit, red tie and his signature cheek-to-cheek smile.

Chávez always entered like a tidal wave because of the massive circle of people around him. It was a bee swarm of presidential guards, plain-clothes counter-intelligence guards, assistants, advisors, Cuban doctors and everyone else trying to get close enough to him to win his attention. He politely made his way through the crowd, greeting his cabinet members one by one, shaking hands and tapping the shoulders of the ambassadors and giving a few hugs and kisses here and there. When he reached me he gave me a hug and kiss on the cheek, but I could tell he was rushed and tense. He took his seat alongside the heads of government and signaled for the event to begin.

The baritone voice of his presidential announcer introduced the event. 'The State Event In Defense of National Sovereignty,' he bellowed forcefully, as though this act were a declaration of war. He acknowledged the President and all the other important members of government present in the room one by one. Then he called me up to the podium. I took a deep breath before I began talking, taking a moment to absorb how far I'd come. The only other American who had ever spoken in that majestic Elliptical Salon before was John F Kennedy, nearly 50 years earlier in 1961. Me and JFK. I was deeply honored and humbled. Here I was before the most powerful people in this major oil-producing nation all waiting for me to speak, to hear my voice, my words, my ideas. I had their attention. Most of all, I had Chávez's ear and his confidence.

I greeted everyone in the room and, trying my best to skip the crossed-out lines on my paper, spoke my prose. I denounced what I considered clear violations of international law, primarily by the US government. I cited specific examples of meddling in Venezuela's elections, the channeling of millions of US taxpayer dollars to anti-government groups engaged in regime change efforts and covert CIA operations aimed at undermining Chávez's government and political movement. I praised the Venezuelan people's resilience in the face of threats and their brave defiance and refusal to bow down to powerful interests. It was a righteous and idealistic lecture, delivered with passion. And I profoundly believed every word of what I said. I ended by proposing the enactment of legislation to protect Venezuela from foreign intervention in internal political affairs. The 'Golinger Law', it was later called, after Chávez heeded my words and instructed the National Assembly to institute it.

Everyone in Venezuela saw the speech. They had to, since it was broadcast on all the public and private airwaves in what was known as a *cadena*, or an obligatory transmission. Any television or radio channel that failed to broadcast a *cadena* would be fined and potentially shut down by the government. So everyone saw and heard me. If I wasn't already a household name in Venezuela, I definitely became one on that day. I was the *gringa* beloved and paraded by Chávez.

When I finished speaking, after a fist in the air and passionate 'Viva Venezuela! Viva Chávez', I got a standing ovation. Chávez walked over to me and took both my hands, bowing down almost as though he was going to propose. Whatever stress or hastiness he had entered the room with before had dissipated. He seemed invigorated and proud, showering me with kisses, hugs and laudatory words. He spoke the final words of the event, a call to arms to defend Venezuela's sovereignty and right to self-determination.

Trending on Twitter

I was a worldwide trending topic on Twitter for hours. Most of it was not good. The trolls were out in full force, calling me every obscenity that came to mind and threatening me with everything from rape to the gas chamber. By then I was used to it. I didn't care anymore what anyone said or thought about me, especially those who didn't even know me at all. When I wasn't in public, I mostly kept to myself. The ups and downs of my life were stranger than fiction. I went from brandishing the sword of liberation in the halls of history alongside Chávez one day, to hopping on a plane to New York the next to cook meals and clean house for my convalescent father, relishing my anonymity.

That is, until the call came from Caracas and my bipolar world was once more forced to reconcile. It was Maduro again. Wikileaks had just released a trove of documents from the US State Department and the President wanted me to analyze all the ones mentioning Venezuela to see if there was anything useful for his strategizing. My time as a caretaker was up. I had serious work to do. Chávez needed me.

I returned to Venezuela to a huge surprise. The Cuban Ambassador in Venezuela had left me several messages on my local cellphone asking me to stop by the Embassy as soon as I could. It was urgent, he said. I had a package and he said it was perishable.

I drove over there as fast as I could with no clue as to what I was picking up. The security guards at the Cuban Embassy told me to pull the car up to the front gate and pop the trunk. Then they loaded two large and heavy nondescript cardboard boxes into the car and handed me an envelope. Inside was a card wishing me a Happy New Year. It was signed, Fidel Castro.

I raced home and lugged the boxes into the elevator and up to my apartment. I couldn't open them fast enough. Inside the smaller box were approximately ten pounds of green and red apples. Apples, from Cuba. Fidel had sent me ten pounds of apples. The larger box had a giant basket inside packed with seven different bottles of Havana Club rum, ranging from the darkest aged straight up to the lightest white that's used commonly in mojitos and daiquiris. Interspersed between the rum bottles were varying boxes of Cuban chocolates, several bottles of Spanish red wine, candied almond bars, panettone, two packs of the darkest, most delicious Cuban coffee and two sealed wooden boxes of the finest, fat Cohiba cigars. The kind Fidel himself smoked.

Apparently, Fidel had liked the speech I'd given a few weeks earlier and this was his way of showing it. I had officially been put on Fidel Castro's holiday gift list.

2

From rebel to truth-teller

I had always fantasized about being part of a revolution, but I never imagined that the revolution would be thousands of miles away in Venezuela, or that I would become a household name there. For my senior yearbook picture at Sarah Lawrence College, I superimposed my head on the body of Sarah Connor from *Terminator 2: Judgment Day*. You know, the one where she's all buffed up as the Mother of the Resistance, holding an AK-47? I craved radical change, despised injustice and always regretted not being born in time to have played an active role in the social and political movements of the 1960s and early 1970s in the United States. I was born at the tail end, just as the Vietnam War ended in 1973, though the societal turmoil was still brewing.

Far from having radical or leftist roots, I was born on an Air Force base in Langley, Virginia, where my father had been stationed during his mandatory military service as a surgeon in the armed forces. The irony of being born on Langley Air Force base haunts me to this day. Once a Cuban friend asked me where I was born and, when I told him the truth, he blurted out in shock and partial disgust, 'You were born in the CIA?'

Of course, Langley Air Force base in Hampton, Virginia, is not the same place as the Central Intelligence Agency headquarters in Langley. But to foreign ears, thanks to the successful export of Hollywood culture to every inch of the planet, Langley means the CIA. Because of that, and because of the fact that practically every other person in my family had been born in New York City or the New York metropolitan area, I rarely talk about my true birthplace. When my mother, a born and bred New Yorker, was in labor and on the verge of pushing me out of her body, she screamed at the top of her lungs to my father, the doctors and everyone within shouting distance at the hospital: 'Put me on a helicopter and fly me to New York! I won't let this baby be born in Virginia!'

While it's true we share a common birthplace, my relationship with the CIA does not stop there. In fact my obsession with the world of espionage and intelligence operations started when I was around eight years old. I played spy games, not Barbie. Growing up, my fascination with covert operations expanded into the world of politics. I watched every spy thriller I could find and read every book by a former agent or intelligence officer that was available. It was the Cold War in those days, and tensions were high between the US and its enemies.

I remember when my mom, brother and I gathered around our small television set in 1983, when I was just 10 years old, to watch *The Day After*. The scene in which all the people disintegrated as a result of nuclear radiation still spooks me to this day. At 11, it was the movie *Red Dawn* that turned my neighborhood friends and me into the resistance fighters against the evil commies as our cul-de-sac became a war-torn battleground for freedom. I never imagined that, decades later, I would be living and working with Cuban and Russian comrades like those portrayed in that blatantly propagandistic Cold War film.

When I was about 13 years old, nuclear warfare seemed once again to be becoming an increasingly terrifying possibility with the 1986 bombing of Libya. I prepared an escape plan with a neighborhood kid two years my junior. We would stock his mom's beaten-up old station wagon with supplies and head north to Canada. I'd drive. That was about the extent of the plan, but the main goal was to escape the fallout of war. I might not have grown up with bomb-shelter drills in my childhood like my parents had, but the threat of war and warmongering was always all around us. How could I have foreseen that, a couple of decades later, I'd be dining in a tent with Libyan President Muammar Qadafi in one of his many secret compounds in Tripoli?

Activist education

Despite the heavy influence of pro-American propaganda on television and film, and my fascination with the CIA, I became highly suspicious of the US government and its policies. This skepticism and critical view of government and politics evolved primarily from observing my mother, who throughout my early years of political awakening was an avid feminist activist working with the National Organization for Women to pass the Equal Rights Amendment. I was marching in the streets for women and children's rights from the time I was five years old, proudly wearing my 'Children Are People Too' button.

My mother held consciousness-raising meetings in our home in the late 1970s with her feminist friends, to my father's horror. The fighting between them began soon after that and didn't stop until well after their divorce. So, while my family was falling apart, I was becoming politicized at a young age and aware of the injustice all around us, even at home. I was taught in school that we lived in the best, strongest, freest country in the world, the purest of all democracies, but I was seeing the cracks in that image. Women were not equal and they weren't going to be any time soon, despite my mother's persistence. When the Equal Rights Amendment failed to pass in 1982 for want of a mere three states, my mother was devastated. Her political activism had cost her years of hard work and dedication, time away from her family, extremely low-income earnings and an ugly divorce from my father, who blamed it on her feminism. But what I saw was my mother fighting hard for our basic right to be recognized as equally valuable human beings while the unjust world we lived in, including the government charged with our protection, failed us. Unsurprisingly, I repeated this pattern years later when my own marriage fell apart after my husband gave me an ultimatum: my political work or him. But I'll get to that later.

The last straw that led my mother to decide it was time to give up being a full-time activist and go back to working as a nurse was when the bomb squad arrived in full force at our townhouse in the suburbs of Washington DC, where we had moved after my parents' divorce. She had been working on the highly volatile pro-choice campaign in support of women's reproductive rights while so-called 'right-to-lifers' were violently harassing and threatening the lives of women defending abortion rights and those having abortions. It just so happened that one of our neighbors was a leader in the anti-abortion movement and forced me to sit through horrific videos of aborted fetuses every time I went to their house to play with their kids. My mother was always anxious that I would be swayed by the anti-abortion propaganda, but I assured her that would never happen, I knew where I stood on the issue. I might have been only 12 years old, but I already had strong principles of justice and a very independent mind.

One day when our mail was delivered my mom found a large manilla envelope with a big bulge in it from an unknown sender. She immediately called the police and alerted them to the suspicious package. Minutes later, the bomb squad arrived at our modest home, bomb-sniffing dogs and all. The package was placed on our postage-stamp front lawn and examined first by the dogs and then by a bomb-squad expert in a hazmat suit who poked and prodded the envelope. It was quite a spectacle for the neighbors in our small cul-de-sac. Finally, after determining there were no apparent explosives inside, they opened the envelope. It was a Statue of Liberty medallion that my mom had been sent by some not-for-profit for her work on women's rights. That's it, she said: she was done with the risks of political activism. As a single working mom struggling to feed, clothe and house her two growing kids she had enough to deal with; fears of our house being blown up were a bridge too far.

Rebel rhythms

As I grew more aware of the injustice caused by US government policies both at home and abroad, I became more rebellious and critical of authority, and my interest in the CIA evolved to enlightened suspicion. Espionage was portrayed glamorously through the media and it was thrilling to watch or delve into in a novel or non-fiction tell-all, but the real impact of intelligence operations began to pique my concern. Who were the people the CIA was undermining and overthrowing, and what about the citizens of those countries who had elected those leaders? Wasn't that a violation of their rights and a grave injustice? And did the victims of all those romanticized CIA undercover missions really deserve what they got? These were all questions I began to explore as the turmoil within my family and my adolescence peaked.

Let me just stop here and assure you that this is not a book about my entire life. This is just to offer a little context that might explain how someone like me ended up being showered with flowers, perfume and cigars from Fidel Castro, dining on camel (just the cheese for me, please) with Muammar Qadafi, hiking the Syrian countryside with Bashar al-Assad and his wife, and joking with Vladimir Putin about testing our martial-arts skills.

As a teenager, I rebelled against everything and everyone and had utter disregard for authority and for anyone who tried to tell me what to do. Maybe it was just normal teenage behavior, or maybe it was the resentment I harbored after witnessing my mother fight for women's basic rights and lose everything, while the system carried on as though nothing had happened, flicking us off like pesky flies.

I spent many free afternoons and evenings singing the rebellious lyrics of Bob Marley songs and playing them over and over again on my acoustic Yamaha guitar out on busy streets in DC, collecting the change and dollar bills of people passing by. At 15 years old, it wasn't the worst way to earn a few extra bucks.

My mother and I had moved into Washington DC after my brother had left for college. But the nation's capital was no safe haven at that time. There were frequent drive-by shootings and the AIDS epidemic was rampant, plus it was the peak of crack cocaine and the nation's capital was the hub. I remember when our mayor, Marion Barry, got busted on camera for smoking crack. As crazy as that probably seemed to outsiders, it appeared to be the norm within Washington. Politicians were corrupt, the city was in shambles, racial tensions were at a frightening high and the city felt permanently on the verge of eruption.

At 14 I became a vegetarian after seeing what I believed was an umbilical cord in meatballs I was making from ground beef. I nearly threw up in the shiny aluminum bowl full of pink flesh. It was probably just a bloodied vein or some other body part from a poor cow that had been slaughtered, but I'd had enough. I loved animals and believed that it was a grave injustice to massacre them for our food source. More than 30 years later, I've never had another bite of meat.

On the streets of DC I made new friends who were more like-minded. They were rebellious and unconventional, independent and free-spirited. When I was 16, a group of us pooled together our resources and bought a 1974 yellow school bus from a junkyard for about $400. We tore out the interior seats, filled it with second-hand couches and mattresses and painted the exterior green, purple and yellow. It barely ran, but we took it as far as it could go that summer, starting out with nine of us, all minors, and ending up with about 24 people as well as several dogs and cats picked up along Route 50 across the heartland of America. I was the main chauffeur steering that big clunky hippie rig, pumped up on cheap watered-down Truck Stop coffee and sugary hostess cupcakes, but I left the bus somewhere after Indiana. I knew the joyride would end soon and my intuition told me to get out before it all fell apart. That was true of my later adventures as well: I always seemed to know in my gut when it was time to move on.

The following summer, at 17 and finally graduated from high school, I did it again, but this time with just two friends and a cute little orange kitten we had rescued from a shelter. We named him Zerbert. For about $650, we bought a used 1970s VW camper with a pop top that had a sleeping hammock and a fold-out double bed in the back, comfortably sleeping the three of us plus kitty. We stocked it with a small fridge, a cook top and our gear, painted the outside yellow and purple and set out from DC up the east coast to Maine and then cross country to San Francisco, where we eventually broke down and spent three weeks sleeping on the streets trying to raise the funds to get the camper fixed. We then traveled down Route 1 on the California coastline to Santa Cruz, Los Angeles and headed back east through the desert, stopping for a few nights' rest in Boulder, Colorado.

We were young and fearless and wanted to see the world, starting with our own country. Looking back on that time now, it's amazing we made it out alive. Three teenage girls alone, sleeping in an old beat-up VW on the streets or at rest stops in unknown places and far away from our homes. There were no cellphones back then, no GPS for directions, and we were on a tight budget. In fact, we were pretty broke. I'd play the guitar on the streets for gas money, we ate sparingly and showered in the bathrooms of McDonald's and Truck Stops along the way. We saw the underbelly of the American heartland, the poverty, drugs, desolation and overall suspicious attitude towards anyone who didn't belong. We were stared down by waitresses and patrons in the cheap diner in Kentucky where we had one of our few hot meals. 'Ya'll not from around here.' It wasn't an invitation to stay.

Learning from the law

The rebelliousness and street smarts I developed early on became a fundamental part of me. I honed my distrust and questioning of all authority into critical thinking skills later on while at Sarah Lawrence College, my alma mater. My travels across the United States throughout the heartland, rust belt, deep south, midwest and coast to coast had deepened my understanding of the vast diversity coexisting in my country, as well as the ingrained racism, misogyny, social decay, despair and egocentrism.

The summer after I was 18, I volunteered at MADRE, a Latino legal clinic in Washington DC that was aiding Central Americans to apply for Temporary Protected Status (TPS) and political asylum in the US. TPS had been extended to citizens from El Salvador, Honduras and Nicaragua due to the role the US government had played in the wars in those nations during the 1970s and 1980s. Tens of thousands of people had been killed and hundreds of thousands displaced, in addition to all those tortured, raped and persecuted by their US-supported regimes. TPS was a way for Washington to redeem itself by mitigating the collateral damage of its foreign policy. After arming and supporting murderous rightwing mercenary armies that violently suppressed and destroyed any leftist, socialist or communist influence south of the US border, Washington decided it could wash its hands by providing refuge to the thousands of terrified and traumatized families forced to flee their homelands.

While filling out their asylum and TPS applications, I learned the horror of their stories, the indiscriminate torment suffered by women, children and men who were beaten, tortured and robbed of their safety and stability. It was humbling to witness the fear that had driven them to leave everything they knew behind and head northward on a treacherous and dangerous journey, risking their lives to escape warfare, landing in a nation not their own, immersed in a different language and unfamiliar cultural norms. One after the other, the stories of hardship, terror and suffering filled the pages of immigration paperwork. I did my best to write down their experiences as vividly as if they had been my own.

Comprehending that my own country had caused their turmoil and pain was disconcerting, but it only further affirmed my inherent distrust of authority and my suspicions about the real intentions behind the CIA and its covert activity. I had seen injustice up close, both inside and outside of the United States, and the burning anger and passion within me began to transform into a determination to fight the system.

All the same, I little imagined that, around 20 years later, I would become a close confidante of one of the world's most controversial presidents, who professed to be leading a real revolution. Spending almost a decade in the inner circle of Hugo Chávez in Venezuela gave me a privileged, insider view of the real world of power and politics, for good and for bad. I saw the struggles of an unconventional, nonconformist president who genuinely desired to change the system. I witnessed how he came up against the impenetrable obstacles of bureaucracy and corruption, and ultimately was overcome.

The rise and fall of his movement, which has deteriorated dramatically since his untimely death in March 2013 from an aggressive leiomyosarcoma cancer, holds undeniable and essential lessons for any and all movements that seek to change the establishment and transform a traditional, power-locked political system. The trend of unexpected electoral results breaking with established elite structures has appeared to reach even the United States, with the election of Donald Trump.

Don't get me wrong, Donald Trump is no Hugo Chávez. Chávez, unlike Trump, was eloquent in his discourse and genuine in his revolutionary vision for his country and the planet. He believed in building a better and more just world, eradicating poverty and misery and rebalancing global power to create equilibrium and multipolarism. Chávez had empathy, he cared about people. Trump is a malignant narcissist with no similar grand vision. But both movements demonstrate that we cannot underestimate the detrimental impact of political demagoguery, and need to be wary of any leader who exploits the cult of personality. Systems with deeply ingrained, institutionalized injustice – racism, economic inequality, misogyny, widespread exclusion – may need to be deconstructed and rebuilt in order to create a fairer society. As I witnessed in Venezuela with Chávez, this process can be highly disruptive and vulnerable. However, it must be conducted in a collective manner – of, for and by the people – with checks and balances, and not left subject to one person's whims. When one man believes he alone is the conduit for change, the slippery slope to authoritarianism beckons. The corrupting force of power must never be underestimated.

3

How I met Hugo Chávez

I first met President Hugo Chávez on an airplane; actually, it was *his* official presidential airplane. The day was 11 April 2004. I was 31 years old and trying to get my bearings as an attorney when I decided to dive head first into the world of global power and clandestine operations. I had flown to Caracas from Brooklyn, New York, just days earlier with the hope of personally telling the President of Venezuela the results of my year-long investigation into the US government's role in the 2002 coup d'état against him.

In 2003, a year after that briefly successful coup, I had decided it was time to see if Washington had a real hand in trying to overthrow the leftist South American President. After all, it was the era of George W Bush's hardline Republican politics, which had brought the crafters of US dirty wars in Latin America during the 1970s and 1980s back to the White House. I knew of other investigations that after decades had uncovered US government documents proving CIA involvement in coups and other clandestine activity, as in the overthrow of Chile's Salvador Allende in 1973. I wanted to see if it was possible to do it in real time and actually have an impact on the current political climate. Could we prove a CIA role in a modern coup that had happened just a year before?

I called on the help of Washington DC-based investigative reporter Jeremy Bigwood, who had been referred by a mutual friend I'd met during law school. Jeremy was a former wartime photojournalist turned expert researcher in hard-to-find government documents. When I reached him by phone and explained what I was looking for, he agreed to help. He too was interested to see if we could obtain any relevant documents so close in time to the actual event. Together we submitted hundreds of requests under the Freedom of Information Act (FOIA) to obtain declassification and release of any documents US government agencies had on the coup against Chávez. This was back before Wikileaks existed when using FOIA was one of the only tools available to uncover classified government activity. The results were overwhelming.

Bigwood and I began the FOIA requests in October 2003. The first results came in early 2004 – pretty speedy for US government bureaucracy. We received hundreds of documents from the National Endowment for Democracy (NED), a relatively unknown, congressionally created agency funded through the State Department that finances political groups supporting US interests in over 70 countries worldwide. Curiously, these documents, primarily consisting of grant agreements between the NED and a variety of Venezuelan organizations, showed a clear pattern of funding to the very same groups that had executed the coup against Chávez a mere year and a half earlier – funding that was apparent before, during and after the coup.

The evidence was damning. This US agency had intentionally given hundreds of thousands of taxpayer dollars to anti-Chávez organizations inside Venezuela that were working to overthrow their government, which, like it or not, was a democratic government supported by a clear majority. The documents dated after the failed coup showed a US government role extending beyond that initial failed attempt to oust the leftist president. The pattern of funding appeared continuous and was even expanding.

At that time, in January 2004, Venezuela was immersed in yet another tense political moment. Opposition groups were collecting signatures aiming to oust President Chávez through a recall referendum. Venezuela's young constitution, written and ratified by the people through a national referendum in 1999, included in Article 72 the possibility that any elected official could be subjected to a recall vote after reaching the halfway period of his/her term. Certain requirements had to be met to convene the recall referendum, including a petition drive proving that 20 per cent of the electorate was in favor of holding the plebiscite.

The Venezuelan organization at the head of the recall drive was a newly created group named Súmate (Join Up). Led by a small board of wealthy, connected Venezuelans, this 'out-of-the-blue' organization had a sudden massive campaign machine, well geared and seemingly well funded. As Súmate became the face of the anti-Chávez movement and the recall vote, something caught our eyes in the NED documents we were reading. There was Súmate on page after page, as clear as day, receiving tens of thousands of US taxpayer dollars to run its campaign against Chávez.

This was huge news. Not only did we have irrefutable evidence of US government funding to groups involved in seeking to overthrow President Chávez during the April 2002 coup, but we also had ongoing, real-time proof that those leading the continuing efforts to oust the Venezuelan head of state were backed by Washington, and were getting big bucks in aid. This information had to get out – we couldn't just sit on it. This type of revelation could have a major impact on Venezuelan politics in the here and now. We could potentially prevent another attempt to overthrow a legitimate democratic government. Besides, what right did the US government have to fund an electoral campaign in another country? The whole concept seemed outrageous to me. If it were to happen in the US, it would be considered an act of war.

Breaking the story

Bigwood and I sent the documents to some contacts at the Venezuelan Embassy in Washington DC, requesting that they be given to President Chávez. Simultaneously, we set up a website and began uploading the original NED grants documents together with Spanish translations that I was hastily doing. We sent out a press release in Spanish and English. We had the proof: Washington had funded the coup against Chávez and now was trying to oust him again through a recall vote.

The news reached Chávez quickly and, in early February 2004, he showed the NED grants documents on live television. 'Here is the proof that Súmate is supported by the US government. They are getting thousands of dollars from the US to do their dirty work against us,' he said, outraged, but thrilled that he had the hard evidence to hand. The news exploded in Venezuela, making major headlines. Súmate was a US government creation and had been publicly exposed.

Our modest website got more than 20,000 visits after Chávez's announcement, and we knew we were on to something big. We kept analyzing, translating and uploading documents to the site, but I felt like it wasn't enough. The story didn't stop at Súmate – it was much larger than that. The funding network from the US government extended through anti-government political parties, newly created NGOs and projects aimed at undermining the Chávez government. There were dozens of groups receiving this financing with the sole purpose of building up opposition to Chávez. I decided to go down to Venezuela and take the more than 2,000 documents we had so far directly to the President. Of course, at the time I had no realistic way of personally reaching him, but I was determined to find a way, no matter what it took.

I spent days making copies, translating the most important documents and preparing the information in a comprehensible way so it could easily be seen for what it was: clear and indisputable proof of US government meddling in Venezuelan affairs. American taxpayers didn't know hundreds of thousands of dollars of their money were being spent to undermine a democratic government in South America and most would probably oppose such misuse of public funds –money that could be better spent on infrastructure, jobs creation and social services inside the United States. What right did the US government have to undermine the will of the Venezuelan people? None. So, why was this happening? One word: oil.

Venezuela just so happens to be the country with the largest oil reserves on the planet. Believe it or not, they have more than 300 billion barrels of certified oil reserves, exceeding that of any other country on earth, including Saudi Arabia. And we're not talking about somewhere halfway around the world like the Middle East. Venezuela is right here, in the same hemisphere, and just a quick trip under three hours from Miami.

So here's Venezuela, sitting on all this oil, of which the United States is the principal consumer and investor, and now they've gone and elected a leftist president who talks of socialism and nationalization. No, no, no. How could this be? After all that work during the Cold War to rid the world of communism and anything that reeked of it – including really anything 'left of center'. And now, here comes this guy, raised in poverty on the far plains of Venezuela, a soldier in the army, under-educated and with dark skin, who talks of socialism and giving power to the people, and has no political experience. This was just plain unacceptable to Washington.

As a recently graduated attorney who specialized in international human rights during law school, I found Washington's funding of groups trying to overthrow and undermine Venezuela's democratic president a clear and present injustice. It was plain wrongdoing and my knowing that it was happening in real time gave me an obligation to do what I could to stop it. I was determined to act fast.

I gathered up the copied documents, put them in the little brown-leather briefcase my mother had given me as a present when I graduated from law school and I caught the next plane to Caracas. I had a few leads up my sleeve from my prior experiences with Venezuela and I started with a young woman I had met the year before in New York, a photographer working for the presidential press team that had accompanied President Chávez to the United Nations in January 2003.

I had attended a pro-Chávez rally outside the UN headquarters and she had been there to take pictures and document support for Chávez outside of Venezuela. She was introduced to me by some of the other activists as a famous photographer who had exposed the truth about the 2002 coup against Chávez. Wendys (the 's' is correct, despite what you are thinking), who was actually named after the American fast-food chain, had captured the key photographs during the coup. She had been a photographer at the time for Venpres, a now obsolete state news agency, and had been out on the streets near the presidential palace during the violent events that day. Wendys had taken photos of the opposition-controlled metropolitan police of Caracas firing on Chávez supporters with long-armed and automatic weapons while wearing gloves to cover up their fingerprints. She had risked her life to take those pictures, and had hidden the film while she was briefly detained. Her photos and testimony were later key in bringing those same members of the metropolitan police force and their bosses to justice.

When we spoke on the phone she immediately understood the importance of the documents I had brought to Venezuela. She offered to help get them to Chávez. 'Meet me tomorrow at two o'clock at La Carlota Air Force base. You can come with me to the *Aló Presidente* show where Chávez will be,' she said. I eagerly agreed. In fact, I was ecstatic.

Well, that was much easier than I had imagined. I had barely been in town more than a day and already had practically secured the chance to meet President Chávez. Was it too good to be true?

At the air base

With my briefcase inscribed with my initials 'EWG' in tow (it was practically chained to my arm), the following afternoon I took a taxi to La Carlota Air Force base in the eastern part of Caracas. I had never been on a Venezuelan military base before, so I was a bit nervous and it didn't help that I had no idea where I was actually going. At the gates, I told the uniformed, armed guards in my gringo-accented Spanish that I was supposed to be on the president's press team plane. Just like that, with no security revision or further questioning, they let me through and directed the cab driver down a windy road alongside varying military aircraft. We maneuvered through air fields and finally found the one where Wendys and about a handful of other journalists were standing around with their camera equipment. There was a small military propeller plane painted in camouflage on the runway.

I was jittery with excitement when I saw Wendys. We hugged and I launched into an explanation of the revealing documents I was carrying tightly in my briefcase. Her eyes opened wider as I told her how I had actual paystubs with the signatures of current opposition leaders, accepting their thousands of dollars from the US government. 'This has to get to the President,' she affirmed. We boarded the small camouflaged plane and took two seats about halfway inside. There were only about 12 seats in total and there was no door separating the pilots from the passengers. I had never been on a military plane before, or a plane this small, and it was both nerve-wracking and exciting. My adrenaline was to the moon and all I could think about was meeting President Chávez and personally explaining to him the importance of the documents.

As Wendys chatted with her fellow journalists as they boarded the plane, I stared out at the military base beyond the window, my mind racing with the possible scenarios that could occur when I finally met Chávez. My thoughts were abruptly interrupted by a shrill voice asking Wendys who the hell I was. Wendys explained that I was an American lawyer from New York who had all these US government declassified documents in my briefcase revealing support to the Venezuelan opposition and their efforts to oust Chávez, and how we planned to give this information to the President during his show the following day.

The person asking who I was turned out to be the chief of the presidential press team and, suffice it to say, she was not happy with my presence. A woman who looked not a day older than me, she scanned me up and down with a furrowed brow and declared, 'Girl, you are not coming with us.' She ordered me off the plane immediately. 'Go,' she barked. Wendys' protests were met with 'you could lose your job for this' and a stare that basically said 'shut up now before you're off the plane, too'.

The tiny woman (I'm only five foot two, but she was several inches shorter than me) escorted me to the edge of the runway, making sure I was as far from the plane as physically possible. And there she left me, on the edge of the runway, giving me a 'Fuck you' shrug as she got on the military plane. I watched the plane ascend into the blue sky, briefcase tight to my chest, tears rolling down my cheeks. I had been so close!

I had no idea where I was or how to get out of there. I had no one to call, and no phone to call with anyway. I had no roaming on my New York cellphone so it was useless. I started to walk, figuring I'd eventually find the exit from the military base and then look for a taxi before nightfall.

As I walked away from the runway, head down and feeling sorry for myself, a young uniformed soldier pulled up in a car. He leaned out the window and offered me a ride. 'I saw what happened and the way you were treated by that lady. That's not how we Venezuelans are. Can I give you a lift somewhere?'

I don't usually accept rides from strangers, especially armed ones, but I figured he was a soldier and I could trust him, and in any case I really had no one else to help me get out of here. I got in his big old rusty-brown Chevy and we drove off the base.

As he drove, I began to pour out the whole story of my visit and the documents and that tiny, evil lady kicking me off the plane. He seemed genuinely upset about the way I had been treated. His name was Bolivar, a sergeant in the Venezuelan Air Force, and he had a kind, handsome baby face. That's all I remember now, though at the time a ride from someone named Bolivar seemed mystical. Simón Bolivar was the great independence hero of Venezuela and also a founding father of Colombia, Bolivia, Ecuador and Peru, a true fighter for justice and freedom until his death. And here was Sergeant Bolivar, my savior in a moment of deep grief and despair. And here I was, with information that could save this country from severe instability and turmoil.

Bolivar suggested we have lunch before he drove me to wherever I needed to go and, while I wasn't hungry, his eagerness to cheer me up made me accept. We went to a nearby food court in a mall right near the military base. As we ate, I filled him in on the details of my investigation and my current purpose in Venezuela. Bolivar agreed that the President needed to see the information. Like Wendys, Bolivar reacted with urgency, understanding the importance of the documents. He began making calls on his cellphone, and then he let me borrow it to call anyone and everyone I could think of.

I tried calling an acquaintance I had met the year before when he was giving a lecture on Venezuela in New York City who now worked as the President's chief of staff. That's how things were in Chávez's government – people with no experience in government, but who were diehard loyalists, were now in high-level roles. Still shaken from the morning's events, I left tearful messages on his office phone to the tune of, 'I was thrown off a plane, severely mistreated and abandoned on a military base by the presidential press team'. Maybe a bit exaggerated, but in my state that's how I felt, and anyway I figured a touch of Latin American soap opera couldn't hurt. I continued to call every contact in the government I could think of, but I only got their voicemails. I left dozens of messages.

Sergeant Bolivar offered to take me wherever I wanted to go. Feeling utterly defeated, I could only think of going back to my friend Piki's apartment in El Valle, a working-class neighborhood in Caracas where I had been staying with him and his mother, Diana. My uniformed savior dropped me off at the door of the dilapidated high-rise, shaking my hand and wishing me well. 'Remember me, Sergeant Bolivar, when you meet the President. I know you will,' he said encouragingly. I forced a smile from the depth of my despair and thanked him for his kindness.

Second chance

I sulked up to the smog-crusted building, lugging my briefcase, which seemed heavier as each moment passed, and knocked on my friend Piki's door. Diana, a big-hearted, caramel-skin-colored hardcore communist, answered and let me in. She saw by my frowning, pale face that things had not worked out. We sat down at the kitchen table and she made *cafe con leche*. Over coffee and cookies, I filled her in on my dream-turned-nightmare. She felt my pain, but held out hope. 'You never know what can happen in Venezuela, Eva. Have faith,' she said, comforting me.

Hours passed as we sat at the table talking politics and analyzing the most recent attempts to overthrow Chávez and their impact on Venezuelans' daily lives. My mind kept going over and over possible people I could reach out to about the documents. If there were any chance that I could prevent further instability in the country by passing on the evidence I had uncovered, I had to reach the President. I couldn't take my eyes off the telephone, which was sitting on the center of the table so we wouldn't miss it if it rang. And, just as I was ready to throw in the towel and head off to bed, it rang. Diana answered. '*Aló? Un momento*,' she said and handed me the phone. I thought it was one of the people I had contacted finally getting back to me. '*Hola*,' I said in my accented Spanish. A heavy male voice responded. '*Doctora Golinger?*' he asked. In Venezuela, lawyers are referred to as 'doctors'. We do, after all, have a Juris Doctorate, at least those of us who got our degrees in the United States.

'*Si, soy yo*,' I said, as my heart skipped a beat.

'*Doctora Golinger,* I'm calling on behalf of the President of the Republic. The President requests your presence tomorrow morning on his airplane to accompany him on his television program'. *Whaaaaaaat?* My mind was exploding and my heart was racing a mile a minute. I muttered a meek 'Okay' and the voice then said, 'We will pick you up at 7am'. I gave him the address and said thank you to the click on the other end.

Umm, okay, well, I guess things do work out after all in Venezuela. 'The President invited me to go on his plane tomorrow,' I told Diana. She hugged me and gave me an 'I told you so' grin.

I barely slept that night. I had laid out my clothes for the morning and prepared my briefcase with the documents, checking them all over and over again, highlighting the most important ones and making sure I could clearly explain them to the President and look decent and serious at the same time. Let's just say that, during that period of my life, my look was not so professional. I didn't wear much make-up and my hair was short – usually tied up in little pigtails with colored ties, as I was growing it out at the time. My clothes were short on glamor, to put it nicely.

The next morning I was up by 6am. After I had showered and put on a plain, light-green J-Crew sleeveless dress, tattered brown-leather sandals and tied my short hair into uneven pigtails, Piki, a dreadlocked musician over six feet tall and not exactly an Armani man, took one look at me and asked 'That's what you're wearing?' I laughed and responded, 'Look, this is who I am and I'm not going to pretend to be anyone different just to meet the President.'

Briefcase in tow, I went downstairs and out to the street entrance of the building, half expecting no one to be there on that quiet Sunday morning. After all, the whole thing could have been my imagination or plans could have changed and the President could have decided he no longer wanted me on his show. But, lo and behold, a car was there waiting for me with two soldiers dressed in presidential guard uniforms, green with red berets and black high-top boots starkly contrasted with crimson-red laces. '*Buenos días, Doctora Golinger,*' said the guard who opened the back door to let me in. He couldn't have been over 18. I could see the braces on his teeth in the 10 seconds he spoke to me.

During the 30-minute ride to Maiquetía airport down the

winding road through Caracas' voluptuous, ripe-green mountains that opened to the vast, blue Caribbean sea, I went over what I would say to the President in my head and how I would explain the hundreds of documents I had in my briefcase in the shortest time possible. I figured time would be tight. Really, I had no idea how it was all going to play out. I actually thought that Chávez wouldn't be on the plane, because I had heard he had been on a trip to Havana the day before and in all likelihood would fly directly to the program, which I understood was to be broadcast from the western Venezuelan state of Zulia.

As we approached the airport, the car veered off onto a side road that led to a private entrance. 'Rampa 4,' a sign said. After we came to a halt, the young red-bereted guard opened the door for me to exit the car. I was standing on the tarmac in front of what seemed to be a private terminal. Venezuelan flags flew high above the doors, the wind whipping them back and forth like welcoming arms. Bomb-sniffing cocker-spaniel dogs were mulling around alongside plain-clothed security officers. Off to the right, I saw the plane. An Airbus A319CJ with a white body streaked with the colors of the Venezuelan flag – yellow, blue and red – and *República Bolivariana de Venezuela* (Bolivarian Republic of Venezuela) emblazoned on the side. The modern aircraft had caused a stir among critics for its $65-million price tag when it was purchased in 2002. The previous presidential plane had been in constant need of repair and Chávez had made the decision to replace it after decades of use due to its unsuitable and outdated conditions. But it was a hefty price tag in a country still grappling with high poverty rates.

I turned and walked up the stairs as the glass doors opened and entered what now appeared to be the presidential air terminal. Presidential guards topped with red berets lingered everywhere along with a few civilians or plain-clothed security officers. I was invited to sit on one of the squishy, black-leather couches by a soldier who checked my passport. I sat down, hugging my briefcase to my chest, and waited for someone to tell me what to do next.

I didn't see the President anywhere but, if the bomb-sniffing dogs were here, I thought, then he was probably coming. And anyway, I reasoned, it was *his* plane, after all. If he had still been in Havana that morning then his plane would have been there, too. I watched and waited as very official-looking people came in and out of the terminal, some of whom I recognized from television as government officials and cabinet members. Finally one of the guards gestured for me to board the plane. I had no idea if the President had arrived or not, but I certainly hadn't seen him.

Inside the presidential plane

As I walked out onto the runway towards the Airbus with the other passengers, I saw most of them walking to the back entrance of the plane. Only what appeared to be certain high-ranking cabinet members climbed the stairs of the front entrance, so I followed others towards the back. '*Doctora Golinger*,' called a guard. 'Please, this way,' he said, signaling towards the front entrance. *God*, I thought, *what am I in for?*

I reached the top of the stairs and entered a small cream-colored hallway with soft leather padded walls. I'd only once been on a private plane in my 31 years, a charter jet that one of father's wealthy friends had hired for his 25th wedding anniversary.

The guards inside directed me through the hallway and motioned to a set of big, cream soft-leather cushiony seats. There were eight seats in total, facing each other in sets of two in what appeared to be a more luxurious 'first class' area of the plane than the regular passenger area. A curtain sealed off the back area accommodating most of the staff, assistants and other passengers.

The big seats had name tags. One had golden letters spelling out 'President of the Bolivarian Republic of Venezuela' with the seal of Venezuela in the middle and the colors of the flag. I definitely thought I had to be in the wrong area until I looked over at the seat next to the President's. It had a small tag with 'Doctora Eva Golinger' written in cursive on white card stock. I felt my heart drop into the pit of my stomach. *Okay*, I thought, *calm it, calm it, get a hold of yourself and breathe. Just sit down and be cool, you can do this.* A few people had already taken the other seats in front and across the aisle from me. They just sort of raised their eyebrows as I sat down, thinking, most likely, 'who the hell is she?'

An older brown-haired woman with a pleasant face across

from me smiled and nicely asked the question they all had in their minds. 'I'm Yadira, the science minister; so, who are you?' As I began telling her about my investigation and the documents I was carrying, she got that same wide-eyed look as my photographer friend Wendys had when I'd told her about the NED grants and the paystubs signed by leading opposition figures.

'You've got to tell this to the President,' said Yadira, immediately understanding the importance of the information.

'Yes, that's why I'm here, I hope,' I responded.

All the seats filled up except for the President's next to me and the plane geared up for take-off. *Oh well*, I thought, *it was too good to be true. He must not be on the plane, which is why they probably sat me next to his empty chair.* I was, after all, an unknown *gringa* from New York and they hadn't even searched my briefcase when I came on board. *I'll see him at the show and just hope that we'll get a chance to talk.*

Then, about 10 minutes into the flight, dressed in an olive-green military shirt with matching pants, a smiling President Chávez came out of a private room in the front of the plane and began to greet his cabinet members and close advisors who were sitting around me. After exchanging words with his defense, science and communications ministers, his eyes turned to me. 'You must be Eva,' he said, reaching out his hand.

'Yes. Hello, Mr President,' I blurted out nervously, shaking his thick hand. And, before I could say anything else, he turned and walked back to his private room. *Damn*, I thought, *did I just blow it?*

I looked at Yadira, who gave me a sympathetic nod, and I asked, 'Do you think he'll come back out again?'

'*Vamos a ver*,' (We'll see) she replied.

About 20 minutes before landing on the hour-long flight, most of which I spent reviewing and selecting the most important documents to show the President, a young lieutenant named Morales, tall and well groomed, appeared and motioned to me with his finger, saying, 'The President wants to talk to you.'

Holy crap, this is it, I thought. *This is my one chance to show him everything and explain it all coherently and the plane's landing gear is about to drop!* But I couldn't complain. At least

I *was* getting the chance. I scrambled to gather up my bulging briefcase and followed the lieutenant down the narrow hallway to the private room. The door opened and Morales motioned for me to enter. He closed it behind me, leaving me standing there by myself in my little green sleeveless dress holding my briefcase tightly to my chest. I looked across the room. President Chávez was sitting alone at a small table reviewing paperwork and sipping black coffee from a tiny white cup with a little handle, which he held in his long fingers. Despite the luxury of the plane, the room was modest and sparse. A table and two chairs in the middle and a small couch off to the side. Nothing seemed overly opulent or even particularly 'presidential'. There were no bells and whistles, just a regular room with a man reading at the table and having his coffee. 'Sit down,' he gestured with his hand and spoke in an inviting voice.

I sat in the chair opposite his and didn't skip a beat. I immediately began pulling documents out of my briefcase and spread them on the little table. 'Wait, wait,' he said, waving his hand for me to put the documents to the side. 'Have you had breakfast yet?'

Breakfast? I hadn't had breakfast, but frankly eating was the last thing on my mind. My stomach was in knots and I was overly anxious to use the few precious minutes I had with the President to tell him as much as I could about the goldmine of evidence in my possession. 'No,' I responded meekly. But before I could say, 'But, I'm not hungry,' he had pressed some invisible button and called the waitress in to order two breakfasts.

'*Tráenos dos desayunos,*' he told the tall attendant, who looked as though she could have been a beauty queen. It was possible: after all, Venezuela was a country famous for winning more Miss Universe pageants than any other.

'Let's talk first and get to know each other,' suggested the black-haired, stocky head of state sitting before me. I stared at him in a daze. Was this really happening? Wasn't the plane about to land? Would I ever be able to tell him about the documents?

'Are you a Christian?'

'What? No,' I admitted, not wanting to spend my few minutes with the President's attention going into a whole explanation regarding my lack of religious beliefs or the fact that my family

43

heritage was actually Jewish. I knew that Chávez was a proud Christian and he talked about Jesus a lot but all I wanted was to talk about the documents I had lugged down from New York and jumped over hurdles to bring before him.

'How is your mother?' he continued, making genuine small talk. 'She's fine, thank you,' I responded impatiently, and then I dove right into my speech explaining my investigative work and the documents I had brought to show him. His eyebrows raised slightly and I could tell I had piqued his interest. As I started to pull the documents out again and put them on the table, breakfast arrived. He motioned for me to clear them away again. *Jesus.*

'This is a military barracks breakfast. I hope you don't mind,' said Chávez with a smile. 'Simple, just as I like it.' He was so relaxed about everything. I wondered if he could tell how nervous I was and was trying to put me at ease.

We were each served a modest plate with Venezuela's traditional cornmeal patty, the *arepa*, together with a slice of white cheese, two anchovies and a small crescent of melon. The meal came with a cup of sugary black coffee. I tried to eat a few bites so he wouldn't be offended, but really my stomach was churning. I knew the clock was ticking, so I kept talking. By now he had given up on persuading me to eat and make small talk, so I rattled on while he ate, sprawling the documents out over my uneaten breakfast. As I detailed the paystubs, grants and numerous internal reports clearly evidencing the financial and political relationship between his detractors and the US government, the President got that same wide-eyed expression as had the others after I had explained the content of the documents in my hands.

He pressed the magic button again and called for his communications minister. Jesse Chacon, a close ally and brother-at-arms during the President's military years, joined us in the private room, pulling up a little stool to the side of the table where breakfast had been served. Chávez told him to listen to what I had to say and then co-ordinate a strategy to use the documents in the most advantageous way. For the next 15 minutes I spoke. I showed document after document and explained, in the best way I could, the intricate web of funding from Washington to the Venezuelan opposition that I was beginning to unravel. Before any kind of strategy or plan could be devised for using the documents, the plane began to descend.

There was no time to go back to my seat as we prepared for landing, so I stayed in the room with the President, fastening my seat belt in the chair while still at the table. I shoved the documents back inside my briefcase.

Live TV, pigtails and all

We arrived on a rustic airfield and were immediately escorted off the airbus and towards two large black military helicopters with their engines running. I had never been on a helicopter before. I climbed on with the President but, while I sat on one of the cushioned benches in the back, Chávez went into the co-pilot's seat and took control of the craft. The doors were left wide open so we could see the terrain below. I sat clutching my briefcase to make sure none of the cherished documents would fly out the open hatch.

It was a short, noisy trip, just under 20 minutes. We landed at Fort Mara military base in Zulia state, the site chosen that week for Chávez's Sunday television and radio program, *Aló Presidente*. As we descended from the helicopters and walked towards the big white tents where the set for his show was ready to air live, I stayed right behind the President, keeping pace with him. My eyes caught the face of the woman who had kicked me off the press plane the day before. She looked at me with shocked horror – her face had turned a ghostly white. I think she thought right then and there that she would be fired.

Her automatic assumption that I had told on her to the President, who would fire her, was similar to my reaction in thinking she was evil. In the end, I understood she was just doing her job, even though I disagreed with her 'method'. If I were her, I probably wouldn't have let some strange foreign person on a presidential press plane headed to a presidential event, but I might have handled it differently. Nonetheless, I had no intention of getting anyone fired.

Chávez took his seat at his desk on the set and I was escorted to the front row of the audience. The show always had a live audience, generally a mix of supporters and government officials. To my surprise, in this case the entire audience was full of uniformed military personnel. We were on a military base, after all. At least I was wearing green!

Just a week earlier, several soldiers had burned to death in a detention cell on Fort Mara and the media were having a heyday with the story, trying to say Chávez had ordered the soldiers' execution. The President had chosen to have the show there that day to set the record straight and debunk the rumors about an alleged military uprising in the barracks.

It was hot day and, even though we were under a big tent shielding us from the blaring Zulia sun, I was seriously sweating. Some of that perspiration probably came from my nerves and the rush from the Black Hawk helicopter ride. And I still had no idea if I would be asked to speak on the live, nationally broadcast program.

About halfway into the hour-long show, Chávez caught my eye in the front row and began recounting our conversation on the plane. 'This young woman has all these declassified US government documents she's carrying around that prove major funding to the opposition. I saw the paystubs with their signatures on them!' he exclaimed. 'Eva, tell us about it,' he gestured to me.

I stood up and a microphone appeared out of nowhere, thrust right in front of my mouth. I began to tell the story of the investigation, the documents, the evidence. 'This is the proof of not only Washington's role in the coup two years ago, but also of the ongoing meddling of the US government in Venezuela's affairs, and its close relationship with the opposition. We're talking millions of dollars in funding efforts to oust you, President Chávez. These documents even show the opposition's current funding from the US government for their recall referendum campaign against you, Mr President,' I explained.

'Eva is a brave woman, this young woman, strong and brave. Thank you, Eva,' said Chávez, and everyone clapped. The uniformed military audience even stood up to applaud my work. I felt humbled and a bit embarrassed. Imagine being surrounded by dozens of decorated military officers and all of them looking at you and applauding. And there was little ole me, in my plain green

J-Crew dress and uneven pigtails, standing amongst them looking like I was about 12 years old. It must have been quite a sight.

After the show ended, some of the local media ran over to interview me before I was rushed to the big black military helicopters which had remained on the grassy field beyond the mobile television set. Once we were nestled back onto the plane and in the air, President Chávez came and sat in his seat in the passenger area next to me. He talked with his cabinet members about some pending internal matters and I just quietly observed. A simple lunch was served, which I just pushed around on the plate. My nerves hadn't yet settled.

When we landed in Caracas, he kissed me on the cheek, as Venezuelans do when they greet each other or say goodbye, and he thanked me for coming. He instructed his assistant to help me with anything I needed. I asked to accompany him during the events commemorating the April 2002 coup d'état that were taking place over the next couple of days. 'Of course,' he said, instructing his assistant, Morales. 'Make sure Eva is invited to participate in all the events.'

As I walked down the stairs exiting the plane I turned and looked back at the presidential Airbus with its gold, blue and red stripes on its big white body and I wondered to myself, will I ever ride on this thing again? It was 11 April 2004 and, although I didn't know it yet, my life had been changed forever.

4

Before Chávez,
or how I met Venezuela

The first time I went to Venezuela was the summer of 1993, more than five years before Hugo Chávez was elected president. It was the summer before my senior year in college and I was ripe for adventure. I had never been to Latin America, with the exception of crossing into Tijuana, Mexico, which I didn't really count because it's a border town catering to southern Californian tourists (no offense meant to the Tijuanians).

During my junior year at Sarah Lawrence College, an introspective and enriching small liberal arts university right outside of New York City, I had joined a close group of friends exploring the very difficult issue of white racism. We had attended a special workshop on the subject and those of us who wanted to continue analyzing and understanding the profound roots of racism in the United States decided to form a small, intimate group to delve head first into our own personal fears, feelings and desires. It was hard work, often embarrassing, tearful and scary, but the circle of trust and blatant honesty we created really helped us to understand and break down the deep roots of racism embedded in the 'whiteness' of our society. It was a reality we had to deal with, accept and deconstruct if we wanted to rid ourselves of beliefs and feelings we never asked for and didn't want to carry for the rest of our lives.

As part of our exploration, we each had to map out our family trees in as much detail as possible with the goal of first discovering our own roots. You have to really know yourself and where you come from in order to understand the world around you and your own, unique perspective. Let me just say that one side of my family is victim of the traditional 'New York Jew' syndrome, which means that, when it came to the past, 'I don't wanna talk about it' was always the answer. Or, when an elder family member was asked about another absent relative, the response might be: 'I lent her my fur coat once and she never returned it, so I never talked to her again. Ehh.' If, for some reason, you didn't show up at a family event – a wedding, funeral or other engagement – that's it, you were cut off for good.

So, I only knew bits and pieces of my family's past, infused with vague memories of birthdays or visits when I was a little girl and faces that seemed lost in time. No one talked about the family members who weren't around, even if they were still alive. Maybe that level of denial was due to the hardships so many Jewish families faced after World War Two and the difficult process of emigrating to the United States, leaving everything behind. It was a harsh and cold way to treat family, but the trauma suffered by millions of Jewish people and their families during the Holocaust made more loss intolerable. It was better just to cut someone off for a perceived betrayal than to deal with their eventual loss.

At that time, I didn't even know if my own grandparents on my father's side were born in New York or somewhere in eastern Europe. Nobody talked about it. And of course, no one wanted to talk about those who had passed and left us for the great beyond. The only details I really knew were that one of my great-grandfathers on that side was from Romania and the other was from Austria and had invented the men's toupe and brought it to America. He made a million dollars, had a thriving wig shop on Fifth Avenue in Manhattan, The House of Louis Feder, and was even featured in the book, 'How I Made a Million Dollars'. Unfortunately, he spent every hard-earned cent gambling in Havana, Cuba, and left not a penny for the family. So, even though my people were proud of his fame, they were bitter and resentful about being left with nothing, not even a little chunk of that million bucks.

The other side of my family was even more obscure. Out of respect for my mother's privacy, I won't enter into all the painful details of the severely abusive situation she grew up in. Both her parents died young and there was a lot of secrecy, emotional and physical abuse and denial. My extended family in total was limited to four cousins, three aunts (one died when I was 12) and one uncle – and that's from both sides. And I had just one set of grandparents, my father's parents. Through the family-tree process, I did learn that I had Romanian, Austrian, Russian and Polish origins, as well as, surprisingly, Venezuelan heritage, or so my mother believed.

I knew about the eastern European part before from my Jewish side of the family, if not in detail, but could we really have Latin American family? That was big news to me. Could it be that all these years I had Latino blood in me? Could that explain my unbridled passion and revolutionary fervor? Did that explain why I always felt different and out of place around my mainly white American friends?

The man my mother knew as her father, Antonio Calderon, was born in Caracas, Venezuela, at the end of the 19th century. His parents had emigrated from the region of Malaga, Spain. There were several brothers and sisters, though one died as an infant and was buried in the Caracas central cemetery. The Calderons lived in Caracas until the early 1900s when Antonio's father was allegedly assassinated by the dictatorship of Juan Vicente Gomez. His mother took the children and fled by boat to Cuba, where he and his siblings were raised into adulthood. Around 1919, Antonio Calderon left Havana for Miami then made his way north to New York. He became an airplane pilot and worked as a print cartoon artist, until he met my grandmother, a first-generation Polish-American with blond hair, blue eyes and a voluptuous body. She was very Marilyn Monroe, an enchanting, artistic woman who changed her name many times over her short life, and he courted her with cheesy romantic poems and drawings of them dancing together. They fell in love and started a family, hoping to live happily ever after. They had my mother and her younger brother, Anthony, named after his father. Sadly, Antonio Calderon developed bone cancer from a melanoma on his leg and he died when my mother was just five years old. He was in his early fifties. My grandmother then married an abusive, Polish drunk and the story goes downhill from there.

In search of my Venezuelan heritage

I decided to go on a mission to find my roots in Venezuela. To me, learning this part of my family history was life changing – I just didn't realize how much. When I began researching travel to Venezuela I discovered that few people from the US went there as tourists. In fact, it wasn't really an official tourist destination according to travel books and tour agencies. Except, of course, for Margarita Island, a Caribbean resort where cruise ships would dock for a few hours for some duty-free shopping and fun in the sun, but nothing else notable.

What was strange was that Venezuela did appear as a tourist destination for Europeans, particularly the Germans and Dutch. And most seemed to go either to the pristine, semi-wild Caribbean beaches, or they went trekking in the Andes. I couldn't even find an exchange program at the university level between the US and Venezuela – none existed at the time. No language schools in Caracas, the capital, advertised for Americans. The only program I found was a six-week Spanish-language school in Merida, a small university city in the Andes Mountains. So I took a chance and enrolled.

The program included a home-stay with a local Venezuelan family. I had taken high-school Spanish, but really all I remembered was '*Hola*', '*Buenos días*', '*Como estas*' and '*Me llamo Eva, como te llamas?*' I figured I'd pick up the rest out in the field. I was sent a brochure about Merida that included a list of warnings and rules about safety. I felt like I was regressing back to my early teenage years when the dangers and risks of drugs, sex and alcohol were lurking everywhere. 'Do not go out at night', 'Do not talk to strangers', 'Do not attempt to go near the university', 'Do not walk around alone', 'If you see a protest, return home immediately', 'Do not drink the water', 'Do not flush toilet paper in the toilet' and 'Do not eat any fresh fruits or vegetables because they could have been washed in the water'.

I was going to have some serious problems because I'm a vegetarian who was looking forward to eating all those fresh tropical fruits and vegetables, who also likes to walk around alone and explore things instead of being accompanied by a pack of gringos who stick out like a sore thumb, and, most of all, I like to throw my used toilet paper into the toilet. Where else would it go? I also had a *very* keen interest in checking out those protests.

The flight down to Caracas went from Miami, where I met up with the other students and the co-ordinator, a Venezuelan woman with accented but perfect English, and her two completely bilingual gorgeous children. There were fewer than 10 of us in total. Most of the other students came from the heartland of America and were very blond. I was the only New Yorker.

We landed at the international airport in Caracas after a mere two-and-a-half-hour flight; then we were quickly shuffled through immigration and customs and taken to the national airport next door where we were put on a plane to Merida. 'Caracas is dangerous,' the co-ordinator told us. 'Never go there.' Basically, as we understood it, if you went to Caracas you would be killed.

The flight to Merida from Caracas took a little under one hour. As we approached the small city, the luscious green mountains towered above us on the plane. We could see the peaks covered with ice and snow. I had never seen anything like it in my life: it was breathtaking.

And then my magical moment, immersed in the exotic beauty of a foreign land with the largest and most beautiful mountains I had ever seen, was abruptly interrupted by extreme terror. All of a sudden the plane was circling inside the mountain valley and dropping lower and lower. I could see the Spanish-tiled rooftops below me getting closer and closer. It seemed as though we were going to land right on top of them. And then I saw the runway laid out before me. It looked the size of a hot-wheels car track. I could see it from beginning to end. I didn't think the plane we were on was much smaller than the runway we were apparently about to land on. And then I saw a gas station with big gas tanks perched right at the start of the runway. Houses and shops surrounded the whole strip, as though it served as a walkway for locals. Who the hell had designed this airport? It was a giant death trap and I was terrified. Either we were going to crash into the gas pumps and explode, killing us and all the people in the dozens of houses and shops nearby, or we'd just crash at the end of the shortest runway ever right into the residential buildings positioned conveniently at the edge.

Passengers on the plane began crossing themselves and reciting prayers in Spanish. I thought, this is it, we're going down. I guess, instead of finding my Venezuelan roots, I'll be buried with them.

Our co-ordinator could see the fear in our eyes and tried to instill some tranquility. 'Yes, it's a small runway, but don't worry, the pilots are used to it. If they can't make the landing, we'll go to another airport in the next town,' she said as she crossed herself and recited a Hail Mary, as though that would calm our growing terror and fear of imminent death. The last thing I would have believed at that moment was that I would make that trip dozens of times over the next few years – each time experiencing the same imminent fear of death when approaching the moment of landing.

Today, that airport no longer allows big jets to land there, like the one we were on that day and the ones I flew on during the following five years on my many trips back and forth between New York and Merida. But that day, we landed, with brakes screeching all the way down to the very end of the runway, and I mean barely. It was a sign of how, even with poor planning, Venezuelans find a way to make things work.

Culture shock

That first arrival was my initiation into Venezuelan culture and the stark differences that exist between the orderly, law-abiding, disciplined lifestyle I was used to in the United States and the unbridled chaos of Latin America.

Venezuela was a country where seat belts were non-existent and traffic lights were optional, where little kids hung their heads out of car windows and everyone smiled. People not only stood and crouched on crowded buses, but also sat on crates next to the driver, or on the windshield, with their butts plastered to the glass. The safety regulations I had known my entire life as obligatory were brushed off as restrictive measures attempting to control freedoms everyone really wanted to enjoy, no matter the risk.

I saw danger and imminent death or injury everywhere I looked. People rode with entire families on a motorcycle, wearing no helmets, little kids and babies squashed between parents, weaving in and out of traffic, driving up on narrow sidewalks and the wrong way down one-way roads. Cars drove on shoulders, passed on the right or the left, and engaged in what appeared to me to be a permanent game of 'chicken', especially on curvy one-lane, two-way mountainous roads with no shoulders or sidewalks. Stop signs were unknown, aging buses emitted the most nasty black fumes I'd ever seen or inhaled, drivers held visible beer bottles or slugged unlabeled homemade liquors at all hours and pedestrians were a rarity.

Most people drove, hitched rides, took taxis or squeezed into makeshift buses, despite what seemed to me as incredibly uncomfortable and humiliating positions (especially for those with their rear ends smushed against or sticking out of the windows). Fuel is cheaper in Venezuela than anywhere on the planet, and that's something that hasn't changed today, even during the Bolivarian Revolution started by President Chávez. You can fill the tank of a large car for under one dollar. That is cheaper than cheap. A tank of gasoline costs less than a bottle of water, or a tomato, or a mango, which grow on trees there everywhere.

According to Venezuelans, the price of fuel is the one thing you can't mess with – ever. Try to raise the heavily state-subsidized, ridiculously low gasoline price and riots break out. It had already happened once in February 1989, when then President Carlos Andrés Pérez suggested that fuel prices could go up. He hadn't even implemented the measure when the riots began. People protested, went on strike, hoarded, speculated, looted and staged a mass uprising against the government. President Pérez responded by suspending all civil rights and quashing the protests with brutal force, killing thousands, mainly in poor communities. Pérez hadn't just threatened to raise gasoline prices, he had also announced he would be leading the country on the path to privatization despite the fact that he had been elected just months earlier on a platform opposing exactly that. Pérez had lied to win office and Venezuelans were pissed off. The fuel-price rise was the straw that broke the camel's back.

The events of February 1989, four and a half years before I arrived in Venezuela, reflected widespread discontent in the country due to the rapid increase in poverty, inequality, mass corruption and economic policies that clearly were not designed to benefit the majority. The February 1989 popular uprising, known as the Caracazo (The Big Caracas Explosion), was the first big protest against privatization and globalization, a trend that quickly spread around the planet. Think Seattle, 1999. And those events in Venezuela, particularly because of the government's brutal response and direct violent attack on the people, changed the nation forever and set it on a path to irreversible transformation. Most of the thousands killed in February 1989 were never accounted for. The Pérez government had dug mass graves and hurled the bodies in. It was his perverse way of 'reducing poverty'.

Fast forward four and a half years and at that time in Merida it seemed to me that no one walked. Walking was treated almost as a form of punishment. People would rather have their ass smashed against a window in a small van passing for a 'bus' to go two blocks rather than walk. I mean, why walk if fuel is so cheap? Even today, a tank of gasoline costs the same as a dozen rides on the Metro in Caracas. So, people reason, if you do have a car, or can get one, why not use it?

So, walking was (and still is) a rarity in Venezuela. To me it made no sense. Coming from a walking city, I would much rather walk than take transportation. Plus, I liked the fresh air and exercise. And Merida was absolutely gorgeous, if you could get past the pollution from car and bus exhausts. A village in the middle of those enormous green snow-capped mountains with the most perfect spring-like climate year-round. It was never hot or cold, just perfect. In the seventies Fahrenheit in the day, and in the sixties at night – what more could you ask for? Tropical fruit trees were everywhere, mixed with Andean pines and flora I had never seen in my life that looked straight out of a Dr Seuss book. It was beautiful. How could I not want to walk every foot of it?

And therefore, I did. Besides, I like going against the current. People stared at me out of buses and cars, and offered me rides and just couldn't understand why I would rather walk than go in a car. I was totally weird to them. A weird *gringa*.

The language-school program had arranged for me to stay with a family in what I would have considered an upper-middle-class neighborhood of Merida: El Carrizal B. They were a typical nuclear family, tropical version, with a mom, dad, daughter, son, live-in maid and three parrots who constantly cackled and cracked up laughing, which made me think they were always making fun of me. I guess I was a little insecure. The daughter and son were both much younger than me and spoke some rudimentary English. The parents neither spoke nor understood English, although I think the parrots did. Those parrots really got to me.

They had a big house, white with a Spanish-style red-tiled roof, as did all the others in the gated community. Yes, it was a gated community with guards at the entrance who also frequently patrolled the streets. I was told not to go out at night, period. Both parents were professors at the university and they appeared to make a nice living. The kids were still in secondary school. They were all very pleasant to me and the mother, a proud Venezuelan, made some seriously good hot chocolate. It was thick and creamy, made with fresh whole milk and dark chocolate melted right in. Just the right amount of sugar was added so it wasn't too sweet and you could still taste the bitterness of the local cacao.

It's rather unknown outside of gourmet circles, but Venezuela has some of the finest cacao beans in the world. Belgian and Swiss chocolatiers use Venezuelan cacao to make their delicate and delicious world-class truffles. International gourmet chefs use Venezuelan chocolate to bake their scrumptious, refined desserts. I can smell its exquisite chocolatey odor now as I write this and taste it melting in my mouth...

Back then, before Chávez's Bolivarian Revolution, few Venezuelans ever really ate their own chocolate. They much preferred the status boost of eating Nestlé or Hershey products – after all, imports cost more than local products, which meant the more imported foods you consumed, the wealthier you appeared. Believe me, that bizarre line of reasoning still applies today among the Venezuelan middle and upper classes. Paying higher prices means you have better class status. Forget bargaining, raise the prices please! It's better to look good than to feel good and it's better to look rich than actually to be rich.

After Chávez was elected president in 1998, one of his main initiatives was to invest in national production and development, first and foremost for Venezuelans. The Chávez government provided micro-credits and loans along with skills training and machinery to small chocolate co-operatives in the coastal cacao regions of Barlovento and Chuao, which had previously sold their raw product at cheap prices to foreign transnationals that then turned it into pricey, gourmet chocolate sold for top dollar on the international market. Under Chvez, Venezuelans began making the final product for national consumption and, for the first time, Venezuelans began opting for their own delicious chocolate instead of a Nestlé bar.

Happiness – and political turmoil

Merida was a lovely, small city, nestled in the mountains, and I immediately fell in love with it, despite all the crazy dangers and contradictions I saw everywhere. People were nice, gentle and seemed happy all the time. In fact, most Venezuelans always seem happy, except for the lighter-skinned upper-class ones who always seem angry at the government and blame it for everything from the rain to a pimple on their face. There is actually a World Happiness Index and as recently as 2010, Venezuela ranked #1, so this was not just my own perception.

In 1993, Venezuela was also a country in major turmoil. When I was told, 'Don't go out at night', I thought everyone was being over-protective since I was a foreigner in an unknown land. I didn't realize there was actually an obligatory national curfew in place.

After the Caracazo in 1989, when Carlos Andrés Pérez began to privatize everything from communications and electricity to healthcare and education, and thousands of people died in the resultant repression, the country never recovered. The Pérez regime's popularity ratings dropped severely to less than 20 per cent by 1992. In fact, the State Department's United States Information Agency (USIA), a propaganda arm which no longer exists, conducted a poll in Venezuela in January 1992 that determined 84 per cent of the population had a negative view of the Pérez government's policies. Nevertheless, State Department documents (which I obtained through my freedom-of-information requests) revealed that the US government would publicly back Carlos Andrés Pérez as an important ally and 'model democratic leader' in Latin America, no matter what he did. In the same breath, State Department also admitted Pérez was 'one of most corrupt politicians in the region'.

The US was interested in maintaining Carlos Andrés Pérez in power. He was busy privatizing everything and giving the sweet deals to US corporations. And he was completely subservient to US interests. With his sleek townhouse in Manhattan's posh Upper East Side, his luxurious estate in the Dominican Republic and his mansion in Miami, Pérez was more interested in preserving his own US interests than in doing the right thing for his country.

In early 1993, Pérez was brought up on impeachment charges after an internal investigation discovered he had embezzled over $20 million in public funds, amongst other corrupt deeds. He was forced to step down from the presidency and was placed under house arrest. Pérez later escaped and fled to Miami, where he remained until his death in December 2010.

But, before the 1993 impeachment, another major event had occurred – a military rebellion to overthrow Pérez's corrupt and murderous government. Although the strategic planning of the coup attempt was meticulous, the uprising failed after the rebels were unable to capture Pérez and secure control over the presidential palace of Miraflores in Caracas. The soldiers involved turned themselves over to the authorities. One stood out from the group. He was Lieutenant-Colonel Hugo Chávez. That day was 4 February 1992.

As he was taken into custody, the young Chávez was swarmed by television cameras, microphones and journalists begging for any declaration or explanation of what had happened. Chávez responded by doing something no other politician had done before in Venezuela, at least as far as people could remember. He looked into the cameras and said directly into the microphones: 'I take responsibility for this failed rebellion. We tried, but did not achieve our objective, *for now.*'

Did he say 'responsibility'? Politicians never took responsibility for failures in Venezuela, especially not during those days, which were full of wrongdoing and injustice. And here was this confident, young officer, who had just tried to overthrow the President of the Republic, talking on television about Simón Bolívar, the fight for justice, equality, building a better nation, working with and for the people. People liked it, and they liked him. The villain quickly became a hero.

Hugo Chvez and his fellow brothers-at-arms were sent to prison, but Chvez's words resonated deeply with the Venezuelan people. His phrase 'for now' was a sign of hope that he would continue to fight for change in the future, that he wouldn't give up, despite having suffered a setback. People saw him as honest, genuine and sincere and they began to express those feelings publicly. Yes, Chvez did try to overthrow an elected president but, many reasoned, that president was thoroughly corrupt. Venezuelan citizens flooded the Yare prison with letters for Chvez. He had countless visitors, including many from the country's leftist parties that hadn't given up on some day winning power, despite being frozen out by the nation's closed two-party system.

I arrived in Venezuela in the early 1990s just as these conflicts and crises were unraveling. In fact, while I was there that summer, the nation's second-largest bank, Banco Latino, defaulted. Its customers' life savings had been squandered, embezzled or misused by the bank's directors. The state tried at the last minute to intervene, but it was too late. Thousands of mostly middle-class Venezuelans lost everything they had. Most of those responsible for the collapse fled to Miami, further plummeting the country into economic crisis.

Student demonstration time

Even though I did not know all the causes at the time, I felt the resulting tension around me – the national curfew, the heavily armed national guard presence on the streets, the forced military draft of young men, and the constant student protests at the University of the Andes in Merida. It seemed to me I was in a nation where something big was about to happen.

Nearing the forbidden university campus one day, I saw smoke billowing from the street. As I got closer, I could see police in riot gear toting some pretty serious weaponry. They were shooting teargas into the campus. Then I saw masked students with t-shirts covering their faces running out from behind the buildings, throwing rocks and other hard objects towards the police. I was in the middle of a Latin American protest, rebellious students against 'The Man'. Or at least that's what I imagined.

I came back the next day to see if the demonstrations were continuing. They were, and so, defying my language school's warnings, I returned with my camera loaded with black-and-white film. In those days, needless to say, we didn't have digital cameras or cellphones. I thought I'd document the protests visually, interview the students and maybe even write a book about social movements in Venezuela.

I voluntarily embedded myself with the rebellious, masked students by simply walking onto the campus and finding them. I had figured out that, according to Venezuelan law, the police were prohibited from entering university grounds, which were considered autonomous from state authority. So, technically, the students protesting weren't as rebellious and brave as I had envisioned. They were protected by the campus lines, from behind which they hurled rocks and other potentially harmful weapons at the police. They covered their faces so the police wouldn't recognize them when they left the university grounds to go home. And they always called a time out for lunch.

At first I couldn't decipher why, all of a sudden, the protests stopped around noon and then started back up again between three and five in the afternoon. But I guess everyone has to eat, even rock-throwing, masked students. Apparently there is an unspoken truce between the police and protesting students during the lunch hour and on holidays.

I do not intend to demean or minimize the importance of the student protests, movements and demonstrations in Venezuela during the 1990s. For decades, student movements and leaders fighting for social justice had been treated with harsh repression by governments. Many were killed, persecuted, arrested, tortured or disappeared. Several of those former student leaders later became high-level members of President Chávez's government, such as Elias Jaua, Tareck El Aissami and Ricardo Menendez. Many students have risked their lives for real change, but there are also some who have turned out to be opportunists, often with other, less clear, agendas.

After spending a few days with the Merida protestors in 1993, I realized these were, unfortunately, the opportunistic type. They had no clear agenda or demands and were simply protesting to disrupt order and gain some sort of power over the university population and local authorities. They didn't appear to be fighting for social justice.

The romantic vision of young rebels fighting for their rights in Merida vanished quickly from my head after I discovered the protestors' lack of real purpose. Their endless 'game' with the police became not only boring but really annoying, because they caused roads to be closed, increased traffic congestion and kept forcing the university to suspend classes. Later I learned this was common in Venezuela, especially in Merida. Students and faculty were lucky if the university was in session for half a semester out of each year. Pay was regularly delayed, which caused faculty members to protest, and then students demonstrated in response to reclaim their right to education. It was a vicious circle.

The wonders and dangers of local food

While I was no longer enthralled with the student protests, I was still captivated by Merida and Venezuela. The delightful spring-like climate made the small city pleasant to reside in, and the tropical mountain scenery with its vibrant, colorful flora and terracotta-roofed homes never stopped being magical. I delved into the local culture and customs – as much as I could with my limited language skills.

You have never had juice until you've had fresh fruit juice in Venezuela. The options are endless. Papaya, mango, strawberry, raspberry, pineapple, guava, guanoabana, cantaloupe, watermelon, passion fruit and one of my favorites: three in one, a mix of orange, beet and carrot juices. Fresh juice in Venezuela is literally fresh, peeled fruit stuck in a blender with filtered water, pulp included. You can order it with or without added sugar. Heavenly!

After drinking fresh juices in Venezuela, I've never been able to purchase juice anywhere else, especially not if it's 'made from concentrate'. In the United States, you can only get juices like these at health food stores, or the now popular 'juice bars', and they cost a bundle. But in Venezuela, juice is cheaper than soft drinks or other refreshments, and it's all local and natural.

Venezuela's fresh, natural juices highlight yet another national contradiction. While people will drink the fruit blended into juice, they rarely will eat the fruit raw in its natural form. Fresh fruit, or fruit salad, is not served typically for breakfast, snack or dessert – you have to ask for it to be made, and you will get a strange look from the server. I remember I would have to practically beg in restaurants for them to serve me a plate of fresh fruit. Sometimes, waiters would say, 'No, we don't have any fruit', while the juice bar with its array of freshly cut tropical fruit was visible to all eyes.

With vegetables, it was even worse. Fresh salad was generally not a meal item, despite the massive abundance of green leafy veggies, ripe tomatoes, purple cabbage, all kinds of squashes, eggplants, assorted peppers and the largest avocados I'd ever seen. In fact, there was such an abundance of fresh vegetables and fruits in Merida, due to its many farms in the lowland mountain areas, that you could see them rotting on roadsides, on the backs of trucks and in markets everywhere. But apparently, they weren't for eating raw. The only vegetables served were boiled and mixed with mayonnaise or lots of butter, or cooked in soups and casseroles.

The staple foods in Venezuela do not include these desirable fruits and vegetables. Cornmeal patties called *arepas*, stuffed with overwhelming amounts of cheese, beef, seasoned chicken, or all of it together, are the classic Venezuelan food. Occasionally you can get avocado in an *arepa*, but I've never seen or heard of a 'salad arepa'. On the coast you can get fresh fish, but inland it's much more difficult and pricey. Local cheese is white and unpasteurized, and, while a bit tasty, somewhat bland and flavorless. Typical desserts are creamy, eggy and custardy, like the famous *Tres Leches*. I don't know if Tres Leches really has three kinds of milk in it, but it has a lot of creamy stuff and tons of sugar.

Merida did have one incredible food that I basically lived off during my time there: pizza. All pizza in Merida was baked in big, wood-burning ovens, completely fresh, and I don't know what their secret ingredient was, but everyone who has ever had that pizza agrees that it's the best.

As a vegetarian, dependent on others for nourishment and

without my own kitchen to prepare food, it wasn't easy at first to adapt, but I got used to my limited options and made do. Hey, a diet of delicious pizza and fresh tropical juices wasn't all that bad! Another staple of the Venezuelan diet is fried food, just like in the United States. I generally don't like fried foods. However, Merida's special *empañadas* and *pastelitos* filled with fresh white cheese and topped with *guasacaca* (avocado sauce) and *picante* (hot sauce) were addictive. I didn't realize the extent of the fried-food diet in Venezuela until my mother, a registered nurse, came to visit me during the last week of the language program. 'You see all those men limping around?' she asked me, referring to the men in their forties or fifties whom you would see around town limping or with an immobile arm or facial paralysis. 'Those are stroke victims,' my mother affirmed. 'Too much fried food.' Yikes, no more empañadas.

Venezuelan time

While I could experience the food and the gorgeous landscape, my broken Spanish didn't allow me to explore much more. Also, I had to adhere to a 'schedule' set up by the language school. 'Schedule' in Venezuela is a relative, ever-changing and permanently flexible concept. Just because the 'schedule' says a class will start at 9am, does not mean in reality that it will start at 9am. Most likely, it would start at 10 or 11, if it's even held.

The cultural difference over time was particularly difficult to adapt to. It took me many years to fully understand and accept what time means in Venezuela. I suffered bitterly with this issue in both my personal and professional life. Coming from the United States, and particularly from a major city on the east coast, time had always been of the essence. Time was money, time was precious, time was carefully planned, adhered to, taken advantage of and respected. If I was told to be there at 9am, I would be there by 8.45am, if not earlier. Before arriving in Venezuela, I had always considered myself a very punctual person.

Time in Venezuela, however, is ever-changing, flexible and taken lightly. Punctuality is not a particularly admirable characteristic, nor is it required. In fact, unpunctuality is expected, allowed and not considered any kind of offense. I slowly learned that Venezuelan unpunctuality was not generally due to disrespect or laziness. It was actually part of a much larger concept that goes beyond time and includes space. 'Plans', like 'schedules', in Venezuela are not set in stone. There is always room for change, because you never know what can happen. If you close the door to time, you limit your space, which in turn inhibits your personal growth. But if you leave that door open, then you allow yourself a wealth of opportunities and a world of adventures. This was one of the most important lessons I ever learned, which led me to some of the most incredible experiences of my life.

It's actually a very Tao-esque philosophy. Go with the flow, go as your heart directs. It's also incredibly impractical. But who says practical is better?

My first induction into this Tao-like concept of time was the language school's 'schedule', which, although it existed, was impossible to follow. The co-ordinator, a well-intentioned Venezuelan who had lived for many years in the United States, had created the schedule for a bunch of American students, and so it was in American code. But the American code did not jive with Venezuelan culture, and so even if we were supposed to have class at 9am, we never actually could, because all the pieces that had to fit into place to make that happen were acting on their own time and space, on their own code.

For example, even if you wanted to arrive by 9am and you left your house with plenty of time, maybe traffic was heavy because of student protests, or the bus broke down and you had to catch another one, and anyway, the buses don't operate on schedules, you just get on one when it goes by and so you never know when you'll arrive. Or maybe it rained and when it rained, everything temporarily shut down. Actually, in Merida, rain was the excuse for everything. 'It's raining' basically meant, all bets are off. With the rain, whatever little possibility that existed of plans or schedules being complied with completely disappeared. You see, the possibilities are endless. Anything could happen that could alter 'the schedule'. Time and space adapted to the ever-evolving reality.

The conflict of cultural codes meant that we rarely had class and basically ended up arranging our own agendas. I decided it was much more effective for me to stay in El Carrizal B, listening to the parrots cackling and reading the newspaper with a Spanish-English dictionary each morning in order to accumulate vocabulary. And in the evenings, forbidden from going out, I would watch television in Spanish and try to understand. Occasionally, we held class in whatever time and space we could devise, and we, or at least I, began to accept this new dimension.

My mother descends

Before I had left for Merida, my mother had decided she too wanted to come to get to know Venezuela and any roots we may have had there. She had bought her ticket and made arrangements well before I had learned about the Venezuelan code of space and time or really knew anything about where I was going to be and what it was like.

The hair-pulling, nail-biting stress began at the thought of her on the plane, landing at the Merida airport. I don't think anyone who loves their mother would wish that experience on her. I tried to prepare her mentally for it. 'Just close your eyes about 15 minutes before landing and don't open them until the plane has stopped completely on the ground.'

There was also the ever-possible issue of the plane not being able to land at the Merida airport because of cloud cover. In that case, the plane would go to a nearby airport in El Vigia and the airline would allegedly shuttle passengers through the dangerous, dark mountainous roads to Merida, which takes about two hours. Since I had not had that experience, I could only imagine the worst. I did my best to prep her on that possibility, praying to the gods and goddesses that it would not play out that way.

Then there was the issue of where my mother would stay. My host family's hospitality did not extend to my mother so I searched for a hotel. At that time, since Venezuela was not a major tourist destination and really had no tourist infrastructure, hotels generally doubled as brothels, unless, of course, you could afford the five-star hotels. There was not much in between except the *posadas* or youth hostels, which, while fine for me, were not where I imagined my mother staying.

I must have looked at every hotel in Merida, from zero to five stars, before finally settling on one in the most touristy area of town, Plaza Las Heroinas, that had two stars. It had no hot water and a bit of leakage from the bathroom into the room but it seemed safe, relatively clean and was the right price. Anyway, I did remember my mother taking me on a trip to France when I was 12, where we survived off baguettes, brie and liquid yogurt and stayed at least in one *pension* with stained, peeling ceilings, a sunken bed and shared bathrooms down the hall. So I thought she'd survive the crappy little Merida hotel.

On the day of her arrival, my worst nightmare came true as the clouds settled in early over the mountains and that was it, no more airplanes were getting in. She was going to El Vigia. I was a nervous wreck. I sat for hours out on the curb at the minuscule Merida airport, anxiously hoping that every approaching taxi sheltered my mother in the backseat. There were no cellphones then, so I couldn't call her to see what was going on and the airline personnel just kept telling me, 'Vamos a ver,' (We'll see), assuring me all the passengers would arrive before tomorrow. Great.

Finally, after several nail-biting hours, a taxi came whizzing into the terminal entrance and out came my mother, carrying a little tote bag containing all her belongings for the week. I was on the verge of tears, expecting the worst. But she was smiling and happy to arrive and then I realized, of course, that she was my mother, a survivor. And I'm my mother's daughter. Can't speak the language? So what! You'll figure it out, you make do, you survive, you move on.

My mother and I spent the week exploring Merida, walking around, eating pizza, drinking tropical juices and just taking it all in. She came and met my host family, and, while language remained a barrier, the delicious hot chocolate communicated much more than words could have.

After my mother left, I said goodbye to my host family, thanking them and the cackling parrots for their hospitality, and I moved into a *posada* in Plaza Las Heroinas to spend a last week in Venezuela.

The *posada* was run by an expat Swiss polyglot named Tom and his wife Raquel, a Venezuelan from Merida. They had a great little tourist operation going, including not just safe, clean homey rooms, but also actual tours. They offered tourism packages for day trips in the mountains, trekking, camping and even out to Los Llanos, the cowboy flatlands of Venezuela.

I decided it was time to see something beyond Merida, so I spent my last week on an adventure tour to Barinas, a flatlands state which borders the other side of the Andes, and home to Chávez's birthplace, Sabaneta. Although I didn't even know who he was then, it seems a strange coincidence now that, of any place I could have visited in the whole country, I chose his home area.

Led by Alan, a Venezuelan tour guide who spoke perfect English, I and a handful of other foreigners were driven through the mountains, then went by canoe on the rivers, alongside freshwater dolphins, alligators, piranha, hot pink flamingos, and more than 200 other species of birds and animals out there in the wild. We slept in hammocks over the water and got eaten alive by mosquitoes. All those bites were worth it to see a night sky unimaginably full of stars.

While the others ate an alligator we had passed by as roadkill (yes, in the Venezuelan plains, alligators are roadkill) and made omelets out of her eggs (gross!), I stuck with plain spaghetti. But despite my lack of culinary adventurousness, out there in the flatlands, under the wide open tropical sky, I sensed that a major adventure awaited me in Venezuela and that there was still so much to explore.

5

Venezuela: a love affair

Within months of returning to the US I was back in Venezuela. I went there for my college winter break, then for spring break, then again the summer after graduation in 1994. I had been accepted to law school at the University of New Mexico to pursue a joint Juris Doctor degree in law and a Master's in Latin American Studies. I decided I would spend the summer in Venezuela before embarking on an intense few years of study, though my heart had become further and further entrenched in a country that was feeling more like home each time I visited.

During my winter and spring visits, I had made new friends and discovered an eye-opening feeling of liberty and independence in the semi-tropical Andean paradise of Merida. The stereotypes and barriers that had fenced in my existence in the US disappeared in Venezuela, a place where curves on women were expected, not rejected or ridiculed, and personal interactions had few boundaries and seemed lighter and easier. People were warm, friendly and welcoming, and not just because I was a single, foreign woman from the US. This is just how Venezuelan culture is: joyful, affectionate and jubilant, like a giant, cozy bear hug.

On one of my visits back to Merida that year I ventured to the Caribbean coast with Alexander, an artisan friend I had become close to. Venezuela has pristine beaches all along its expansive coastline and, though most do not attract foreign tourists, they are certainly vacation destinations for Venezuelans. It's where they go for Semana Santa (Easter Week), Carnaval, Christmas, August, long weekends, short weekends – in fact, they will take any excuse possible to make a quick escape to the beach for a few hours in the sun and surf, drinking beers and listening to salsa, reggaeton or merengue music. I was soon to find out why. Of course, the trip to paradise was not without difficulty.

Alexander was a handsome young Andean craftsman who made a living by making and selling his leather bags and belts on the streets of Merida. He had honey-brown skin, long wavy brown hair tied in a ponytail, and a bright, wide smile. He lived in a tiny tin shack on a postcard plot of land about an hour's hike up into the mountains. The route there from the city was first by *por puesto* bus (makeshift vans stuffed with passengers that served as local transportation). After about a 40-minute ride through the winding mountain roads, with no side fences or barriers to prevent vehicles from driving off a cliff, we then had a trek further up the mountainside on a dirt path filled with rocks and vines. There was no electricity or hot water in Alexander's house, but there was a standpipe with allegedly clean running water that serviced the small artist community living on the hillside. There was also no bathroom, not even a port-a-potty to do your business, which definitely made me suspicious about the safety of the water supply.

Alexander would work in the daylight on his leather crafts and as the sun set he would make black beans in a tin pot over an open fire for dinner. Black coffee was made by boiling water over the flame and pouring it through a makeshift sieve holding the coffee grounds. Coffee was also a delicacy in Venezuela since it was grown and harvested locally. In contrast to chocolate, Venezuelan coffee is consumed almost exclusively by Venezuelans. I would argue that it's actually the best coffee in the world, a statement that will most definitely provoke responses from Colombians and Cubans. Like so many other things in Venezuela that were forgotten or abandoned in the oil boom, the thriving coffee industry of the 19th century dwindled to the point where it only produced for the domestic market. Pity for the rest of the world, but at least deliciously rich and strong coffee was still produced for Venezuelans and available everywhere in the country.

Alexander and I had decided to go to the beach in the coastal state of Falcon, home to Morrocoy National Park, an expansive 50-square-mile coastal wilderness full of mangroves and little islands with pristine, petite beaches. Tucacas was the least glamorous of Morrocoy's local tourist destinations, while

Chichiriviche was the most popular, with its dozens of little islands accessible only by small boats crewed by local guides and fishers. They take you out for the day and pick you up at dusk before the mosquitos settle in to feast on your blood and sometimes leave you with the gift of dengue or malaria.

We had planned to stay at a small, modest *posada*, paying around $15 a night. I had offered to treat Alexander, since he had no money anyway, and he would act as my guide and translator. My Spanish was not yet perfect and accents and dialects vary from region to region in Venezuela. Plus, we had a little thing going and he was pretty darned cute. It was about an eight-hour ride on the bus.

An encounter with the National Guard

It was spring of 1994 and Venezuela was still in a state of emergency with a national curfew imposed by the government and a continued suspension of all constitutional rights. By now a new president had been elected and conservative politician Rafael Caldera had won on a platform of reconciliation. But things had yet to change, and a forced military draft remained in effect, with Alexander just at the riskiest age, late teens to early twenties. We boarded the bus in Merida and paid the full fare to Tucacas. There were no other foreigners on the bus but me, but I blended in because of my coloring, dark hair and unpretentious look.

The ride was long, bumpy and very uncomfortable. For some inexplicable reason, buses in Venezuela are so cold that they make you feel like you're at the North Pole. The drivers crank up the air conditioning so high that the windows frost over from the inside. The extremely cheap subsidized gasoline probably contributes to this wasteful, hazardous practice that baffles and annoys Venezuelans as much as foreigners. Everyone gets sick after a bus ride in Venezuela because of the insane temperature spikes from the frost-bitten interior to the sweltering heat once the doors open and you step outside. Alexander slept as the bus bumped along and I tried to read a book. The lights were on inside the bus so there was no way I could sleep and the driver had badly dubbed B-movies blasting from a television set located just above his seat.

It was some time in the middle of the night when the bus stopped at the side of the road. The doors opened and the driver stepped off. There was commotion towards the front of the bus and passengers looked noticeably anxious, some quickly trying to look as though they were deep in sleep even as they peeked out of the frosty windows. I shook Alexander awake and asked him what was going on. '*Es la guardia*,' he said. Two uniformed National Guard soldiers had stepped on board the bus and were asking passengers for their national ID card, the *cédula*. I was a little nervous since I was way out of my comfort zone – this was the first time I had been on a back road in a bus full of strangers with a guy I barely knew at my side.

One of the soldiers approached our seat, looking suspiciously at Alexander, with his long hair and hippie look, and asked for our IDs. Alexander gave him his *cédula* and I showed my US passport, which the soldier took from my hand. He looked at our documents and up at us several times. Then he walked over to the other soldier and showed him our IDs, exchanging words we couldn't hear but that made us very worried. They signaled to us to stand up and get off the bus. Alexander obliged but I spoke up in my broken Spanish. Why did we have to get off the bus? Could I have my passport back? Where were we going? They said nothing and just pushed us along until we reached the door and ordered us to get off. The soldier followed us and told us to stand over on the side of the road. He handed our IDs to another military officer, probably his superior, and pointed at us. He then boarded the bus again to continue checking the documents of the remaining passengers. At that point I was freaking out.

I went up to the officer holding my passport and asked for it back. He looked at me and said they had to check my passport to make sure it wasn't fake. 'Fake?' I said, 'are you kidding? That's a US passport, I'm a US citizen and I want my passport back.' They had no right to take it from me, or so I thought. I had never been in a country before with a suspended rule of law and martial order in place. Actually, the military, under authorization from the government, could do whatever they wanted and I had no way of stopping them. Out there in the middle of nowhere I was completely powerless. My sense of injustice and American arrogance was likely only to make the situation worse, so I did what any woman would do under the circumstances and cried. I appealed to their macho side. I cried and sobbed and told him I was scared, I was just a tourist going to the beach with a friend, we had done nothing wrong. And that was when things took a turn for the worse.

They had decided Alexander was going to *la recluta*. He was the right age to be drafted, had no real job or family and he wasn't in school. The officer said they were taking him right then and there. That's when I really let go and started begging for them not to take Alexander. I knew no one else. How could they leave me all alone on this bus to some place I didn't know when I hardly spoke the language? Alexander was my guide, I appealed to the officer, I needed him. And just then, in the midst of my heartfelt appeal, just as I could see the officer bending and considering letting Alexander go, the bus drove off. 'Wait!' I screamed, 'what about us?' The bus sped off as fast as it could, leaving us in its dust cloud on the side of the road with the National Guard, who were still holding my passport and Alexander.

I put my head between my hands and sobbed. This time I was really crying, and this time it worked. Of course, all this time what they really wanted was money. I'd never lived in a culture where corruption is rampant at every level and bribery is the norm, so I didn't even pick up the blatant hints. Had I given them money when they first pulled us off that bus we would doubtless have been on our way to the beach, laughing the whole thing off. But I was clueless and Alexander said nothing, plus I really only had enough money for our trip. By the time I figured out that this was a shakedown, I already had the officer on my soft side and, on principle, there was no way I was giving them money to get my passport back. I can honestly say that, to this day, despite having since been in numerous situations where bribery was clearly in play, I have never paid off anyone for anything.

Finally they agreed to let Alexander go and they gave us back our IDs. We were relieved, but still stuck on the side of the road with nothing nearby. 'Now what?' I asked them, 'what are we supposed to do, how do we get out of here?'

'You have to wait for the next bus to come by,' the supervising officer said, and that was it – they left us standing there and walked away. I was grateful we were free and unharmed, and not a penny poorer. But I was furious that the whole thing had happened in the first place, and now we were stranded on the side of the road with not even a service station around for miles. So much lawlessness and injustice everywhere. It was hard to understand how a country could function this way. Corruption seemed embedded in the culture and everyone just pretty much accepted it as a way of life. We sat down on our bags and waited. Two hours later, another bus came by and we signaled for it stop. Thankfully it had empty seats and we were able to make it to Tucacas, a place I was happier to see than I could have ever imagined.

Artistic revolt – and falling in love

After that adventure with Alexander, I returned to New York, finishing my senior year at Sarah Lawrence College and pledging to return in the summer.

When I did go back that summer, as a fresh college graduate set to enter law school in the fall, the country was still in turmoil. By then, Hugo Chávez had been pardoned for his crimes and released from prison. In Merida his presence wasn't as strong, but he was already building a political movement nationwide that was to take him to the presidency within four years. Protests continued in Merida and the University of the Andes was still the centerpiece of the action.

I went back to the Posada Las Heroinas, owned by my friends Tom and Raquel, and lived and worked there during my extended stay. Just a few blocks away was the university's art school, a vibrant cultural center in a colonial-era building that shared space with the national government's local housing and development division. Walking by there one afternoon I saw a performance-art installation taking place involving lavish costumes and body paint. There were signs and placards protesting against the decision to evict the art school from the building and put the entire program at risk of closing. Students had taken over the building and refused to leave in a *toma* (literal translation: a take, an occupation).

At that time in Venezuela, local arts were neither a priority nor considered valuable, with many preferring US film, television and music over the country's own. There was no cultural ministry supported by the national government, just a small grants organization that catered to an elite, well-connected group of artists in Caracas. The government of Hugo Chávez eventually changed this profoundly, creating a Ministry of Culture with vast resources that supported Venezuelan artists in many fields and genres, rescuing Venezuelan traditional music and culture and incorporating it into the mainstream as an enriching, necessary part of society.

Chávez's government also created and funded book publishers, community libraries and book distributors, and launched a literacy program that was so effective that Venezuela was declared a territory free of illiteracy by UNESCO in 2005. His administration also provided resources to create national record labels that supported Venezuelan musicians, performance spaces for theatre groups, and awards for artists across the cultural spectrum.

Back in the mid-1990s, though, the scene for artists outside of the capital was bleak. In conservative Merida, performance art was a rarity and seen as a cultural aberration. So I was delightfully surprised to find an enclave of protest, activism and art just around the corner from my residence and I went by there daily, photographing the amazing and colorful artistic performances and talking to the protestors. They were a group of creative, committed young people who might not have had a completely clear vision of what they wanted to accomplish, but who felt there was an injustice happening and fought against it. I admired their courage to express themselves artistically and to protest creatively.

On several of my visits, one attractive, long-haired student held my attention. He was a sculptor, a visual artist and an artisan who made the most beautiful ceramics I had ever seen. Ruben was an artist in the purest sense, with a brilliantly creative mind and a provocative personality. His art was his identity and his only pursuit in life. Ruben didn't function in conventional parameters, he lived completely on his own terms, well beyond the box. He was definitely my kind of guy. We immediately hit it off, though he was wary of gringos and didn't want to be seen as a local taking advantage of a foreigner for monetary gain, which was a common occurrence in Merida. The locals that preyed on foreign visitors were known as the *caza-gringos* (gringo hunters). Usually they weren't ill-intentioned or violent, but just used the foreigners to get free meals, gifts and trips, providing company and guidance in return.

Initially, Ruben kept his distance from me on some days and then on others would spend hours talking to me about literature, politics and art. I would hang out with the other student protestors in the hopes of seeing him. Some days I would stay for hours and he wouldn't even show up. One day, after a particularly intense and passionate political discussion, he boldly kissed me. From that point on we were inseparable. When we weren't at the art school, he would take me to his parents' house where he still lived and I would accompany him as he made his sculptures and ceramics that had been commissioned by local galleries or collectors. His mother was also an artist and had a large, successful studio in their house. Ruben was her prodigy and his talent was known and respected nationwide. Like most incredibly talented artists, he was completely disorganized, unpunctual and unreliable. I still fell madly in love with him.

We spent the rest of that summer together and of course I didn't want to leave when it was time for me to head back to the States and law school. I told him I would stay but he convinced me to go back, citing several reasons, including his not wanting to interfere in my career and my future, and his fear of commitment. I left reluctantly, tearful and lonely. Ruben was the first man who had loved me for who I was and not what I looked like. He adored and cherished my mind and my body, despite my being overweight. In fact, his sculptures, made well before I met him, tended to feature women with curvy bodies. He admired the female body in all its different shapes and sizes. I credit him for helping me to overcome many of the insecurities and difficulties with my own body that had plagued me for most of my life. He even convinced me to work as a model at the art school, where the students would practice drawing my body. It was definitely a life-altering experience for me and I became much more secure in who I was and what I looked like. Of course, everything has a flip side, and this one eventually turned out to be devastating.

A New Mexican episode

I started law school at the University of New Mexico in Albuquerque that fall. I had moved to a city I had never been to where I knew nobody – not even one person. I had rented an apartment over the phone, a fully furnished studio in town and biking distance from the law school. I didn't have a car so I rode my bike everywhere. For some reason I had thought New Mexico's large Latino population would make it a more comforting place for me, reminding me of Venezuela and being in a community that had become a familiar, safe space. But Albuquerque was no Merida, and the culture in the law school was cold, competitive and far from accepting. My rebellious nature was not an asset at that law school, which kept to the Socratic method of hierarchy and competition, making students feel vulnerable and embarrassed if unprepared. I didn't really care about that, since I was prepared and not afraid to speak out, but I felt suffocated by the rigid learning method, which was unwaveringly insipid and full of drudgery.

When I wasn't writing love letters to Ruben, I wrote opinion articles for the local newspaper, *The Daily Lobo.* My columns focused on issues of racism, civil rights, comparable political systems and constitutions, and even on Cuba, debating the pros and cons of free healthcare and education under a socialist government. I received dozens of letters from readers each week, mainly hate mail. Email was a limited resource back then and I only had an internal law school inbox, but it quickly filled with hate-ridden messages from fellow students telling me to leave the law school and give my space to a more appreciative student. Some even implored me to leave the US entirely. One day coming out of class I found my bicycle wheels filled with nails and both tires flat. I had to walk a few miles home that day, but I didn't stop writing. I've never been one to fold in the face of intimidation.

It was a fairly hostile environment in my classes. My professors didn't appreciate my critical view of the way they taught the law and my questioning of legal education methodology, which I argued was responsible for turning the practice of law in our country into a money-making machine run by detached and insensitive lawyers, instead of advocates for the people in the interests of justice. One professor took me aside about a month into classes and politely suggested I consider transferring to a different law school. CUNY Law School in New York would be better for you, he said. It has a different methodology, focused more on the interests of people and justice. He thought it would be a better fit and that I would thrive there and, after checking out the school, I decided he was right. But that didn't happen until much later. New York was not on my radar for the immediate future. I heeded the call from my classmates to leave the US, not because they wanted me to but because I decided it was what I wanted and needed. I put in for a transfer to CUNY Law School, where I had been accepted, and then deferred for a year. I was going back to Venezuela, back to Ruben. Weeks after I completed my semester and took my final exams at UNM Law School I received a call from the Dean's Office. I had won the Merit Award for receiving the highest grade in Contracts. Of all subjects, I had excelled at the one most emblematic of the capitalist system. The irony was biting.

Crushed by love

My return to Venezuela was not as welcoming as I had expected. Ruben met me in Caracas, where we stayed a few days with some friends of his, but was aloof and strange, no longer the same affectionate man I had known. The distance had wedged between us and he had drifted. He sent me back to Merida on the bus and told me he was staying for a few more days in Caracas to meet with gallery owners about his art. I would soon come to see a different reality than the one I had experienced with him months earlier, and my entire world was to be turned upside down. I had thought I was in a long-term, deep relationship with a man I might marry and have children with. But, just as I was learning that Venezuelan culture was unreliable and unpredictable, those tenets also seemed to apply to Ruben.

Ruben had been living in a Buddhist Center that had recently opened in Merida, run by an Englishman. I had hoped we would move in together somewhere but he convinced me that he was better off there for the time being since he was staying there rent-free and was without a steady income. I felt like something strange was going on but I convinced myself that I should shrug it off and just enjoy the time I had with Ruben.

One day, however, the Englishman from Ruben's Buddhist Center called me and asked if we could grab a coffee together. Sure, I responded, though it seemed odd for him to invite me out for any reason. Hours later, we met in a local café and he asked me straight out what my relationship to Ruben was. We're in love, I responded. We plan to marry and have kids someday. His jaw dropped and he went pale white. He asked me how long Ruben and I had been together. About a year and a half, I told him – why? He took a deep breath and then shattered my world into tiny little jagged pieces. He told me he had been in a serious, committed relationship with Ruben for two years and that they lived together.

What? I couldn't believe what he was telling me; I thought he must be delusional. I laughed. Two years? That would mean they were together before I even met Ruben. How could that be possible? Then everything fell into place. We went through weekend by weekend and figured out what excuses Ruben had made to each of us for why he couldn't be with us that day or that night. Of course that was why Ruben couldn't stay with me or commit to deepening our relationship any further. He was bisexual and in a committed gay relationship with a man. That sank in, hard. I had been duped.

We decided to call Ruben, who we knew was at his parents' house working in the studio, and tell him we needed to talk with him together. I thought Ruben would surely clear everything up and tell the Englishman that he had fallen in love with me and would explain that his relationship with him wasn't serious. When Ruben came to the phone I spoke to him first and told him what I had just found out. It wasn't true, was it? He went silent and after a few moments said he would come and meet us, then he hung up. We waited for two hours and he didn't show up. The Englishman decided to go back home and wait for Ruben. He said he would call me as soon as he got there so we could all talk about what had happened. He and I saw things more logically but, as for Ruben, we had discovered his big dark secret and he couldn't face us. I called his parents' house again but he had left. His mother told me he had gone to visit his best friend Julian in San Cristóbal, a city close to the border with Colombia about six hours from Merida.

Not wanting to disappoint either of us and not wanting to face up to the implications of his own deception, he had made a run for it. Any normal person would have just sobbed their heart out and tried their best to move on, but I wasn't a normal person. I couldn't accept the deception and needed an explanation. I couldn't just let it go. I knew Ruben's whole family and most of his friends, and they all knew me as his girlfriend. The whole thing seemed crazy and I needed to see him face to face to figure out what was going on. I called his older sister and asked her for Julian's contact information in San Cristóbal. I told her that I was supposed to meet Ruben there and I was taking a later bus. She had his phone number, but not his address. All she knew was that Julian was a doctor and lived in an apartment building down the hill from a plaza somewhere in the city. It was not much to go on and I had never been to San Cristóbal, but all I could think about was getting there.

To say I am persistent is an understatement. My persistence and determination have always been both my biggest assets and my gravest defects. I can be persistent to a fault, and I know that it can seem abrasive, overbearing and extremely annoying. Whatever I decide to do, I pursue it until it gets done, no matter how difficult it can be. I don't give up, I don't get intimidated and I don't take no for an answer. I went to the bus station and got on a bus to San Cristóbal the first thing in the morning with nothing more than myself, my passport and wallet, and a destination: Julian's house, an apartment down the hill from a plaza in the city.

San Cristóbal is a city of about 300,000 people and a bustling commercial hub between Colombia and Venezuela. It was bigger than Merida and I knew no one there. When the bus arrived at the terminal I went looking for a map of the city so I could identify all the plazas and start walking through them one by one. I hailed a taxi and asked the driver to take me to the first plaza. When we got there I looked for apartment buildings and asked the cabby to drop me near one. 'What's the address?' he asked me. I didn't have one, I said: 'I'm looking for an apartment building that's down a hill from a plaza, but I don't know which one. A doctor lives there – Julian.' I asked if he knew him. I knew it was a long shot but figured I had nothing to lose. No, he didn't know the doctor but he did know which plazas had hills and apartment buildings at the bottom. We narrowed it down to two plazas and started at the first one.

The cab driver didn't want to leave me on my own, so he offered to wait as I went door to door in the buildings, asking if Julian the doctor lived there or if anyone had heard of him and knew where he lived. After knocking on a few dozen doors and getting nowhere, I was ready to give up. It had been three hours and we had covered both plazas and still hadn't found the house. Finally I decided to try one more small building off a corner of the plaza. There were only about a dozen apartments in the building and some had ground-floor entrances. I knocked on a few doors but no one answered. I sat down on the front steps of the building, held my head in my hands and cried. What the hell was I even doing? Was I completely nuts? I had come there not even knowing where to find Ruben and, in any case, he had gone there to run away from me. As I was just about to get up and go back to the cab and tell the driver to take me to the terminal where I could catch a bus back to Merida, the front door of the building opened and a brown-haired woman came out looking startled at my presence on her walkway. 'Can I help you with something?' she asked.

'I'm sorry,' I said, 'I'm trying to find Julian's house, he's a doctor. Do you know him, by any chance?' I held my breath, feeling defeated. She looked at me, taking in my accent and noting I was a foreigner and literally said, 'there's a doctor named Julian who lives in 2B, but I don't think he's home now.'

I couldn't believe it. I thanked her and told her I would wait there for him. She hesitated, then shrugged and walked away. I ran over to the cab and told the driver I was staying, I had found the doctor's house. I paid him his fare and thanked him for all his generous assistance, and waved him off as he tried insisting on staying and keeping me company. I went back to the front steps of the building, sat down and waited. It was about two o'clock in the afternoon.

I must have sat there for about three and half hours before I finally saw Ruben coming. At first he didn't see me sitting there as he was striding along, laughing and talking to a man in glasses whom I assumed was Julian. As they approached it was Julian who saw me first and, though we had never met before, our eyes locked and he said, 'you must be Eva!' He came over and greeted me with a big hug and kiss on the cheek. When I looked at Ruben I saw he was in shock. The last thing he had expected to find there in his getaway pad was me, yet there I was. 'What are you doing here?' he tried to ask in a normal voice. 'I came to find you,' I said. 'We really need to talk.'

Julian waved us inside the building, saying how wonderful it would be for us all to have dinner together and get to know each other. His jovial attitude gave me a glimpse of hope that maybe I had been right, that Ruben really did love me and the thing with the Englishman was just some sort of fling.

We sat down in the living room and Julian offered us drinks while we chatted lightly, though the heavy burden of Ruben's deception hung over us. When Julian's wife came home they went to make dinner in the kitchen, leaving Ruben and me alone for the first time.

'Is it true?' I asked him.

'Yes, it's true,' he said. He tried to explain how he had fallen in love with me and was confused and unsure about what he wanted to do. He really did love me, but he also loved the Englishman and felt more comfortable with him. 'Have you always been gay?' I asked him, knowing he had had a long-term girlfriend before me whom he had almost married, but had left her just before the wedding (that should have given it away, I suppose). He said he was bisexual and loved both women and men. After dinner we continued our conversation for hours. He chose the Englishman instead of me. I cried the whole night.

That experience with Ruben – my first true love and a love that I have never again experienced – became symbolic of my entire relationship with Venezuela. It was passionate, profound and unexpected but also unreliable, disappointing and sadly deceptive. But it was very raw and real, and it made me hesitant to fully trust anyone again.

Singing in a band

Rejected by Ruben, I went back to my childhood dream and began singing in a local band with Venezuelan musicians. A few nights a week I would sing and play my guitar at a local bar that by night transformed into a roaring gay club where local married men and well-known politicians would convene to live out their fantasies. It helped me to better understand Ruben and Venezuelan culture. The religious conservatism and homophobia were so repressive that men had to live double lives in the dark of night. Because they couldn't reveal their sexual preferences and secret lifestyles to their friends and family, and were forced to remain closeted and live a lie, many of them died of AIDS-related diseases due to unsafe practices with multiple partners in dark corners. I was able to help support one artist friend to come out of the closet and celebrate his true self in spite of his family's resistance, and, even though he contracted HIV, he was able to get the medication needed to prolong his life. Another close friend, Fabio, sadly died of AIDS a few years later.

Music became my passion and I was relieved to channel the energy and intensity I had put into Ruben and our relationship into something else. Our band grew more popular and was something of a novelty with me as the lead singer, a foreign woman in a small town performing original Latin jazz-rock music in both Spanish and English. We called ourselves *Color de Hormiga* (color of ants), which in Venezuela was a very politically charged phrase meaning things are heating up. The times were still very turbulent and state repression was rampant. The National Guard frequently showed up at our gigs and would shut them down, dispersing the audience and taking a few of the young men to the *recluta*. We might have provoked them just a bit with our flyers and posters placed around town advertising our performances. On some of them I recklessly used excerpts from *The Anarchist Cookbook* as a way to draw in the crowds. I guess the National Guard thought our 'How to Make a Pen Bomb' flyers were serious attempts to promote an underground anarchist insurrection against the state. Looking back now, it probably wasn't the best idea to associate our band and music with violent anarchism, but the tactic certainly helped to draw in huge audiences.

By that time, Hugo Chávez's movement was growing nationwide and building up support for his presidential bid in 1998. In Merida, in rebellious student circles, there was a healthy suspicion and distrust of Chávez because of his military background. No one wanted another dictatorship in the country and having a military officer as president was seen as a sign of regression, not progress. I came to know numerous people in Merida who had trained with the leftist Colombian guerrillas, the Armed Revolutionary Forces of Colombia (FARC) and the National Liberation Army (ELN), as well as diehard members of the Venezuelan Communist Party. At that time they were still planning for possible armed revolution in the country. The economy was bottoming out, the middle class was disappearing and party politics had completely run amok. Only those with cards identifying them as members of the political party in office, a *carnet*, could get jobs and services from the state. Corruption had penetrated every sector of Venezuelan society and the country had become a completely lawless state.

Police, National Guard, government officials and bureaucrats had all made a habit of shaking down anyone and everyone they could. It was so bad that the police or National Guard, who were still prominently out in the streets, could stop anyone at any time and shake them down for a bribe, with absolutely no cause. And either you had to pay or risk being imprisoned on false charges. I had never experienced life in a state system so corrupted and broken. There was no trust or confidence in the government or any authorities, which meant laws were rarely enforced, were widely disrespected and basic tenets of order and civility were undermined.

When you have a government in power that openly violates and disregards the law, or degrades and belittles judicial and law enforcement institutions, much as Donald Trump has recently done in the US, then the system erodes and succumbs to chaos. Nothing and no one can be relied upon. No one is accountable or responsible. Dysfunction becomes the new norm. In Venezuela, it was a way of life.

Eventually I knew I would have to leave Venezuela and return to the US and my responsibilities and obligations as a member of that society. I had deferred my student loans from college and it was time to pay up, and law school was waiting for me to return and complete my degree. I had taken a lengthy leave of absence after feeling compelled to spend more time in Venezuela. But I knew my days abroad were numbered and soon I'd have to go back home, get a job with a salary in US dollars and pay my debts.

Just as Venezuela was gearing up for the 1998 presidential elections, with Hugo Chávez as a candidate, I decided I had had enough of the disorder, disarray and lawlessness in the country. It seemed as though the vibrant social-justice movements in other Latin American nations had gained no purchase in Venezuela. One of the leading candidates in the presidential race was a former Miss Universe, Irene Saenz, and she was polling high. She already held office as the mayor of the wealthiest enclave in Caracas, Chacao, and it didn't seem too much of a reach for a beauty queen to become president in a nation that treated its beauty pageant as the most important annual event. I was also fed up with the political apathy and the obsession with Hollywood culture I saw in Merida, and I had begun to feel asphyxiated in such a small city. Did I forget to mention that I was also having an affair with the married guitarist in my band and things got a bit scandalous? Yes, there was that too. I felt like I was living out a *telenovela* (Latin American soap opera) and I was ready to leave it all behind.

6

Prelude to a coup

After nearly four years of living in Merida I was fed up with small-town living where everyone knows your business. I had had high hopes during my first years in Venezuela of being engaged in vibrant social-justice organizations and writing books about revolution in Latin America. Eventually, though, I realized there wasn't much to write about since apathy and overall lack of interest in and distrust of politics were so widespread. Ironically, less than a decade later things would change so profoundly that I would end up writing more than a handful of books on that very same topic.

I wasn't able to find the right fit for myself in Merida and realized I was yet again an anomaly, a misfit and an outsider, so I left for the US, but I remained deeply attached to Venezuela and its people.

I was especially attached to my guitarist, Gustavo. About six months after my return to New York he wrote to me asking if he could come to visit. He had separated from his wife, he told me. I got him a ticket and a visa and he arrived, guitar in hand and ready to take on the Big Apple. But, as many visitors to our wonderfully complex city soon learn after landing here, it's a tough town to make it in. We moved into a one-bedroom railroad apartment above a hair salon and a cockroach-infested Chinese take-out in Brooklyn that was double the space of the tiny studio I had been renting on the Upper East Side in Manhattan. I was paying all our expenses, though it was not luxurious by any standards. The kitchen cabinets were half-unhinged, the old wood floor creaked liked a haunted house, but the vibrant street scene out front gave us a quick escape from being cooped up inside and the area was flush with parks and playgrounds nearby. Gustavo had brought his two-year-old son with him from Venezuela to start a new life in America, though I wasn't fully convinced of my role in it all. I realized after a while that I wasn't exactly ready to alter my lifestyle at age 26 to become a step-parent to a toddler. Love and passion can be blinding, and I guess I hadn't fully thought it through.

By then Hugo Chávez had won the election in Venezuela and become president, breaking with a 40-year tradition of two political parties taking it in turns to hold power. Chávez had run on an anti-corruption populist platform, promising a social revolution that would regain Venezuela's sovereignty and control over its massive oil industry and redistribute the profits from oil to decrease poverty and misery. He was able to garner over 56 per cent of the vote as a first-time candidate running on a new political party platform. His failed rebellion against former president Carlos Andrés Pérez in 1992 had made him wildly popular amongst the nation's lower classes, which had come to see the soldier as a strong leader, unafraid to speak truth to power.

When he was elected, Chávez hadn't yet spoken of socialism as a path forward for Venezuela. Rather, he advocated the idea of a 'third way', as proposed by Britain's Tony Blair – an unlikely ideological model for a Latin American leftist leader. Not capitalism, not socialism, but something in between. He did promise revolution, but a Bolivarian revolution based on the ideals of Venezuela's founding father Simón Bolívar: sovereignty, independence and equality. Chávez was a patriot, a nationalist and an advocate for the underclass. He came from poverty and embodied the majority of Venezuelans who had become marginalized and felt betrayed by the corrupt political class that rotated governmental power, treating the country as though it were a private enterprise. He initially seemed moderate and flexible, far from the radical leftist he became years later. Venezuela's oil industry, though it had been nationalized decades earlier, was on the verge of being privatized as Chávez won the presidency in 1998. He immediately rolled back those plans and threatened to overhaul executive management and entrenched bureaucracy within the state-owned oil company, Petróleos de Venezuela, SA (PDVSA).

As he was settling in to his new role as head of state, Chávez retained close advisors who represented reformist visions of the country, yet held strong ties to the elite political class. Those advisors would soon betray his trust and attempt to undermine and obstruct his presidency as it moved further to the left. But before the threats from within grew against him, Chávez embarked on his most ambitious and popular campaign promise: the writing of a new constitution. He needed a broad coalition to form the constitutional assembly that would draft the nation's new Magna Carta and put it to a popular vote in a national referendum for approval.

Prominent roles in the constitutional process were given to Chávez's closest advisor, Luis Miquilena, who became president of the constitutional assembly, and Chávez's wife, Marisabel Rodriguez. Nepotism was common in Venezuela and not prohibited by law. The rest of the 131 members of the assembly included loyal members of his Bolivarian Fifth Republic movement, including Nicolas Maduro, and a coalition of politicians from leftist-leaning parties. Five seats were reserved for indigenous leaders, who had traditionally been excluded from the political process in Venezuela. The drafting of the new constitution was historically participatory with input from communities nationwide through local meetings and forums run by members of the designated assembly who would then incorporate comments and feedback into the document. After a year-long process to create and elect the constitutional assembly and then to draft and revise the final document based on citizen input, the new constitution was overwhelmingly approved by over 80 per cent of the vote in a national referendum that took place in December 1999.

A landmark constitution

I had regular contact with friends in Venezuela, and also through Gustavo, who was required to return every six months with his son for his ex-wife's visitation rights. We got copies of the draft constitution and followed the entire process with great interest. The new constitution was a masterpiece of human rights and participatory democracy, with 350 articles that detailed the inclusion and protection of all classes, genders, races, ethnicities and individual citizens. It even had an entire chapter dedicated to the protection and defense of indigenous people's rights, which included language, cultural and land rights.

Venezuela's constitution was now leagues ahead of the US and other Western democracies in its participatory, inclusionary and egalitarian vision. But would the country be able to transform sufficiently from its corrupt, dysfunctional system and turn such an ambitious vision into reality? I found the process of creating this new constitution fascinating and inspiring. Not only did I delve further into Venezuelan politics and the rise of Chávez's Bolivarian revolution, but I also decided to finally complete my own legal education. It was hard to believe that the apathetic, depressed and disengaged country I had left just two years earlier was now becoming one of the most vibrant, pro-active, progressive places on Earth.

Venezuela held general elections in July of 2000 under the newly ratified constitution, which extended the presidential term to six years, and Chávez won easily, with nearly 60 per cent of the vote against his former (and later) ally, Francisco Arias Cárdenas. His party also won a significant majority in the new legislative body, the National Assembly, with 91 seats. The next-biggest party in parliament was the traditional Acción Democrática, with a mere 33 seats. With a secure mandate and a new, publicly supported outline for his transformative government, Chávez set to work to implement the rights and guarantees articulated in the constitution, which also changed the name of the country to the Bolivarian Republic of Venezuela in recognition of Simón Bolívar's importance to the newly minted Fifth Republic movement. In addition to the vast array of human rights guaranteed in the constitution, state control of hydrocarbons and other natural resources and the redistribution of profits from them so as to reduce poverty were also now the law of the land, to the dismay of the traditional elite.

After his new cabinet was installed and the other four branches of government filled their seats (the new constitution created five branches of government instead of the traditional three: Executive, Legislative, Judicial, Electoral and Citizen Power), Chávez requested that the National Assembly grant him executive powers under the Enabling Act, which would allow him to surpass parliament to decree laws. Even though his party had a majority in the legislature, he wanted to avoid wasting time on lengthy debates and bureaucratic obstacles that could delay implementation of the new constitutional mandate. That raised eyebrows, since it meant bypassing the basic democratic process and arguably signaled increasingly authoritarian tendencies. His popularity had not waned, however, and he was given the mandate to draft a package of controversial laws that would upset the political order in Venezuela so much that it led to his detractors attempting to overthrow him only months later through a coup d'état. But first, as Chávez was pushing through his package of 49 laws, including the controversial Land and Agrarian Development Law and a Hydrocarbons reform that impacted the wealthiest interests in the country, the world was rocked by the horrific terrorist attacks on September 11, 2001, in New York and Washington DC.

The new me

Gustavo and I, along with five-year-old Marcelo, were still in Fort Greene, Brooklyn. I had found a much better-paying job as a senior paralegal in an immigration firm in Manhattan, and was pursuing freelance work with other attorneys. This had enabled us to move into a larger apartment, a beautiful duplex in a turn-of-the-century row house off the still un-gentrified Myrtle Avenue. As things were transforming in Venezuela, I also went through a personal transformation. Tired of being overweight for my entire lifetime, I decided to focus on losing all my extra baggage. I hadn't dieted since I was forced to as a child and had come to accept being overweight, though I had always hated my body and had never felt comfortable with how I looked. It's hard to say what triggered the switch in me that turned all my persistence and determination on to myself, but perhaps it was the challenge ahead of law school, which I was starting again that summer of 2001, and I went full force. I followed a diet, increased my exercise, and lost 30 pounds that summer and another 20 pounds that fall. I had my hair cut short in a pixie cut and felt liberated and fantastic. I was running over seven miles a day from Fort Greene up to and around Prospect Park and on weekends doubled my mileage. I could wear clothes and sizes I had never thought were possible for me in the normal range. I had finally gotten myself to a point where I felt good not just about who I was, but also what I looked like. After a lifetime of suffering with my weight and hating my body, it was finally over. Unfortunately, Gustavo didn't see things the way I did.

He didn't like my going back to law school and focusing on politics, and he was suspicious of my hard-won new body and self-confidence. He became resentful and jealous that I was no longer solely focused on him, his music and his needs. He accused me of losing weight to attract other men, despite my assurances to the contrary. I had done it for me, but he took it as an affront to him and our relationship. His machismo began to show through his generally passive demeanor. It disappointed and shocked me that he couldn't celebrate my empowerment, and instead viewed it as a threat to his masculinity and power. The same injustice, mistreatment and inequality I had seen my mother experience when I was a child was now front and center in my life, on the most personal level. I should have seen the signs then that this relationship, doomed and cursed from the beginning, had no future, but we got wrapped up in and distracted by the events unraveling around us.

New York and 9/11

By mid-August I had quit my job at the law firm in order to focus on law school, which was starting a week later. The firm I was working at was located in the Financial Center of Manhattan on Exchange Street, about two blocks from the World Trade Center. I would ride my bike from Fort Greene over the Brooklyn Bridge and up past the Twin Towers every morning slightly before 9am to go to work. Had I not quit that job, on the fateful day I would have been right below the Towers as the first plane hit. I still think about that, take a long, deep breath of relief and count my blessings. Instead, that morning I had dropped Gustavo's son off at his charter school in Bed-Sty and was in my old car driving to the law school out in Flushing, Queens. I had the radio on, tuned to WBAI, a local progressive station.

When I heard the announcers say a plane had just crashed into one of the Twin Towers it sounded like a bad joke. They were saying it with such disbelief and shock that it didn't seem real, almost as though their shrieks were laughter. At that moment, most reporters thought the plane that had hit the towers was a small aircraft, not a commercial jetliner. I began switching the stations on the tuner to see if others were reporting the incident, which of course they were, on every channel. Live on the radio I heard them screaming with horror as the second plane hit the south tower and I abruptly pulled the car off the road and came to a stop. I stepped out and turned around to see off in the distance the Lower Manhattan skyline in flames, the two towers burning and swelling with fire as a steady stream of dark grey-black smoke billowed out the side. My immediate thought was that this was no accident. One plane maybe, but two?

None of us want to live through that horror again, but we shall never forget that day. Those of us in New York City not only witnessed the burning and destruction of the World Financial Center and the atrocious images of people jumping to their death, but also lived, smelled and breathed the pungent odor of death for more than a year as the remnants simmered at Ground Zero. I felt the chickens had come home to roost and that our country would never be the same again. Decades of interventionist and aggressive foreign policy had finally felt its deadly consequence at home. I feared for the lives of my family and our future, and fully expected rioting and looting to overtake our city. Thankfully, New Yorkers showed their strength, unity and solidarity and the city came together as never before to support, defend, protect and rebuild our identity and sense of security. But still, every day ashes and debris would float in the air, landing in the streets where we walked and lived, as a reminder of the death on our doorstep and the imminent threat facing us all.

That day I got back in my car and continued on to the law school in Queens, arriving just as the towers came crashing down. Students and faculty were gathered watching the distant image live in horror, sobbing in despair, while broadcasters on television tearfully narrated the terror before our eyes with shaky, wavering voices. My mind raced with images of what might come in the following hours – a state of emergency, suspension of rights, curfews, more attacks, looting, massive uncertainty and general disruption – all things I had already lived through in Venezuela. I ran back out to my car and drove as fast as I could back to my stepson's school and rang the bell for them to let me in. I was the first parent to arrive and the school's director looked shocked when I told him I was there to pick up my stepson and take him home to safety. 'We haven't been notified by the mayor's office of any early closures,' he said, questioning my hasty decision. 'You will be,' I responded, 'but in the meantime I'm taking my child to safety.' Just as I was buckling my stepson into his car seat the radio was broadcasting Mayor Rudy Giuliani announcing the immediate closure of all schools, universities and educational institutions, and the shutdown of all public transportation and bridges in and out of Manhattan. We were on lockdown.

For days we watched the images of the planes hitting the towers and we could see the stream of billowing black smoke from our kitchen window in Brooklyn. There were no additional direct attacks after that day, but I knew things would get bad in the country and abroad, as they rapidly did. President George W Bush quickly rushed the Patriot Act through Congress just weeks after the attacks and an authorization for a blanket war on terror was given with just one dissenting vote, that of Congresswoman Barbara Lee. When the bombings began against Afghanistan a month later, we were still digging bodies out of the rubble in New York City, trying to breathe again. At law school I began to focus more on human rights and international law. It was the dawn of a global war at home and abroad and basic rules and rights of democracy were hastily being brushed aside in the name of national security. I told my contracts professor I couldn't see the point any longer of sitting through a class on the market economy when precisely that concept was the driving force behind the atrocities we were living through. He understood my perspective and generously gave me the choice to come to class or not, though he counseled me to attend and contribute my opinion instead of silencing myself into retreat.

'No longer the only devil'

Meanwhile, in Venezuela, things were heating up. Chávez was already an outspoken critic of US foreign policy and its interventionist role throughout history in Latin America. He had initially tried to develop a respectful bilateral relationship with President Bill Clinton in early 1999, even obtaining a meeting at the White House during his first international tour after winning the 1998 presidential election. But, after refusing orders by the US State Department to cancel his visit to Cuba to meet with Fidel Castro, Chávez was received 'through a back door' at the White House, with no formal reception or bells and whistles. He knew from that point on that if he didn't play ball and bow down to US power, he would become its enemy.

At this point Chávez felt invincible, that he had a strong mandate from the people of Venezuela to regain his nation's independence and sovereignty and to revamp its political and economic system. As he was beginning his revolution inside Venezuela, he also began to make his voice heard internationally. During September 2000, Venezuela was host to a historic summit of OPEC in its role as rotating chair of the oil-producing nations' organization. It was the first time in 25 years that heads of state and high-level representatives from OPEC nations had met, and oil prices had dropped to an all-time low. Chávez's leadership in the organization strengthened and united OPEC, providing it with a new purpose and force to regain control of oil production and pricing worldwide. His defiance towards the US resonated with the Arab leaders who had been subjected to US humiliation and aggression. In Chávez they saw an ally who envisioned a great alliance that could alter the balance of global power and make OPEC a powerful force in world affairs. Chávez later embarked on a tour of OPEC nations, and was the first head of state to officially visit Saddam Hussein in Iraq since the Iraq war in 1991. Clearly that rattled desks back in Washington.

In the spring of 2001, after oil prices had tripled and Chávez was building momentum for changes at home that were already causing ripples amongst the elite, he had his first in-person encounter with the new president of the United States, George W Bush.

During Clinton's final year in office, Washington had maintained a 'wait and see' policy in relation to Chávez and Venezuela. No one thought he would really follow through on his rhetoric and actually implement real change in the country. Chávez hadn't yet harmed or threatened US interests, despite his empowering OPEC, driving oil prices up and meeting with Saddam Hussein and Fidel Castro. It was inconceivable to traditional State Department and intelligence-community bureaucrats that Venezuela could change course from being a relatively stable, élite-controlled democracy that was favorable to US interests. They believed Chávez was more bark than bite, so they waited and watched.

When Chávez openly challenged Bush at the Summit of Americas meeting in Quebec City that April of 2001, rejecting Bush's plan to expand the Free Trade of the Americas Agreement throughout the entire region, his defiance was duly noted in Washington. Chávez later told me how Fidel Castro had called him after that meeting and said how happy he was to 'no longer be the only devil' at international summits. In response to Chávez's defiance, the US government began ratcheting up financing for Venezuelan political parties and NGOs that were building opposition to Chávez's policies. In fact, as evidenced in the US government documents I obtained under the freedom-of-information legislation, funding for anti-government groups in Venezuela doubled in 2001 and US political consultants began working closely with opposition politicians to build an anti-Chávez coalition inside the country. But it wasn't until Chávez forcefully criticized the US bombing of Afghanistan that October, referring to it as 'fighting terror with terror', that the 'wait and see' policy became 'regime change'.

I was back in Merida that December for the Christmas holidays, accompanying Gustavo and his family. Chávez had barely settled in to his role as president and the political turmoil had begun again in the country. Television programming had become increasingly critical of Chávez and there was suspicion amongst his followers that the media were taking sides against him. They seemed to be uniting behind the anti-Chávez coalition that was building. Strikes were popping up throughout the country, causing disturbances in the workforce and educational institutions – not that this had ever been an uncommon occurrence in Venezuela.

The media dominated public opinion and everyone seemed to take note of their powerful role in the growing movement against Chávez. Curiously, it wasn't just regular programming on the country's main broadcast television stations that was blatantly anti-Chávez. The channels were also running well-prepared commercials against Chávez and his policies, similar to campaign propaganda, except there was no campaign in progress. Most of the opposition was to the implementation of the Land Reform law, which proposed a reorganization of the country's vast fertile lands that were not being used for production, but were owned by wealthy landowners, and to the Hydrocarbons Law, which planned a redistribution of oil-industry profits to reduce poverty, increase social services and rebuild infrastructure.

With the Hydrocarbons Law came the reorganization of the state-owned oil company, which had been run like a private corporation, with an elite executive board syphoning off lucrative commissions and benefits. The resistance internally to Chávez's reforms began to grow and several high-ranking military officers joined forces with the opposition coalition – which now included the chamber of commerce and the leading union federation – to demand that the President either resign or cease attempts to restructure the establishment. Behind the scenes, the US Embassy, Defense Intelligence Agency and the CIA were quietly working with the anti-Chávez forces to push towards a coup. Chávez was treading on the wrong toes and would soon pay the price for his defiance.

7

From coup to revolution

On 11 April 2002 we received a frantic call from Merida. I answered the phone in our Brooklyn apartment and heard Gustavo's mother yelling on the other end, 'It's a coup, they've taken him: he's gone!' I quickly turned on the television and flipped through the channels but saw nothing about a coup d'état in Venezuela.

'What happened?' I asked her, though I wasn't too surprised since we all knew a coup was in the works. The question was whether or not the opposition would actually go through with it and what would happen if they did.

'He's gone, they've taken him away! There are protests everywhere. Eva, what are we going to do? They've taken Chávez!'

It was impossible to calm her down so I passed the phone to Gustavo and kept changing the channels on the television. Finally I saw a ticker tape at the bottom of the screen on CNN that read: 'Venezuelan President Hugo Chávez resigned after ordering shots fired on peaceful protestors, dozens killed.' That sounded completely different from the story told by Gustavo's mother, who was actually in Venezuela and relating what was happening on the ground. I told him to ask her whether Chávez had resigned or not. 'No! It's a coup, they took him!'

When a full report came on CNN about what was going on Venezuela, they kept to their storyline: Chávez had resigned the presidency after ordering his supporters to open fire on peaceful opposition protestors and dozens had been killed and injured in the streets. Something was way off. One story was being told on television, which blamed Chávez for the violence and implied he voluntarily resigned his office as a consequence, and another reality was happening on the ground in Venezuela which seemed more complex and volatile. Which one were we to believe?

I started calling friends in Caracas to get more information, first reaching my friend Piki, the musician from a working-class neighborhood whom I had met in Merida years earlier. I could barely hear him on the other line because of all the background noise. He was in the streets near the presidential palace, Miraflores.

'It's a coup! They're killing us in the streets, it's the opposition, they're shooting us with snipers from the rooftops. They kidnapped Chávez.' I asked him if Chávez had resigned and told him that's what CNN and other news sources, including those inside Venezuela, were reporting. 'What? No way! The generals took him from Miraflores and we haven't seen or heard from him since. The metropolitan police are repressing us in the streets, but we're fighting against them. We can't let this happen!'

I had been there less than five months earlier and had personally witnessed the growing propaganda in the media against Chávez and knew they were one-sided. The media had become a principal channel of anti-government opinions and positions, and rarely, if ever, presented anything to the contrary. I also knew that behind the anti-Chávez movement were very powerful forces inside Venezuela, though I hadn't yet discovered the US government's role in the unfolding events. From that moment, everything happened fast.

The opposition was forming a coalition government that would assume power temporarily until elections could be held. Images were broadcast around the world of Chávez supporters, visibly defined by their red berets and red shirts, firing guns, while spliced in were scenes of bloody bodies on the ground, identified by the media as peaceful opposition marchers. But something was not adding up.

First of all, Chávez had not been seen or heard of since he was taken away from the presidential palace by armed generals. It was completely unlike him to remain silent in the face of such a desperate situation. A letter that he had allegedly signed was circulating in which he announced his resignation, but, again, it was highly suspicious that he would not publicly address the nation before making such a grave decision. Reports were also coming in from the ground claiming that it was actually snipers and metropolitan police, under the control of the Caracas mayor who had joined forces with the opposition, who had fired the first shots. Furthermore, it appeared that numerous Chávez supporters had been hit in the head and upper areas of their bodies from gunfire above the bridge they were on, not below in the streets where the opposition march had taken place. In addition, many witnesses attested to the fact that the opposition march had never actually arrived at the presidential palace, despite its leaders having called on protestors to head in that direction. In fact, the Chávez supporters near the palace never came within range of the opposition marchers, but they *were* near the metropolitan police.

It was later discovered and admitted by the media outlets involved that footage from the events of that day had actually been edited and spliced together to make it appear as though Chávez supporters were firing on opposition marchers when in reality that never happened. Foreign snipers who had covertly entered the country in the preceding days shot at Chávez supporters and opposition protestors from nearby rooftops, killing dozens and creating chaos. The incident was then used to justify Chávez's ousting, and he was shuffled away by high-ranking military officers who had defected to the opposition. The alleged resignation letter was a fake – Chávez had never signed it – but it enabled the opposition coalition to install their temporary transitional government, headed by the president of the chamber of commerce, Pedro Carmona. As Carmona was sworn in as president in a bizarrely dictatorial ceremony, where his designated attorney-general announced the dissolution of all of Venezuela's democratic institutions and constitution, White House spokesperson Ari Fleischer publicly gave President Bush's stamp of approval.

In a statement read on the White House lawn on 12 April 2002, Fleischer repeated the same line touted in media reports, that Chávez had ordered the violence and subsequently resigned his office and an interim government had assumed power, supported by the United States. The dust hadn't even settled in Caracas from the violent events just hours earlier and Washington had already green-lighted the 'new' government. Their contempt for Chávez was obvious. Fleischer went so far as to affirm the

Bush administration's support and willingness to work with the transitional government to restore democracy in Venezuela.

Diplomatic celebration – then Chávez's liberation

From New York it was hard to follow everything happening on the ground but, through constant contact with friends and relatives in Venezuela, we knew that resistance in the streets was growing. People were unwilling to let the president they had elected, who represented them, be overthrown by the elite political class of the past, backed by Washington. Millions took to the streets in Caracas and throughout the country to demand Chávez's return. We drove to the Venezuelan Consulate in New York, hoping to find other Venezuelans who were as concerned as we were about what was going on in the country, only to see a large celebration taking place inside the fancy diplomatic building on East 51st Street between Madison and Fifth Avenues. They were backing the coup and celebrating Chávez's removal from power. A similar scene was occurring down the road at Venezuela's Mission to the United Nations on East 46th Street and 1st Avenue. Champagne, laughter, tears of joy, they were ecstatic that this loud-mouthed, brazen outsider could no longer alter the course of their nation's history. With so much to do in Venezuela after taking office, Chávez hadn't changed his diplomatic core and it clearly remained in the hands of his predecessors, who reveled in the luxurious lifestyles with which the government they despised provided them.

Gustavo and I had numerous friends within the Venezuelan community in New York and we were forced to distance ourselves from them once they expressed support for the coup. Like your president or not, a violent coup to overthrow him is not the answer in a democracy. It was a dark day for the country and I was horrified at the attitudes expressed by Venezuelans I knew in New York, whom I had thought to be rational, kind people. They hated Chávez and felt he had been ruining the image of their country with what they considered as vulgar discourse and his focus on the poor. These were all middle- and upper-class Venezuelans, of course, who had the financial capacity to move to New York City to study in expensive private universities, rent apartments and frequently travel back and forth to their country. The clear divide between classes in Venezuela was even more heightened outside of the country.

Back in Venezuela, Chávez was being held captive in a remote military base off the coast. While the plan was to assassinate him, there was disagreement about that within the opposition and he was kept alive. He managed to hand write a note stating that he had not resigned and was still the legitimate president of Venezuela, which he crumpled up and threw into a trash can in the small cell where he was sequestered. A young military officer, loyal to Chávez, emptied the trash, pocketed the note and was able to pass it on to other loyal forces. At that time cellphones were not as commonly available as they are today, nor was the internet as widely used. The note was faxed to CNN, which posted it on air, placing doubt on the circumstances surrounding Chávez's removal. Chávez's daughter, Maria Gabriela, later called in to CNN, after Fidel Castro had urged her to get the truth out about her father's captivity; live on air she confirmed that it was a coup and that Chávez had not voluntarily resigned as president.

Loyal armed forces then stormed the barracks where Chávez was being held and freed him. As word got out on the streets that Chávez had been rescued and was being flown back to the presidential palace, the millions already demanding his return began celebrating, forcing the opposition coalition members hiding inside Miraflores Palace to flee. The images of those individuals, who just hours earlier had applauded the installation of a dictatorship in the country, fleeing in fear for their lives, knowing they were guilty of treason and other crimes, are haunting. What could lead people to act so outrageously? How and why did Washington so quickly support them? I was soon to find out how deeply involved the US government had been in that botched attempt to overthrow Chávez. One thing was certain, however: despite all the millions of dollars and resources funneled into the opposition, Washington had completely underestimated the capacity and resilience of Chávez and his supporters. He was returned to the presidency and publicly called for reconciliation, holding a news conference from Miraflores on the night of 13 April 2002, brandishing a large blue cross with a crucified Christ figure. One of his palace guards would give me a replica of that cross years later, despite my insistence that I wasn't religious. He wanted me to have it because it was important to Chávez, and he knew that I was also dear to Chávez. Despite their actions against him, Chávez forgave the opposition for the coup and called on them to work with him to rebuild the country, but his pleas fell on deaf ears.

In the US the deafness was bewildering, as the Sunday papers all went to press with editorials applauding the coup and blaming Chávez for the violence and chaos that had ensued. Prominent newspapers like the *New York Times* and the *Washington Post* never apologized for their coup-celebrating, or their brazenly false interpretation and manipulation of the events in Venezuela. Condoleezza Rice, Bush's National Security Advisor at the time, didn't apologize for Washington's approval of the coup. Rather, she warned Chávez he was getting a second chance to show his democratic credentials, or else. This clear US support for the coup gravely eroded an already-poor relationship. And because of their key role in distorting public opinion about the coup, the media became a major source of suspicion and distrust. This led to prompt actions within Venezuela to restructure the media, weakening independent and private journalistic outlets while creating a vast state media complex that would eventually control the media narrative.

To my surprise, a small group of local activists in New York had been organizing support for Chávez, denouncing the coup and the US government's role. We formed a local Venezuela Solidarity Committee that became the basis for my political involvement in Chávez's movement and my investigation of the coup.

General strike

Things soon began to escalate again inside Venezuela, despite Chávez's calls for reconciliation. The opposition coalition, although bruised, refused to back down. They called for a national strike to bring the country to a halt and demand Chávez's resignation. Before the coup, Chávez had removed the executive board of the state oil company, which had been the final straw that had activated the putsch. After his return to power, he reinstated the original board as an olive branch to the opposition, hoping that this would calm their concerns about his plans to restructure the industry. It was one of many moves Chávez made hoping that others would respond in good faith, but it backfired. The oil company went on strike, shutting down production and exports, crippling the country's economy and creating an internal crisis from gasoline shortages.

I was back in Merida in December 2002, just eight months after the failed coup, and the country was more polarized than I had ever experienced it before. The oil strike was taking a toll on everyone. The lines to fill up gas tanks were miles long and drivers had to sleep in their cars so they wouldn't lose their spots. The opposition had declared there would be no Christmas until Chávez was gone. Distributors hoarded products so nothing was available to purchase, while schools and universities were shut down due to striking faculty and staff. Media had declared an all-out war on Chávez, devoting 24 hours of programming to anti-Chávez propaganda on all privately owned television and radio stations.

I had never seen anything like it before. In the US the media were often critical of the government, but not to the point of direct political activism with no effort at objectivity or balance. And this was not just cable TV, this was broadcast television, the main news and entertainment stations that were available to people nationwide. They all banded together in one united anti-Chávez voice, pushing for him to be ousted. The goal was to make the people suffer so much – without access to food, basic consumer products, fuel or entertainment – that even Chávez's supporters would demand he step down so the country could return to normality. But once again they underestimated Chávez's support base and his influence.

Chávez once told the story of how, during the strike, after about 30 days of food and supply shortages due to opposition boycotts and sabotage, when there was no fuel for cooking or transportation, he visited a poor neighborhood on the outskirts of Caracas. As he was walking by one particularly decrepit shack, an old dark-skinned woman appeared in the doorway and gestured to him to come over. He went to her and she grabbed him by the arm, pulling him into her one-room abode. A fire was burning in the middle of the floor, a tin pot hovering over it. 'Do you see that fire?' she asked him. Chávez nodded, noting the intensity and rawness of the old woman. 'Do you see that wood beneath the flames? That, Chávez, is what's left of my bed. And if I have to burn every piece of furniture in my humble home to cook whatever morsel of food I can find, I will. But don't give up, Chávez. Don't give up!' She squeezed his arm firmly and stared probingly in his eyes as she spoke.

Even the poorest of the poor were not willing to give in to the opposition demands, despite the scarcity of goods. These were people who had already suffered years of misery and isolation, and in Chávez they believed they had finally found a voice. They might still have been suffering in poverty, but at least they were seen and heard by him, and they were not willing to give that up. This is why charismatic leaders retain their popularity amongst their bases, even when things have turned for the worse. Rhetoric and empathy can go a long way.

Those in the opposition, who primarily came from the middle and upper classes, along with the politicians and bureaucrats in Washington, never tried to understand who these people really were and why they so unwaveringly supported Chávez. Their commitment to him and his vision for their country was consistently demeaned and underestimated. They were used to mistreatment, exclusion and alienation. They were the underclass, the poor, the miserable, the abandoned. Chávez spoke directly to them. He connected with them and understood them because he came from poverty and knew what it was like to be forgotten while others reveled in the wealth of the nation, treating the poor with contempt and disregard. Chávez made them visible, he empowered their families and communities and elevated them to the status of citizen. He was one of them, and he never forgot that, which is why his support remained so strong and why he won re-election years later even when he was terminally ill with cancer and the system was crumbling around him. Chávez was seen as a savior of the people, and they adored him for it.

The strike failed to achieve its objective and not only did Chávez remain in power, but his position was actually strengthened by

103

the opposition's actions. Because of their mishaps and abuses within the oil industry, his firing of the entire board and high-level management was justified and applauded throughout the country. He now had a mandate for his massive overhaul of Venezuela's institutions and industries, and he pursued it with no holds barred. The private media became the enemy and Chávez began building up a state media apparatus that would continue to grow throughout his presidency, serving as a propaganda tool and validation of his policies. The country descended into an 'us versus them' culture; the Chávez who had once been reconciliatory and moderate became heavy handed and radical; and the efforts to oust him and undermine his government did not stop. And I ended up right in the middle of it all.

8

Cracking the code

I had just begun my investigation into the US role in the coup against Chávez and had obtained thousands of documents evidencing how Washington had financially supported the opposition coalition behind the coup and the oil strike, and was now bankrolling the recall referendum. I had met Chávez, after a few hiccups, and shown him the evidence, but I hadn't yet become his confidante. I was still an outsider and viewed suspiciously by many in the Venezuelan government and amongst his supporters, who believed that, because I had obtained classified US government documents, I must be an agent of the US government or, more precisely, a CIA agent.

I was subjected to accusations and rumors of being a CIA agent from the first time I became publicly known in Venezuela on 11 April 2004. Freedom of information was a completely foreign concept in Venezuela, as no such similar transparency laws existed there, and most people could not comprehend how I could have obtained internal US government documents containing such revealing information. When I received a batch of top-secret CIA documents months later and made them public, while I was lauded by Chávez and many throughout the country, others became even more suspicious of my motives and intentions, convinced that I had to be a CIA spy. Some even referred to me as a 'Mata Hari', a *femme fatale* covert spy who used her feminine charm to deceive her targets and then move in for the kill. Or they called me a 'double agent' and a 'mercenary'. While I found this amusing, it was also a cause of great concern because it put my life in danger, at risk from people on all sides of the political spectrum. I was quickly becoming despised by the opposition for having exposed their relationship to the US government, and even more maddening for them was the fact that I was an educated, professional US citizen. So many middle- and upper-class Venezuelans desired US citizenship and all the perks it entailed that I frequently received email and other messages from opposition supporters demanding I trade my US citizenship for their Venezuelan citizenship, which was obviously not a possibility. Or they would threateningly claim I had no right to live in the US and should renounce my citizenship and move to Venezuela.

After arriving back in Caracas on the presidential airplane that 11 April 2004, I had already become a phenomenon, thanks to Chávez, who had paraded me around and lauded my discoveries. Reporters wanted to interview me about the documents and my investigation, and my face was plastered over newspapers and TV screens throughout the country. As promised, I was invited to the events commemorating the two-year anniversary of the coup and Chávez's return to power. Venezuela hosted an International Solidarity Conference with the Bolivarian Revolution every year on the same date as the coup, inviting left-leaning celebrities, artists, intellectuals and activists from all around the world. I had attended briefly in April 2003 for the first time as part of a delegation from our Venezuela Solidarity Committee in New York, despite protests from Gustavo, who was increasingly acting out in jealousy and anger as my political work became more public and time-consuming. Gustavo had been outraged by my invitation, claiming he should be the one to go since he was Venezuelan. He thought I should stay in New York taking care of his son while he took a free trip to Venezuela, despite not having as active a role as I did in the committee. The arguments between us were only beginning, and even though I was the one who traveled to Venezuela that time, he insisted that I call him on my US cellphone from Caracas several times a day and speak to him for nearly an hour each time. It ended up costing me hundreds of dollars just to calm his concerns that I was having too good a time without him.

When I went down the following year in April 2004 and met Chávez, Gustavo was initially supportive, but eventually he became even more jealous, accusing me of having an affair with the President. It was hard for me to understand how someone could act so irrationally, especially considering that I had supported both him and his son financially and emotionally for over five years and had provided them with a good home and quality of life in my city. But it only got worse. It was when he said he didn't want 'his wife' talking politics with men that I knew things had to come to an end.

Even before I became so heavily involved in Venezuelan politics and was focusing on international human rights at law school, he didn't like it. When I was intensely studying for the Bar Exam he refused to give me the space I needed to prepare myself, so I had no choice but to spend loads of money to stay in a hotel room for an entire week in midtown Manhattan. Even so, he called me and accused me of having an affair, questioning why I was alone in a hotel room instead of at home. It was a difficult time on a personal level, and I chose to delve into my political and professional work instead of attempting to repair our fraught relationship. He made demands of me that were unreasonable and were founded in his own insecurities and cultural machismo. I was the breadwinner, I had more success professionally and now I was becoming famous in his country for my political work. His male pride couldn't take it. Eventually, he gave me an ultimatum: my political work or him. As cold as it may seem to some of you, to me the choice was a no brainer. Imagine a woman giving her husband an ultimatum about his work...

Baby face and bodyguards

Back in Venezuela, I was onstage with Chávez at a huge rally for the anniversary event. There must have been at least half a million people in the streets showing support for him and their Bolivarian Revolution that day. This type of rally remained a constant throughout Chávez's presidency as a way of keeping his supporters mobilized, active and involved. It also projected a public image that conveyed the massive support for him, in case anyone dared think otherwise. The rallies and speaking events occurred numerous times a month and attendance was always huge. Whenever it was known that Chávez would be addressing the crowd, the masses showed up for the mere chance to see him in person.

On this occasion, as I stood near him on stage, Chávez made a point of mentioning me and my work. As the camera zoomed in on my face he commented on how brave I was for speaking out against the actions of my country, despite the risks I was taking, and how disarming it was that I could speak of these dangerous and risky matters with such an innocent, angelic-looking face. It's true, I have a total baby face and I'm not complaining. I look much younger than I am; this can be incredibly useful, helping me get through doors that would normally be closed, but it can also be frustrating and demeaning when I am not taken seriously. Back then, I was milking it.

When the cameras stopped rolling, one of Chávez's advisors pulled me to the side and told me it was too dangerous for me to stay at my friend's house in El Valle. They would move me to a secure location and provide protection. Really? I thought – that's a little exaggerated, isn't it? But he was right. The death threats and vitriolic attacks began immediately. I was whisked away from the stage into an unmarked black vehicle with tinted windows. I had been assigned two bodyguards from Chávez's own Presidential Guard, which is similar to the Secret Service in the US; I also had a driver, Mendoza, and a personal bodyguard, Benitez, who from then on accompanied me everywhere. I only knew them by their last names. They drove me to my friend's house to gather my belongings and then took me to a government-owned hotel in the center of Caracas. I was given a room key and Benitez accompanied me up to do a search of the room before I entered. It was the first time I had ever had bodyguards, but certainly not the last.

I returned to New York about a week later and continued working on the freedom-of-information documents. More were coming in each day and I was doing my best to analyze and publish them on our website, but I wasn't managing to keep pace. Frequently Chávez would call me from his Sunday program, *Aló Presidente*, to comment on the last documents and their revelations about the opposition's covert relationship with the US government. There was an endless supply of information, it seemed, and a lot was falling through the cracks. I decided it was time to compile the key documents into a book, which I began piecing together. I traveled down to Venezuela as often as I could, Benitez and

Mendoza always picking me up from the airport and shuttling me around the city, never letting me out of their watchful eye. On one trip, just days before the recall referendum vote was held in August 2004, I had brought with me a few partially declassified documents from the Department of Defense that referred to the presence of the Colombian guerrillas, the FARC, inside Venezuelan territory. I thought Chávez should see these documents since they also discussed conducting a media campaign against his government to link it to the FARC and narco-terrorism.

Even though I was protected by his bodyguards, it didn't mean I had constant direct and unfettered access to the President. I still had to find a way to him without being obstructed by his staff. Some of those in his inner circle distrusted me and my motives and did their best to keep me out of Chávez's sight. So I again called my photographer friend Wendys and asked for her help in getting as close to Chávez as possible. It seems incredible now, but that was always the most effective way to communicate with him. None of the regular, bureaucratic channels worked. You had to catch his eye and smile, and then he'd call you over.

I met Wendys at a rally Chávez was holding for the closing of the recall referendum campaign in an area on the outskirts of Caracas, in Sucre municipality. It was a large outdoor amphitheater and thousands of his followers were gathered, all hyped up to see him speak. Since I had presidential bodyguards I was able to get into the backstage entrance area and meet up with Wendys and other members of the presidential press team. We stood nearby as Chávez spoke to the crowd, warning that their access to public services would be endangered if the referendum was lost. The opposition would do away with everything, he said – they would plunder and loot the country once again, giving away the oil to the north, to the US Empire. The crowd cheered and applauded him enthusiastically – shouts of '*te amo*' (I love you) could be heard throughout his hour-long speech.

When he finally finished and exited through the backstage where I was strategically waiting, he saw me. 'Eva, how are you?' he asked in his usual personal and casual way, as though we were two friends just meeting up on a street somewhere. As always in his commanding presence, I struggled to organize my thoughts and my words. I told him I had some more declassified documents he had to see. They were from the Defense Department. He asked me where I was going. I wasn't quite sure what answer he was looking for, but before I could respond he said, 'Come with me' and pointed to his black sedan, opening the rear door for me. I got in. Once again no one checked me at all and there I was, alone with the President in his car.

He asked if I was hungry. What? No, I wanted to show him some important documents. His security guard in the front seat was eating a bag of what looked like movie popcorn and Chávez wanted it. He was hungry after that rowdy speech. 'Is that popcorn?' he asked his men. 'Yes, my commander.' He reached for it up front: 'let me have it.' Then he looked at me, 'want some?' It was hard to turn down the offer of movie popcorn from the President in the back seat of his presidential limo, so I took some in my hands. While he munched on the rest of it, I laid out the documents and explained the content.

When we arrived at Miraflores Palace he invited me in through the Golden Door, which was his entrance, with red carpet, fancifully dressed palace guards and all. I followed up to his office. He asked if I wanted some lunch. Always with the food, I thought, but I actually was hungry so I accepted. He showed me to a table and sat me down. I thought we would be dining together, but he went into another room and didn't come back out. A waiter came and brought a plate of food and I waved it away, asking if the President would be back. He didn't know, so I asked for a salad since the food he had brought had meat in it. I sat there eating my salad and one of the President's assistants came out to talk with me about the documents, saying Chávez had sent him to follow up. I explained the content and left him with copies and that was that. The bodyguards were waiting for me outside in the parking area towards the back of the palace, and I went out to greet them, apologizing for skipping out on them at the event, but hey, the President had offered me a ride. Who could pass that up? Especially with popcorn.

By early December 2004, I was back in Caracas for the launch of a new international organization propelled by Chávez. Artists and Intellectuals in Defense of Humanity was officially created with a diverse group from across the Americas and Europe, including celebrities, such as Danny Glover and Harry Belafonte, as well as authors, scholars and well-known intellectuals throughout the region. The idea was to inspire a cultural revolution within Venezuela and find solid, credible and respected voices who could defend Chávez and his Bolivarian Revolution internationally.

Venezuela's Sweetheart

While I was there my investigative colleague back in Washington, Jeremy Bigwood, called me with huge news. A new cache of documents had come in from our freedom-of-information requests, this time from the CIA. It was the first time we had received anything from the CIA since filing our requests back in 2003.

Usually the declassification process from the CIA is lengthy and produces minimal results, especially on a matter so recent. What we got was amazing. I asked Bigwood to email me the documents immediately and when I read through them my jaw dropped. These were top-secret CIA documents dating from the days before, during and right after the coup against Chávez in 2002. They weren't fully declassified – there were solid black boxes splotched throughout the documents, redacting whatever highly secretive and revealing information was there – but still, what was revealed was truly astonishing. Once I read through the five documents, all Senior Executive Intelligence Briefs with Top Secret/No Foreign Clearance, I was floored. Here was the evidence, in my hands, that the CIA had been directly involved in the coup. They had the who, what, where, when and how all written up and circulated amongst high-level members of the Bush administration at least five days before the coup in April 2002. There was no feigning ignorance or denying involvement on the part of the US government. They were deeply involved in the coup and I had the proof.

I picked up the hotel-room phone and called a contact at the state television station, Venezolana de Televisión (VTV), and told him I had a major, exclusive story. He told me to come over right away and they would put me on the air. I notified my bodyguards we would be going to VTV and we got in the car. Once we were live on a national broadcast, I revealed the CIA documents, explaining their content and implications. The story was instantly picked up and covered internationally by major media around the world. I was fielding calls from the *New York Times*, BBC, CNN, Reuters, AP, *Newsweek* and other print and broadcast outlets.

This proof that the CIA had had prior knowledge of the detailed coup plans was the kind of evidence that was rarely obtainable, except through a leak or a whistleblower from inside the agency. The release of these documents might very well have been pushed through by someone inside the agency who was uneasy about the US role in the coup, because they were very selective – just five Senior Executive Intelligence Briefs from the time of the coup. The language left unredacted was sufficiently revealing that I suspected whoever had green-lighted the release of these documents wanted the story to get out. It was practically unheard of to get top secret CIA documents pertaining to events occurring within the past two years and involving a foreign government and head of state in an ongoing, fluid situation. Who knows, maybe we had an ally in the CIA somewhere, our own version of Watergate's Deep Throat.

Days later, one of Bush's top Latin America advisors, Otto Reich, tried to deny the veracity of the CIA briefs, claiming they were fakes. But his allegations were immediately debunked, since the declassified documents had traceable CIA markings on them with file numbers and internal stamps that were affirmed by the agency itself. After this story broke worldwide, I came even more under the spotlight, giving interviews to major media outlets in the US, Europe and throughout Latin America on the implications of the revelations that the US had the coup plans in hand before it happened. Needless to say, Chávez was ecstatic about the new information and was using it to his advantage. His suspicions and accusations about Bush's role in his coup were now substantiated. It was no longer a myth: it was fact.

At the closing ceremony for the artists and intellectuals conference Chávez was the keynote speaker. While railing at the Bush administration for trying to overthrow him, he called me out. 'Eva got the CIA documents that prove the US was behind the coup. This brave woman, she's Venezuela's Sweetheart! Thank you, Eva!'

All of a sudden the camera focused on my face and was

broadcast on monitors around the theater. If anyone there didn't know who I was by then, they sure did now. The entire theater, housing nearly 3,000 people, gave me a standing ovation. I was humbled and honored, and a bit embarrassed, especially as people around me began throwing roses at me and blowing kisses. In all the excitement of Chávez's speech I had missed the part where he had called me 'La Novia de Venezuela', which translates as either 'Venezuela's Girlfriend' or 'Venezuela's Sweetheart'. I thought that was a rather strange way to refer to me, but it didn't matter what I thought of it, I soon became branded as 'La Novia de Venezuela', which many took to mean 'Chávez's girlfriend'. From that moment on I was treated as royalty by Chávez's supporters and members of his government. Because he had spoken of me with great affection, others did the same, for which I was truly grateful though I certainly wasn't used to or expecting that kind of treatment.

Mystery tour of Peru

Later that evening, at a reception with the President and members of the newly created Defense of Humanity group, I decided to seize the opportunity and request an interview with Chávez for the book I was writing on the coup that would detail the evidence I had uncovered. I happened to be seated with US filmmaker Saul Landau, a brilliant storyteller and ally of Cuba and Latin America, and was telling him about my investigation. US actor and Hollywood celebrity Danny Glover, an old friend of Saul's, came over and joined the conversation. I asked Danny if I could give him a note to pass on to Chávez, since he was seated at the President's table and I didn't want to break through the security ring and bother him in the middle of dinner. Danny kindly obliged and walked back to the table directly over to Chávez and handed him my note, saying 'This is from my friend, Eva'. Chávez responded, 'What Eva?' Danny pointed over at me and Chávez said, 'No, she's not your friend, she's my friend!' He gestured for me to come over to the table and put his arm around me. I told him I was writing a book on the documents I'd obtained evidencing a US role in the coup against him and I wanted to interview him about it. What followed was a typical Chávez experience.

'What are you doing tomorrow?' he asked me.

'Uh, nothing?' I responded.

'Then come with me to Peru,' he said and called over one of his assistants. 'Eva's coming with us to Peru tomorrow; take care of it,' he instructed. And that was that. I was going to Peru with the President the following morning. Almost every time I traveled with Chávez after that, which was a fair amount during the succeeding years, it was always a result of that kind of impulsive, spontaneous decision, and often I didn't really know where we were going or for how long, let alone where I would stay or anything else. I came to learn that most of his staff didn't know either. There was a common saying within Chávez's presidential staff and security team: 'All we know is that no one knows'. This led to a significant amount of chaos and disorganization, but somehow it all worked itself out.

Chávez thrived on spontaneity, mystery and unpredictability. He loathed protocol and expectations and operated entirely on his own terms. This made him more attractive to his constituents, who saw him as breaking the mold of the traditional elite. But Chávez was also a military man, a tactical strategist and a visionary. He mapped everything out and used visual aids and statistics in his speeches, and he was a voracious reader with a photographic memory, often citing entire passages from history books to the awe of his listeners. In 2005, a study by the US Army Strategic Studies Institute called Chávez a 'wise competitor'. He was unlike anyone they had encountered before. By the time US military and civilian intelligence experts figured out that Chávez was actually a rather astute and brilliant politician, it was too late. He had already become entrenched in his government, supported by a solid majority that remained permanently mobilized. The US had mistakenly underestimated him, just as the opposition in Venezuela had, and Chávez had gained the upper hand.

In this case, his spontaneous invitation meant I had to rearrange my schedule and race back to the hotel to pack my bag. We were to fly out to Peru at 5am the next morning. That meant arriving at the presidential terminal at 3am. All the passengers had to be there two hours before the President would arrive, even though it was a private flight. It was on this trip that I learned the survival habits of the presidential staff, guard and cabinet: sleep whenever you can and eat whenever and all you can, as you never know when you will get to eat or sleep again. It sounded dramatic to me at the time but, after several trips with Chávez, I took the advice. When we boarded the plane, I was again invited to the exclusive front section one seat away from the President. As was the case during my previous trip on his plane, he was a no show in his seat. By now I was getting to know his inner circle on friendly terms, so I didn't feel as uncomfortable, but still the whole experience was intimidating.

By around 4:30am everyone had taken their seats and we waited for take-off. I chatted with one of the cabinet members seated next to me, inquiring about the purpose of the trip. I had been invited by the President but didn't really know what I was in for. All I knew was that we were going to Peru for a summit of South American heads of state, but I had no further details. After the plane was in the air and the President hadn't come out to sit with us, everyone let their guard down and fell asleep. As a light sleeper, I could hear the snoring around me, some deeper than others, and it was clear that these people were seriously sleep deprived. Chávez kept unusual hours, often working until well past 3am and sleeping just a few hours until morning, though he rarely made public appearances before noon. He was a night owl and would call his staff and advisors at all hours. He drank over 20 small cups of sugary black coffee a day, which kept him wired. While that didn't seem too healthy, his energy was endless. Just as I was finally relaxing and falling into sleep, the exhaustion from the previous day's events and lack of rest kicking in, a loud BRRRIIINNNG jolted me awake, making me jump in my seat. The others around me all bounced up, rubbing their eyes, trying to look alert. It was Chávez, standing there before us in the aisle, playing a Venezuelan *cuatro* guitar. He was strumming the little instrument along with his fingers and singing the lyrics to some *llanero* song from his homeland, with a cheek-to-cheek smile on his face. It wasn't even 6am.

We were all startled and, in our half-asleep state, we greeted him as he went down the aisle playing the little instrument and giggling as the groggy passengers were shocked to see their

President acting as an alarm clock. We still had a couple of hours left to go in flight, but apparently Chávez wanted us all awake, I guess because he was. He called in a few of his team to his private room at the front of the plane while the rest of us were left to try and rest for the remainder of the flight. But as breakfast then arrived it looked like another sleepless night.

At large in Cuzco

The arrival in Peru was in Cuzco, an ancient city high in the Andes that was once the capital of the Inca Empire. The plane arrived on the tarmac and it was the first time I had witnessed up close a presidential reception. A red carpet had been rolled out up to the plane's steps and the sides were lined with uniformed soldiers saluting the President in their colorful garb. A military band played while the flags of Venezuela, Peru and Cuzco were proudly displayed. As part of the high-level delegation, I delighted in being treated as important while marching down the red carpet after Chávez amongst the saluting soldiers and experiencing what it feels like to be received like a president in a foreign land.

Since the visit was for a presidential-level summit with over a dozen participating countries, the reception ceremony was shorter than usual and the president of Peru was not there to greet Chávez, as would normally be the case with an official state visit. This time, we were quickly ushered into a lengthy line of black luxury cars, SUVs and vans and escorted off the airport grounds. The caravan whisked us through the narrow mountainous roads into the quaint old city, where the streets were lined with posters and signs welcoming the visiting delegations from throughout the region. There was bustling activity everywhere, but at a seemingly slower pace. Indigenous women in colorful dress carried babies in wraps on their backs while carting crafts and goods to sell to passers-by and tourists. Taking it all in felt like a dream, with my head spinning to absorb all the colors and cultural delights. I felt funny, as though my brain was clogged and not fully alert, and then it hit me. It was the altitude: Cuzco sits at over 11,000 feet, which means oxygen is limited and your body needs to adjust before you can resume normal activity. I took a few deep breaths and my heartbeat was racing in my ear. We arrived at a hotel in the center of the old city and Chávez was quickly escorted inside and up to the presidential suite. I wasn't quite sure what to do at this point. Was there a hotel room reserved for me? Did I have to pay for it? All of a sudden I realized I hadn't allowed for the expenses of the trip, not knowing we'd be staying in hotels and eating in restaurants. I had been invited by Chávez, but everything was so last minute that maybe I was expected to pay for my expenses – after all, I was there to interview him for my book. Just as I was about to inquire at the reception desk about a room, one of the presidential protocol workers approached me with an envelope.

'Doctora, here is your room key and your *viaticos*.' My what? I took the envelope and found a key with a room number inside and a slender stack of four 100-dollar bills. 'I'm confused,' I said to the protocol employee, 'why are you giving me money?' And that's when I learned about the *viaticos*, the per diem that every member of the presidential delegation receives to pay their daily expenses while traveling with the President. But I was just his guest, and actually, I was there to interview him, so why would I get a per diem? 'It was assigned to you for your expenses on the trip,' they said, and that was that. We were only staying for one night in Cuzco and even the five-star hotel we were in cost less than $60 a night for a room. What could I possibly do with all that money? I asked if I was expected to return whatever wasn't spent on expenses and if I would need to present receipts for all costs paid from the per diem. 'No.' Hmmm. It didn't feel right to just accept the money, but they had no procedure for taking it back, nor any accountability for expenditures.

After several trips abroad with Chávez, I learned that the *viaticos* were a business for many of the staff on his delegations. They would collect the per diem, which was always in dollars, and then spend as little of it as possible by sharing rooms in the cheapest hotels or staying with friends in private homes. For those who frequently traveled with the President, the earnings from this could reach thousands of dollars. When the economic situation deteriorated inside Venezuela, those saved fortunes in US currency became a business opportunity by selling the dollars at elevated prices on the black market. I was very uncomfortable with the idea of receiving money from the government that wouldn't be accounted for or documented. Eventually, on future trips, I stopped taking the *viaticos* and just asked those in charge of logistics to cover my costs directly in the same way as they paid the President's expenses. I have no doubt that those individuals pocketed whatever was left of my designated *viaticos* after paying for my hotel rooms but in my eyes this was a form of corruption and I wanted no part of it.

Cuzco was a lovely city but I was so disoriented from the lack of sleep and high altitude that it was hard to fully enjoy it. It all felt so strange and surreal. I was told by one of Chávez's assistants just to walk around town while the President and his team went to the Summit. There wasn't space for any additional guests inside the Summit so I and several other members of the delegation were left on our own to explore the area. I was still waiting to find out when I would get to interview the President, but I was simply told that he would let me know when he was ready. As darkness fell, I grew concerned that the interview would never happen, wondering if maybe he had forgotten. I hadn't seen him since we arrived in Cuzco and I knew that the way things worked with Chávez was face to face. If he saw you, he remembered and, if he didn't, he either forgot or just moved on to other things. I waited in the small hotel lobby drinking coca-leaf tea, which is known for soothing altitude sickness. I wanted to be there when Chávez arrived so I could greet him and ask about the interview.

When he came through the lobby there was a whirlwind of admirers wanting his photograph and autograph, or just wanting to shake his hand. With Chávez it was always like he was a rock star or major celebrity. The public would mob him for the chance to hug him or shake his hand, crushing everyone in their way to reach him. I tried to get as close as I could and catch his eye, but he quickly went past, blowing kisses at everyone and giving in to the few insistent fans that begged for his hand. I ran after him yelling '*Señor Presidente*' and he turned to see me. 'Eva!' He had clearly forgotten I was even on the trip. I asked when we could do the interview and he said later, or tomorrow, which I knew could also mean never.

The next morning we were up again at the crack of dawn to

head back to the airport. Most of the delegation was flown to Lima on the presidential plane, but Chávez took a private jet to the Andean town of Ayacucho to honor a battleground of his hero, Simón Bolívar. The large jet couldn't land in Ayacucho, so we waited for him in Lima amidst the dense fog and heavy grey sky before heading back to Caracas. Once we had boarded the plane, my chances for the interview seemed to be slipping away. There were no regular schedules or appointments with Chávez and, here I was, waiting again, this time for days while traveling to another country! It was still hard for me to adapt to this part of Venezuelan culture – I failed to comprehend what the benefit was of not planning or being punctual.

When the plane finally took off through the Peruvian fog heading back to Caracas, I just let go and decided to rest. Well, I had had a free trip to Peru, visited one of the most ancient cities in the world and had bought myself some nice gifts (what else was I supposed to do with all those *viaticos?*). Of course, once I settled in and fell asleep on the plane I was promptly awoken by Morales, Chávez's assistant. 'The President wants to see you.' Just when I had thought all was lost, it wasn't. I rubbed my eyes, combed my hair with my fingers and grabbed my notebook, pen and tape recorder.

Chávez bares his teeth

The scene was the same as the previous time. Down the private hall through the door to his private room. Again, it was closed behind me and I found myself alone with the President. He was at the same table, but this time he had papers spread over his desk and was clearly working. Another door was open inside the room and I could see a bed in the back with the sheets unmade, a sign that he had been sleeping just moments before.

I sat down and asked if I could turn on the tape recorder and he nodded in approval. He asked me if I had liked Cuzco and what I had done while I was there, again engaging in personal conversation, as was his custom. He asked if I had bought the necklace I was wearing there and I told him I had paid for it with the *viaticos*. He knew nothing of the way government money was being dispersed with little or no accountability in the form of per diem payments to his staff and, while surprised to hear it, brushed it off as part of the 'old bureaucracy' that still ruled the diplomatic corps and other government institutions. 'We will change all of this in time, we are working on it,' he assured me. I told him how surprised I was that the security seemed so lax on his airplane. Here I was, a foreigner, a *gringa*, yet I hadn't been searched even once by his security team, and now I was in a room alone with him with the door closed. At first he looked at me like I was crazy and then he realized I was right. 'Yes, we are still naive sometimes about the threats against us.' I told him he should at least have a metal detector that passengers go through before boarding the plane. I had been studying the freedom-of-information documents for months and was well aware of the threats against him, even those from inside his own government. At that time, he was still relatively unprotected considering the level of danger around him and the powerful interests that wanted him gone. Anyone could reach him when he was out in public, especially because he was so responsive to those wanting to greet him, and now I had learned that, even in private, he was completely accessible without any precautions. This posed a serious security risk for him and I told him so.

I asked him all kinds of questions about the coup and the evidence of the US role revealed in the documents I had obtained. We spoke for nearly an hour. I had a new set of declassified documents I hadn't yet made public and wanted to ask him about. They were from the State Department regarding a joint program with the Department of Defense to train foreign military officers in the US, known as International Military Education and Training (IMET). The documents I'd received showed a clear pattern of Venezuelan military officers trained in the US under this program who had subsequently betrayed Chávez and participated in the coup against him. One in particular, a General Raul Salazar, was mentioned in the documents as having been recruited by the State Department through the IMET program in the 1990s and subsequently serving US interests by infiltrating Chávez's government and becoming the Minister of Defense, all the while collaborating with the US. Salazar later became a key commanding officer in the coup against Chávez, betraying him publicly and backing his overthrow. The documents I had obtained showed that, even after the coup, Venezuela was continuing to send military personnel to participate in the IMET program. I asked the President why he would send his own officers to train in US military institutions knowing that they were liable to be recruited as US agents.

He was taken aback by my question and didn't like it. 'You know you are talking to the President of the Republic,' he said to me in a firm, commanding voice. 'I make the decisions and I don't have to explain them to you.' After that he turned off my tape recorder with a click and took out a pack of cigarettes, lighting one and inhaling deeply. I was shocked to see him smoke; I hadn't even known he was a smoker. In fact, he was known to be publicly against smoking and frequently talked about how dangerous smoking was to the nation's health and wellbeing. Yet here he was, smoking on an airplane, where it was clearly forbidden. But he was, after all, the President.

The interview was over, and I wasn't sure if I should just leave the room and let him smoke in peace. He looked uncomfortable and began moving his head around to stretch his neck muscles.

'Do you give massages?' he asked me.

'What? Umm, sometimes, but I don't think...'

He gestured for me to walk over and massage his neck, which I surprised even myself by doing, albeit reluctantly and with my hands shaking. Feeling rather demeaned and uncomfortable, I asked him if all his interviews ended that way, trying to make a not-so-subtle joke.

'What did you say?' Thankfully he didn't hear what I had said because I'm not sure we shared the same sense of humor and I wasn't in the best position to be angering him any further while stuck 35,000 feet up in the air on board his plane. I thought it best that I get out of there as quickly as possible. I thanked him for the interview and mumbled that I should get back to my seat. He nodded his head in approval and gave me a kiss on the cheek, lighting another cigarette as I walked out the door, shutting it gently behind me. He clearly needed more rest. And I needed to breathe.

9
Welcomed by Castro

When we arrived back at the presidential terminal just outside of Caracas, all of the passengers were informed that we would be taken to the palace in order to accompany the President in a live television broadcast. Even if I had wanted to go home, I couldn't, because the President's security team had my passport and luggage. We were piled into yet another caravan of black sedans, SUVs and unmarked vans and whisked away via the curvy mountain highway to the valley of Caracas.

At Miraflores Palace, another protocol team accompanied us into the room where the President was to make a live broadcast, along with an audience of around 200 people. He was always hosting events in the palace that were broadcast live on television. Sometimes they were simple ceremonies to sign official documents, while at other times Chávez would hand out titles to houses or cars, or credits and loans to small businesses. He tried to participate directly in as many events with his supporters as possible, and always broadcast them live on television. They often lasted for hours and Chávez would speak for most of it. On this occasion, I was so disoriented from the trip and lack of sleep, as well as the lingering effects of the high altitude on my still-foggy brain and my odd encounter with Chávez, that I really just wanted to leave and go home. The interview hadn't gone as I'd planned and the way things ended had left me feeling uneasy.

I left the auditorium and went outside into the palace grounds to find my suitcase and passport. A truck with an open back was parked out front, piled high with the luggage from the trip. It seemed to be an awful lot of baggage for such a short trip. I asked one of the guards if I could get my bag, which was easy to spot since it was the only little red leather suitcase amongst a sea of black trunks and boxes. He brought it down for me and I asked why there was so much luggage considering we hadn't even been gone for 48 hours. Shopping, he said. Even those Venezuelans who worked for the President used their trips abroad to stock up on duty-free products and whatever else they could squeeze into their bags. Some bought new suitcases to carry all the merchandise they purchased on those trips. They could buy anything and not pay duties or taxes on it when entering Venezuela, because none of the luggage on an official presidential trip went through customs. Yet another form of low-level corruption. I was getting used to seeing it everywhere.

I found the guard who had my passport and finally retrieved it from him. That was actually the last trip I took with Chávez using my US passport. Not only was I fast-tracked to naturalization to become a Venezuelan citizen months later by presidential decree, but I was also issued a Service Passport that enabled me to travel with the President as a member of his foreign-service delegation. I never asked for that passport or that status, but after it became apparent that Chávez would want me to accompany him on future trips, his security team gave me the passport. It made it easier for them to clear the presidential delegation through customs and immigration in most countries around the world, without concern for certain visas or other entry requirements. In the end I was very grateful to have that special passport to use when I went with Chávez to places where US citizens generally don't visit, such as Cuba, Iran, Libya and Syria.

I was too exhausted to return to the event after I had gathered my belongings and wanted to leave, though not with my bodyguards. I called a friend of mine who worked at the Cuban Embassy in Caracas and asked him to come pick me up at the corner near Miraflores Palace. I had begun sneaking away from the bodyguards sometimes. Even though I appreciated their help and protection, I often felt suffocated and just wanted to feel like a regular person. Felipe was handsome and kind with a boyish face and a gentle disposition. He was happily married, so I wasn't expecting anything beyond friendship with him, but he was always there for me when I needed and when I called him that evening he didn't hesitate to come right over.

I quickly exited through the Palace's side doors, waving at the young presidential guard keeping watch. Everyone was so focused on Chávez's event in the main palace auditorium, the Ayacucho Salon, that a young woman leaving with a small bag in her hand didn't merit a second look. Felipe was waiting for me on the corner and I hopped in the front seat of his little sedan, tossing my bag in the back. We kissed on the cheek, as is the habitual greeting in Latin America. When you like the person more, you actually kiss cheeks; when you're doing it more for custom, you kiss the air while pressing your cheeks together. He asked me how the trip had gone. Oh, it was interesting, I told him, but a bit weird. I relayed the stories about the *viaticos* and the neck massage, and also how the President had become angry when I had questioned his lack of action on his military officers training in the US. Felipe laughed. Now you're really on the inside, he told me. I wasn't trying to become a part of Chávez's team, I was just trying to interview him for my book. But Felipe was right: that whole experience had given me a privileged access to Chávez and his inner circle that few people enjoyed.

Felipe was intrigued by the documents relating to the military training programs in the US. He suggested I go to Cuba and check out their Strategic Studies Center on State Security, which had archives with thousands of documents collected over the years evidencing US interference in Cuba and against the Castro government. I told him I had to go back to New York and write my book, but he convinced me that it would be helpful to review other documents that could provide a historical context on the larger issue of Washington's policies towards Latin America. I caved easily, since it was hard to pass up a trip to Cuba. I hadn't been there since my first time nearly a decade before during the 'special period', when Cuba was suffering a debilitating economic crisis after the fall of the Soviet Union had meant the loss of its primary economic partner.

Return to Havana

There were frequent direct flights between Caracas and Havana due to the increasingly strong relationship between Chávez and

Castro. I was able to get on one of the 'exchange' flights that shuffled doctors and medical personnel, athletic trainers, teachers and other Cuban experts providing services in Venezuela in exchange for oil. This was the deal Chávez and Castro had worked out: Venezuela would provide cheap or no-cost oil and Cuba would pay in kind, with services. Just a year earlier the agreement had begun and already there were thousands of Cuban doctors in Venezuela servicing low-income communities in newly built clinics throughout the country. The program was known as *Barrio Adentro,* or Inside the Neighborhood, and was one of Chávez's flagship social programs guaranteeing free medical attention for all. Even Chávez's own doctors were from Cuba, a place known for its medical advancements and superior care services. For years I also went to Chávez's doctors for regular checkups and medical care in an in-house clinic inside the presidential palace. Cuban doctors focused on the health and wellbeing of the patient, and not the bottom line, which is why their care always seemed more humane and genuine than in the US.

I was grateful to get a seat on the flight to Havana the next day and decided to seize the opportunity, despite already being weary from days of travel with Chávez. When I arrived in Havana it was like another world from the one I had seen when I first visited in 1995. New, modern Chinese and European cars lined the streets alongside the colorful vintage American-made cars. Scaffoldings hung everywhere as construction was under way in Old Havana and other parts of the city to rehabilitate the historic and ornate colonial buildings that were in severe disarray from years of poor maintenance or lack of repair. The old double-connected Soviet-era buses were a thing of the past and new sleek Chinese buses now ran the transit routes. The special period was long over and the influx of Venezuelan oil and money had rejuvenated the beautiful city. Havana remained low-key and sheltered from chain stores and mass consumerism but now had a more cosmopolitan air. Markets were stocked with imported products, restaurants and clubs had popped up around the more touristy areas and gone were the depressing, barren shelves of the early nineties. The usual anti-US billboards were plastered on the sides of the roads and buildings throughout the city and surrounding areas, with images of Fidel in green fatigues pointing north, 'Yanqui Go Home!'

I stayed for three days and visited several thinktanks and strategic-studies centers on different topics. On my last day, my Cuban hosts offered me the chance to visit a highly secretive museum located on a military base in the outskirts of the city. It was the State Security Museum, a source of great pride for Cuba's intelligence agency, known as the G2. The museum exhibited and portrayed evidence of the hundreds of assassination attempts against Fidel Castro, many of which had been directed and executed by the CIA. The museum was nondescript and housed inside the military barracks, in a plain building with no signs or announcements revealing its existence. It primarily functioned as a reminder of the multiple assassination attempts against Castro that the Cubans had been able to foil, but it also served as a place to research and understand the varied tactics and techniques the CIA employed against its enemies.

I was escorted to the museum after all the official authorizations were issued allowing me to enter. A simply dressed, pepper-haired, dark-skinned woman, who looked like a kind grandmother, greeted me at the entrance to the exhibits. She was to be my tour guide. She led me into the exhibit area and began detailing each assassination attempt against Fidel that was on display with pieces of evidence to illustrate how the deadly plot was to have been executed. There was the exploding cigar, the poisoned cigar, the poison-lined scuba-diving suit, the pen with a needle filled with poison, the drug-laced creams. The exhibits also included discoveries of CIA spy equipment, dead drops, confiscated secret documents and traps that were set to capture Cuban agents and try to turn them against Castro. It was oddly surreal to have this grandmotherly woman detail these severely treacherous and outrageous secret murder plots in such a matter-of-fact way, as though it were second nature for the Cubans, who were used to decades of hostility and aggression from Washington.

Today a similar version of the State Security Museum has been rehoused off the military barracks and is open to the public so all can see and learn about the vicious attacks against Fidel and the Cuban Revolution that were spearheaded by the United States government and its agents.

The Chávez Code

That December, I gathered all my hundreds of key documents obtained under freedom of information legislation that detailed the most egregious meddling in Venezuelan affairs, backing the coup against Chávez and the subsequent attempts to undermine his government, and packed them all into a suitcase. I spent the holidays at my mother's house, which at the time was in Miami, but I didn't really take part in the festivities. For the entire 10-day break I was behind a closed door, writing away. I came out only to sleep and partake in the family dinners on Christmas and New Year's Eve. Gustavo was not happy at all to see me so wrapped up in my work with no time to spend with him and his anger swelled as he could feel me moving emotionally further and further away. I had a new passion and nothing could stop me from pursuing it, especially not his reprimands. On the final day of our stay, I emerged with my manuscript, my long-labored baby. *The Chávez Code* was complete – now I just had to find a way to publish it.

The name of the book had been decided upon a month earlier in Caracas with a group of colleagues. We were brainstorming on different names that might creatively catch the eye of a broad audience. When *The Chávez Code* was suggested I knew it was the right fit: clever, catchy and illustrative of the book's overall content and exclusive, explosive revelations. I had secured a publishing deal with a small publisher in the US that had promised a quick process and late spring publishing date, but they kept stalling on the prospective release date and pulling back on planned promotion and distribution. By late January, they had completely stopped the editing process and I suspected that something else was going on.

Publishing a book that implicates the US government and its intelligence agencies in a coup against a foreign sitting president in real time is a daunting task and not everyone is up for the challenge and the risk. The publisher had received warnings about pursuing my project from sources they wouldn't name but were easily discernible and opted to back out, despite violating our contract. I was disappointed but set on getting *The Chávez Code* published by whatever means possible, and so decided to take another trip to Havana.

I first landed in Caracas since there were no direct flights from New York to Havana and travel to Cuba was strictly prohibited for US citizens, unless you possessed a license from the Office of Foreign Assets Control of the US Treasury. So I went through Venezuela and from there boarded a Cubana de Aviación plane for the less than three-hour flight to Havana. I carried a full print-out of *The Chávez Code* manuscript, with all the annexes that included the partially declassified top-secret CIA briefs, State Department reports, Embassy correspondence, NED grants, USAID grants and budgets and other clear-cut evidence backing up the claims of US meddling I made in the book. I had contacted Cuba's Minister of Culture, whom I had met back in December at the big celebrity event with Chávez. Abel Prieto looked like he was right out of a 1980s rock band, with a long curly mullet and oversized eyeglasses. He was a poet by nature, an avid chess player and a close confidant of Fidel. After a few tries, I had finally reached him on the phone, telling him I was on my way to Havana and urgently needed to meet with him. He had said to come right over after I arrived, so I had the cab drive me to his office in the Cultural Ministry in the Vedado section of Havana.

Abel was always snacking on something to keep his diabetes in check, and he offered me some slices of crumbling wheat bread when I arrived. I kindly declined and instead took out my manuscript, a block of thick white documents about four inches high, and placed it on the table in his office. I told him what it contained.

Abel didn't need much convincing. 'Eva, this must get published as soon as possible.' He picked up the phone and dialed Fidel's office, speaking to the Cuban leader's chief of staff, Carlos Balenciago. 'I've got Eva Golinger sitting right here in my office with the book that shows how the CIA was behind the coup against Chávez. She's got all the top-secret documents, everything, it's in the book. We need to publish it.' He hung up the phone and told me to quickly draft a one-page summary of the book in Spanish, offering me his ancient desktop computer. He said we were sending it over with the manuscript to Fidel for approval.

My adrenaline was rushing at the thought of writing something that would shortly be in the hands of Fidel Castro and my own hands were jittering like crazy from my nerves. I wrote a brief one-pager that was as concise as possible, including the most revealing and explosive details. I explained the urgency of publishing since similar actions against Chávez were currently taking place in real time. Abel gave it a quick read, slapped it on top of my full manuscript and put it in a large manila envelope addressed to Fidel. Off it went in the hands of a courier who hand-delivered it to the Comandante himself.

The call came less than 30 minutes later. Abel answered with a few quick murmurs as I anxiously waited to find out the answer. Did he like the book? Did he find it worthy of publishing? Abel hung up with a big Cuban 'OK' and looked over at me with a smile. 'It's being sent to the translation service right now. An entire team will be dedicated to having it translated into Spanish as quickly as possible. The Comandante said it must be published immediately!' Wow, Cubans were no holds barred. If they decided to do something, it would get done in the most extraordinary way imaginable, especially if Fidel had said it must be done. Abel thought the translation would be complete within a few days since the team would be working on it round the clock on Fidel's orders.

The lap of luxury

I decided to stay in Havana while the translation was being completed, especially after the Cuban government offered to put me up at one of the exclusive protocol houses in El Laguito reserved for foreign dignitaries and distinguished guests of the government. El Laguito is a gated residential area full of about 120 oversized colonial and classic estates built in the 1920s that belonged to Cuba's wealthy elite before the Revolution. Fidel nationalized all private property, including privately owned homes, after taking power, and the vast majority of those who had lived in those mansions fled to Miami, leaving their houses behind, furniture and all. It was a serene, landscaped neighborhood surrounding a lake in the middle – hence the name. Both Fidel and his younger brother Raul lived close by, making the area ideal for private visits with limited public access.

The homes were spaciously built around the lake, some larger than others, and many had pools and grand entertainment spaces, both outdoor and indoor. The area was also home to an exclusive country club, hotel and renowned golf course, once used by American entrepreneurs and millionaires on their vacations in Havana. I was offered one of the more modest homes, a four-bedroom stone colonial with a large front porch redolent of the US South. Each home came equipped with its own staff for cleaning, cooking and service, and I was also assigned a car and driver, since entry to and from El Laguito was reserved only for authorized guests and their visitors and the area was too remote to reach on foot. It felt a little strange to have so many people attending to me during my stay and I felt bad about using up so many resources just for me, one person. I was also provided with an internet connection, which at the time was a major luxury in Cuba. In my case the internet was a necessity, since I would be editing the book and would need to do fact checking and sourcing.

Despite the luxury of the house itself, basic products were still lacking, as they were throughout Cuba. I had brought my own toiletries, thankfully, so I had shampoo, soap and toothpaste. The en-suite bathroom in the room I chose only had a meager sliver of old soap apparently to be used for both hair and body. There was no hot water, but since it was generally warm in Cuba that didn't matter much. The towels were old and thin, as was the toilet paper, but they all did the job so there was nothing to complain about. I was astonished at how much food I was served and was sure I gained at least five pounds during my stay, if not more. Every meal had several courses, consisting of a plate of fresh tropical fruits such as pineapple, papaya, mango and melons, then a salad of shredded cabbage, carrots and sliced cucumbers and tomatoes. These were followed by a main course, which for me was some kind of fish or seafood since I didn't eat meat. I had never eaten so much lobster in my life, though it was definitely cooked from frozen and came in small pieces, rather an entire lobster or its tail as it's served in the US. After all this food, ice cream was always served. Cubans love their ice cream – it's a serious source of pride for the country. Coppelia ice cream is a centerpiece in Havana, with long lines of salivating customers that stretch out into the street every day. I couldn't pass up this delicious ice cream in the confines of my residence with no waiting required. To top off the ice cream, a handmade Cuban cigar and drink of rum was always offered, though not always accepted.

I was uneasy about staying in such luxury, knowing that beyond El Laguito millions of Cubans struggled to get by, though none were deprived of food, shelter, education or healthcare, all of which were provided and guaranteed by the state. But still, this was one of many times that this contradiction impaired my capacity to fully enjoy my surroundings and the privilege I had been accorded.

The translation was done in less than one week, at the speed of light, and we got to work editing right away. Rogelio Polanco, then head of the *Juventud Rebelde* (Rebel Youth) newspaper and member of the State Council, the high-level Communist Party council that essentially ran the government, and Rosa Miriam Elizalde, a young, talented author, were the dynamic duo assigned as my editors. They were amazingly thorough and detailed, and meticulous in their review of my text and selection of documents. After a week of arduous and intense work, which included layout, design and cover art, the final version was complete and ready to send to print. It was mid-February and Cuba's international book fair was under way, drawing crowds of thousands and literary figures from around the world. It was too late for us to release *The Chávez Code* during the Havana portion of the book fair because the book still had to be printed, but there was still time to catch the tail end of the event in Santiago, at the other end of the island. A date was set, 5 March, for the launch of *The Chávez Code* in Santiago, and before that I needed to go back to New York and the life I had left behind.

I still had to do my paying work as an attorney, now in private practice, and it was utterly impossible to manage from Cuba with the spotty, slow internet service. Plus, I still had Gustavo back at home waiting for me. By now we had moved from our beautiful duplex in Fort Greene, Brooklyn, to my family's home in Long Island. After my grandmother had passed away in 2003 the old house had been left empty apart from occasional use by family members enjoying a few days at the beach. I could no longer afford the hefty, rising rent in Brooklyn and Gustavo was not working at all. I had convinced him to return to college and get a degree in music studies, offering to pay the tuition if he went to a school in the City University of New York system, which had reduced rates for city residents. His campus was in Harlem, so the commute from Long Island was excruciating, but he had no choice. Despite the relative stability we had achieved, our relationship had never recovered from the wounds of the past and his jealousy still hadn't subsided. I had no intention of stopping my work and in fact was increasing my political involvement with Venezuela, especially with the book. It was more than clear that we were heading on two very separate paths.

I flew home through Caracas and spent the next two weeks in New York catching up on my client files and preparing for my book launch first in Cuba, and subsequently in Venezuela. I had secured an editorial deal with a local publisher in Venezuela, Question, that was planning a grand release of *The Chávez Code* in Caracas with some heavy hitters. But first, I went back to Havana to meet up with my editing team, Polanco and Rosa Miriam, and to preview the first printing of the book. Just as planned, it was ready before I arrived.

We traveled to Santiago for the book launch together with Abel Prieto and stayed the night in a local protocol house in the middle of the old city. I must have autographed 3,000 books that day, my first time as a published author, but I wasn't too tired to miss the evening's serenade with famous Cuban musician Eliades Ochoa. Cuba has some of the most talented musicians in the world and they share their craft widely and frequently, and quite often free of charge. Eliades Ochoa became an international sensation as part of the classic Cuban group Buena Vista Social Club, comprising stellar, outrageously talented old-timers. He was from Santiago and just happened to be in town the night we were there, so we all got together at a local bar and sang classic Cuban songs to the strum of his virtuoso guitar until late into the warm humid night. I even got up on stage with him and sang 'Guantanamera' and 'Bésame mucho...'

As if that wasn't enough of a star-struck experience to celebrate the launch of my book, when I arrived back in Havana the staff at the protocol house were giddy with excitement. They were waiting for me at the door, all four of them, with big smiles.

'Come inside, Señora Eva,' they said as they escorted me through the front door, while one of them grabbed my suitcase out of the trunk and wheeled it in behind me. In the front parlor, on an entry console, was a huge bouquet of flowers, full of colorful roses and local tropical species. In the middle was a box of Spanish perfume, elegantly named Passion Seductress, and a card that read, *'Felicidades!'*, or congratulations, and was signed Fidel Castro.

10

Living the revolution

Trying to top the Cuban launch of my book was a difficult task for the Venezuelans, but they sure did try their best. They treated my book launch as though it were a high-level state event. The Vice-President at that time, Jose Vicente Rangel, also a journalist and writer, presented my book and me at the gala, giving an analytical summary of my manuscript and proclaiming it necessary reading for every Venezuelan. Before he spoke, the Foreign Minister, Education Minister and Communications Minister also all said a few words of praise for my book and my revealing investigation. The large room was packed with over 500 people, bulging out of the doors and down the halls. In the front row sat the High Military Command, the heads of all the different components of Venezuela's armed forces, and other important members of the Chávez government. The only person missing was Chávez himself. It was a who's who of his closely knit administration and I was the focal point.

Me, in my flowery petite dress with my short pixie hair, holding the cream-colored Mont Blanc pen that my mother gave me when I graduated law school. 'My pen is my weapon,' I proclaimed before the powerful and intimidating audience, hoisting it up high in the air. I read a speech I had written just hours before, highlighting the importance of the investigation and the book with its irrefutable documentary evidence. It was a manual, a guide, an invaluable map to the interventionism, the execution of a coup in real time, detailed plans and all. I was mobbed by the crowd afterwards, signing book after book with my faithful pen. Everyone wanted a piece of me and by the end of the evening I was exhausted and thrilled, riding high on the feeling of fame and success. I had done it. I was 32 years old and had published my first book, Fidel Castro had sent me perfume and flowers and I was being cheered on by the top brass of Venezuela's revolutionary government. The only one left was Chávez, with whom I'd already shared moments of confidence, and I hoped he would endorse my book and bring me closer in to his circle of trust.

The Chávez Code became a massive bestseller. Chávez lauded it, recommended it and practically ordered everyone to read it. I was being pulled in all directions to do events nationwide, presenting my book and autographing it for thousands at every event. The Cubans kept putting out new editions and shipping them to Venezuela – over 300,000 copies arrived by this route. Meanwhile, three other editions came out with Venezuelan publishing houses and I got offers from France, Germany and Italy to translate the book and publish it in Europe. I was carted around in helicopters, propeller planes, military planes, sleek private jets and bulletproof SUVs from event to event, with my bodyguard Benitez always in my shadow.

I received awards and honors from the Venezuelan Army, the Navy, the National Guard, the Air Force and from governors and municipalities right across the country. It was intense and humbling, and a bit overwhelming to be suddenly thrust into a completely new world where I was seen as a powerful ally and confidante of Chávez. I had become the Girlfriend of Venezuela. My face was plastered on magazine covers and newspapers, and I was interviewed on television practically every day. Everyone seemed to know my face and my name, and, because Chávez spoke fondly of me, I was loved by his supporters and hated by his enemies.

That April at the annual Solidarity Conference to commemorate the events of the coup, I was chosen to be the keynote speaker alongside Chávez. By then I was getting used to being in the spotlight and, while still nervous on stage, I had gained much more confidence and experience as a public speaker. I was passionate about my work and had mastered my subject down to the last number, detail and name. My book was distributed to the nearly 3,000 people in the audience and the event was broadcast live nationwide in *cadena*, obligatory on all channels, which meant it was viewed by millions across Venezuela. Chávez referred to me as a great orator, praising my speech and my work, providing the best publicity an author could ever want for her book as he held it up high and called it required reading for the whole nation.

Another private encounter

Two days after the event Chávez called me into his office at Miraflores Palace. I had asked him for a meeting so I could discuss a proposal I had for an investigative thinktank. I had mentioned it to him during one of our previous encounters and he had put one of his trusted aides in charge of working out the details so as to set it into motion. But, despite my persistence, the person Chávez had charged with helping me ignored my calls and requests to move the project forward. Months had passed and I felt like we were wasting and losing time; plus, Chávez had given an order and it hadn't been implemented. I would soon learn this was the *modus operandi* for much of his staff and close advisors, but I was still a believer back then and thought that if I let him know the project was ready to go he could make it happen. I also wanted to ask Chávez for help with my bodyguards. As petty as it seemed, I was extremely uncomfortable with the team now assigned to me. I no longer had his presidential guards, Benitez and Mendoza. His security chief had needed them back for Chávez's detail, which I fully understood, so a few weeks earlier I had been assigned a male and female duo from the DISIP, the country's political police, which also provided security for foreign diplomats and high-level guests invited by the state.

I hadn't been back inside the palace since the brief encounter I had had with the President the previous year, when he had given me a ride in his car and shared his movie popcorn. The whole experience had been such a whirlwind that I hadn't really absorbed what it was like to be inside the palace itself. This time I had an actual appointment, though I fully expected to be left waiting for a long period of time, knowing that Chávez was never punctual. I arrived and was brought through a different entrance, not the Golden Door or the public door, but a side door that seemed more private. I was escorted through the high-ceilinged hallways filled with portraits of Simón Bolívar and various historical battle scenes, past the inner courtyard with its serene fountains and chirping tree frogs, and into a rather small office. His private secretary greeted me and asked me to have a seat. The President was at an event in the Salon Ayacucho and would be ready for me once it ended. I knew this meant I had at least a one-hour wait, so I prepared myself for two.

It's always nice to wait for less than you'd anticipated so I was delightfully surprised when, before the two-hour mark, his private secretary answered a call, mumbled a demurred yes and looked up at me to indicate it was my turn. Chávez was ready for me. I was escorted by a young man in plain clothes who, typical of the presidential counter-intelligence unit and their nondescript, muted manner, said nothing to me and only gestured at me to follow him. They were the most discreet of all the palace guard, undistinguishable from other palace service workers or the general public, quietly doing their job to detect irregularities or advanced security threats against the President. Nevertheless, I still wasn't even searched before entering the palace grounds, building, private area and now, where the President himself would be. We walked through a series of hallways and doors to an elevator I had never seen before and didn't even know existed. The last time I was inside the palace I was taken up a flight of stairs to a landing, where Chávez had then disappeared behind a door and not returned. This time I went in what seemed to be a private elevator staffed by another plain-clothed guard. He asked the guard escorting me which floor I was being taken to. 'To the second-floor room,' he responded. I had no idea what this meant but figured it was Chávez's office or his private meeting room.

I was carrying a large manila envelope containing the thinktank proposal, budget and project information, and I had also placed inside some of the latest freedom-of-information documents that had recently arrived. Nearly 1,000 pages from the United States Agency for International Development (USAID) had come over the preceding weeks and Jeremy and I were still weeding through them. Standing out on the white page, with dark ink reports and internal US government correspondence, were budget plans and lucrative grants allocated to private media outlets that were vocally critical of Chávez and his government. There were also the usual funds going to anti-government political parties and NGOs that continued their active pursuit of Chávez's overthrow. The USAID office had become a bit sloppy and given us a delightful surprise. Several of the grant documents that had names of the recipients and amount funded had been redacted, but instead of sending us photocopies, the USAID office had sent us the original versions with the correctors' tape still on the document. So we just peeled off the tape and, ta da! There was all the information, revealed in all its glory.

Chávez would appreciate this gift from the US government and would be able to give it wide exposure on one of his public broadcasts, which could possibly help deter the current efforts to undermine his government and provide further justification for the thinktank I had proposed. The elevator doors opened on a sitting room with two couches, a few chairs and a coffee table in the middle. There were several other areas behind closed doors but they weren't visible. This definitely seemed to be a more reserved, private area. Even though Miraflores Palace had originally been built as a colonial home during the 19th century, when it became the official presidential palace the interior was transformed from a residence to a working presidential office full of various meeting and protocol rooms.

The formal presidential residence was located on the other side of town in La Carlota. It was a big ranch-style mansion with a large pool and entertainment area outdoors, surrounded by a tall stone wall and protected by the presidential guard. After his second divorce, when his wife left him shortly after the failed 2002 coup, Chávez, a serial workaholic, had chosen not to live in the residence but had instead given it to his two oldest daughters and their families, along with their mother, his first wife. He had decided that he preferred to live in the actual presidential palace, so part of the upstairs had been converted to a residential space, complete with a rooftop terrace where Chávez had a hammock for relaxing and which housed several talkative parrots and other pets, including a turtle.

I had landed in this residential space, though at the time I had no idea which part of the palace I was in, nor did I know then he actually lived there full time. I was told to have a seat on the sofa, so I did, clutching my envelope and wondering how much longer the wait would be this time. No sooner had I sat down than one of the doors opened and out came Chávez in slippers, a white tee-shirt and sweatpants, holding a small plate in his hand and eating something off it with a fork. I guess he was in his comfort zone. He sat down in one of the large chairs and offered me a bite of his mother's *dulce de lechoza*, a candied papaya dessert that was typically from the plains of Venezuela. His mom had just made it fresh for him, he told me – didn't I want to try it? I felt like almost every time I was alone with him he offered me food. I guess he was hungry from all his public events and could only find time to relax and eat during his private moments.

Not wanting to offend him or his mother, I accepted a bite of the sweet fruit, eating it off his fork. I thanked him and handed him back the fork. I told him about the USAID documents I had brought and he laughed. 'You and your documents,' he said. I handed some of them to him so he could see how the office had erred by giving us the original documents instead of the copies. He was pleasantly surprised and found them very useful.

I told him that the project I had proposed to him a few months earlier had not got off the ground because his people had ignored my calls and requests. He wasn't at all happy to hear that, especially when I mentioned how many times I had tried to contact the person he had put in charge of the matter, who had since become his latest Minister of the Interior and Justice, overseeing the entire state-security apparatus. He picked up his encrypted phone, the *telefonito*, which was used for internal communications between Chávez and members of his cabinet or his closest advisors.

Having a *telefonito* meant you were in Chávez's inner circle of trust and could reach him at any given time, as he could also reach you. He put it on speaker so I could hear the whole conversation. He told the Minister that he had seen me recently, not revealing that I was sitting beside him listening in on the conversation, and said I had mentioned to him that the thinktank project was not going anywhere because his staff had been unresponsive. Chávez said there was no excuse for not returning my phone calls. His minister apologized and said he would call me immediately. Chávez said he had better and then hung up the phone and chuckled. 'He thought I was really mad,' he laughed, taking another bite of his *dulce de lechoza*. My phone rang almost immediately. It was the minister, asking if I could come in to his office the following morning to discuss my project. 'Yes, I'll be there,' I said, and hung up, smiling at Chávez. Well, that was fast. Before I left I had to mention the bodyguard situation. I told him about the male/female duo I had been assigned by DISIP and how the guy had asked for my help in getting him a promotion. He laughed at that and said it was crazy. How could I trust them to protect me if I didn't get him his promotion? He called his personal assistant on the *telefonito*. 'Find Eva new bodyguards,' he instructed, 'and make it right away.' He said he didn't want me with the current DISIP bodyguards for another minute.

I knew that they wouldn't assign me anyone from Chávez's team, since obviously they needed to be with the President, but I was hoping they could find someone else trustworthy who wouldn't ask me for any favors. We said goodbye and he went into his modest bedroom to take a nap. As soon as he closed the door to his room and I was left standing alone in the living-room area, his assistant appeared and invited me into his office. He called the DISIP and said the bodyguards needed to be reassigned to someone else and, in the meantime, they would look for a new team for me. For the moment, though, Benitez and Mendoza would be back with me, since that was the safest option until they could sort through what had happened. Having the President personally complain about my bodyguards was a bigger deal than I had thought. In addition, having the President call his minister to chastise him for not taking my calls was not necessarily going to achieve my objective. Rather, I seemed to be creating enemies within the government who would step up their efforts to push me out. I had underestimated the privileged relationship I had quickly obtained with Chávez. Most of them never had relaxed time alone with him, without other eyes and ears around. And most wouldn't dare to speak their minds to him for fear of his reaction. I felt at ease with Chávez, though, and always spoke my mind without any major fear of reprisal or consequence, which I soon learned was unusual, even within his inner circle.

Return to Cuba – under camouflage

At this point I was practically living in Caracas, and things back home were increasingly difficult and tense between Gustavo and me. He hated that I had become so busy with my political and investigative work, and that I had been propelled into the public eye. He had no interest in moving back to Venezuela and refused even to consider a move to Caracas, which he considered a horrible, unlivable place. I thought he was being ridiculous, since New York City's urban chaos far exceeded that of Caracas. The deeper I delved into the politics of his home country, the more he rejected the idea of returning. I told Gustavo that I planned to move permanently to Caracas, with or without him.

In April 2005 a major event was set to take place in Cuba. Presidents Chávez and Castro would formalize the Bolivarian Alliance for the Peoples of Our America, known as ALBA – a co-operation agreement between Venezuela and Cuba that went far beyond the traditional concept of trade. ALBA was premised on barter and trade – the exchange of goods and services to the mutual benefit of all parties involved. Venezuela had oil; Cuba had doctors. Venezuela had oil; Cuba had agricultural and food sovereignty experts who could revive Venezuela's long-abandoned agricultural infrastructure. Venezuela had oil; Cuba had internationally renowned educators and athletic trainers who could help build a solid educational and recreational system in the country, free and accessible to all. It was Venezuelan oil in exchange for anything and everything Cuba had to offer, including intelligence and military officers to help improve Venezuela's lax state-security apparatus and inadequate level of protection for the President.

I had been invited along on the trip by the Cubans, who wanted to showcase my new book during the Chávez-Fidel encounter. *The Chávez Code* had not only been published by a Cuban publisher upon Fidel's instruction, but it had also become the go-to book backing up Venezuela's claims of US government meddling. This time, instead of traveling with the President on his airplane, I had to arrive a day earlier to set up my book event, so I was offered a seat on the plane with Chávez's 'advance' team.

I headed down to Maiquetia airport on the outskirts of Caracas, down the windy mountain road. I was expecting to fly on a regular airplane, since the older presidential airplane that Chávez had replaced with his more modern, luxurious jetliner was still in use by presidential staff. Known as the *camastron*, or 'double', the plane looked similar to the new presidential jet with the seal and colors of Venezuela emblazoned on the side. Since it was older and in need of constant repair, it was generally used for spillover staff traveling with the presidential delegation or advance teams. To my surprise when I arrived at the presidential airport terminal, the *camastron* was nowhere in sight. Instead, a very large military aircraft was waiting for departure – a huge camouflage-colored plane with four propellers on its wings, two on each side. I had been on the military helicopter with Chávez, but this was a whole other ballgame.

The advance team was loading up the plane when I arrived and a guard signaled for me to bring my suitcase so he could load it into the rear cargo area. I handed him my small bag. Were we really going to fly in this thing to Havana? He laughed at my anxious question. 'Never been on a Hercules before, have you?' he asked with a knowing smile. 'You do know that there are no seats, don't you?' Umm, no I didn't know that. 'Or bathrooms.' What? 'There are no bathrooms on the plane. It's a cargo jet,' he explained, 'used primarily for military cargo and transport of military personnel, especially parachutists.' Para, what? I hoped I wasn't expected to jump off the plane with a parachute, because that was where I would have had to draw the line. 'No, no,' he said, 'but beware, because the plane has no internal climate control and can get real cold; also it's slower than a normal jet and so takes double the time to get there.' Oh, that was just great. I was really looking forward to spending nearly six hours on a military cargo plane freezing my ass off with nowhere to pee or sit. Thanks for the ride, guys!

I had little choice in the matter since I had to get to Havana and everything had been pre-arranged. When I boarded the massive plane, the interior had two rows of fold-down benches with stretchy material for seats, rather like hammocks. I was told to find a spot and sit down. I put my handbag under my legs on the floor and clenched it tight between my feet before strapping on the over-arm belts. There was a handful of other women on board, among them members of the presidential guard and press team, and the rest were men, primarily military officers belonging to the advance team. Once we had taken off and were in the air the loud hum of the motor never dissipated. It was so noisy that it was impossible to have a conversation even with the person sitting next to me. The constant shaking of the plane prevented my reading or doing anything other than sitting there, clutching the arm belts and hoping to make it there alive. There was no getting up to stretch my legs and no bathroom to pee in – at least for the women. The men, I soon realized, had a ready solution for their bathroom needs. They simply opened the flight door and peed out the window. Remember that next time you feel drops from above on a sunny day.

After a grueling five-and-a-half hours, we landed at the José Martí International airport in Havana. As we disembarked from the plane, all the women went running to find the bathroom. The men, on the other hand, happily accepted the tropical cocktails offered by the Cuban welcoming committee in front of the terminal entrance. I was just happy to arrive and unload my bladder in a proper bathroom. The humid Cuban heat was also a welcoming relief after being half frozen on the Hercules.

The Hotel Nacional – and meeting Fidel

We were all loaded up into vans and driven into the city, where I was given a room in the historic Hotel Nacional, overlooking the Malecon, right in downtown Vedado. Hotel Nacional is a grandiose venue that was once the center point of Havana during its days as a casino gambling hub for wealthy US businesspeople. From its extravagant cabaret dancers at the famous Tropicana Club to its back-garden luxurious lounge area with breathtaking views of the Caribbean Sea and plush furniture perfect for relaxing with a Cuban cigar and a mojito, Hotel Nacional was a true tropical paradise. It also became a go-to place for me during my many trips to the island over the following years.

The room I was assigned on that April 2005 trip was literally like a time capsule. It was very pink, but a vintage, sun-faded pink, with thick, gaudy, beige drapes and worn-down brass adornments right out of the 1940s. It smelled a bit moldy, the mattress was old and sunken and the shower was tepid and leaked, but it was still the Hotel Nacional. Who cared what the room was like? Just walking into the lobby was a treasure. On this particular trip, the lobby was filled with life-size posters of Fidel and Chávez embracing to welcome the Venezuelan delegation to Cuba. Once Chávez arrived the following day, the bilateral meetings began, as did the heightened security measures. Even though we were all a part of the delegation, there were significant restrictions on access to both presidents. Since I was tagging along and had no official role in the event, I took all this in my stride.

We walked through a large Cuba-Venezuela expo in the convention center on the outskirts of Havana, where companies from both countries showcased the products that were being traded and produced under ALBA. I walked close behind Fidel and Chávez during the tour of the expo, huddling close with Chávez's brother Adan, who often joked about our names, Adan and Eva (Adam and Eve). Then it was off to inaugurate the new office of PDVSA-CUBA, which would begin operations on the island with a new refinery. Since oil was a major part of the ALBA deal, having a refinery on the island was vital. The office was located in a historic building in old-town Havana, *la Habana Vieja*. There were so many people packed into the building that it was nearly impossible even to make it up the stairs to the floor with the PDVSA offices. I was able to squeeze through the crowd just in time to see both Chávez and Fidel cut the tape together, to the sound of a loud chorus of *Viva Cuba, Viva Venezuela*. From there, the whole delegation piled out into the plaza below, which had been cleared by Cuban security. The two presidents had decided to stroll through Old Havana on foot to the site of the next event, the Casa Bolívar, where they would formalize an ALBA agreement.

Chávez and Fidel wandered through the streets, waving at the people leaning out of their windows to salute the two leaders. The walk was slow-paced and quiet, as though it were just an afternoon stroll through town, nothing out of the ordinary. When we arrived at the Casa Bolívar the crowd was substantially reduced, and just a small group of us accompanied the presidents inside. I was escorted through with Cuban security, who had clearly been given orders to keep me close to the presidents. I was just in awe the whole time: it all seemed so surreal. Had I really just strolled the streets of Old Havana with Chávez and Fidel Castro?

After the two leaders signed the agreement and official photos were taken, things seemed to relax for a while. All of a sudden Fidel's chief of staff, Carlos Balanciago, grabbed me by the arm and pulled me with him. Before I knew what was happening, I was standing in front of Fidel and he was looking down at me. Larger than life, he towered over my short frame. He was dressed in his usual olive-green military uniform with a big belt around his waist. His hair was greyish white, to match his beard, and his voice was deep and husky as he spoke, evidence of years of drinking rum, smoking cigars and giving long, impassioned speeches.

'I've seen you a hundred times,' he said to me. 'I've watched your interviews and read your writing. What do you think about Luis Posada Carrilles?' he asked me, as though we were just having a casual conversation. He wanted to know if I thought the US government would allow the extradition of the most notorious Cuban terrorist in history, who had just resurfaced and taken refuge in Miami.

Venezuela had submitted an extradition request to bring Posada back to Caracas, alleging that he had masterminded the bombing of a Cuban airliner back in 1976, killing all 73 passengers on board. Posada had been imprisoned in Venezuela after the attack since he had planned it from a Caracas hotel. He had escaped from prison in 1985, had fled to Miami and been given residence in the US, since he had also worked as a CIA agent. He later went on to execute dozens of additional bombings and violent attacks on Cuban interests until he was arrested in Panama in 2000 after planning to assassinate Castro during his visit there. Posada was discovered in Panama with 200 pounds of explosives and a plot to blow up a university where Fidel was scheduled to speak. Had he executed the attack, he would have killed hundreds, if not thousands, of people. Though he was imprisoned, Panama's rightwing president Mireya Moscoso pardoned him in 2004 just before she left office.

Since relations were so poor between Washington and Caracas, and the Bush administration was still backing efforts to overthrow Chávez, I knew it was impossible that they would extradite one of their own to Venezuela. After all, Posada had served the US government as an intelligence agent; there was no way they'd send him to an enemy nation to face life in prison. I told Fidel my opinion, but he believed the case against Posada was so strong that Washington would have no choice but to extradite him to Venezuela. I thought that he seemed very optimistic in his old age and told him so. He laughed. His idealism had never waned, even as he neared his 80th birthday.

Just as our conversation was continuing, Chávez showed up and brazenly interrupted. He put his arm around me and told Fidel that, while I looked like an angel, he should be careful: 'She's actually a red devil, a red rocket!' The bodyguards and presidential aides around us all laughed and smiled. Later, one of the Cubans told me that, in Cuba, the term rocket, or *cohete* in Spanish, also has a sexual interpretation when used to describe a woman. Oh, great, I thought to myself. Thanks for tarnishing my special moment with Chávez and Fidel by telling me that. I knew Chávez hadn't meant it that way, but still...

I appreciated Chávez's compliments, but was a little disappointed that my first moment with Fidel had been interrupted. But who was I to complain when two of the most revered Latin American revolutionary leaders of modern times vied for my attention?

We were all shuffled back onto the streets of Old Havana, but this time the caravan was waiting out front. The presidents got inside their cars and the rest of the delegation started piling into the remaining vehicles. I was completely confused about what was happening and what I should do. I had no car assigned to me and no means of transportation to get back to the hotel or wherever we were going. I caught one of Fidel's aides and asked him what I was supposed to do. There was some scrambling around amongst them and then he said Tony would take me. Who was Tony?

He was waiting for me with the passenger door open like a knight in shining armor: Antonio Castro, Fidel's hunky son. I had no clue who he was at the time and gratefully accepted the ride. We ended up at the protocol mansion where Chávez was staying. When he dropped me off he gave me his card. He was also a sports doctor, and a very handsome one at that, with his sculpted body and sandy brown hair falling across his gorgeous eyes. Later on in the trip, some of the Cubans teased me about Tony and asked whether we had a thing going, since I was the only one he had offered to drive that day in the caravan. Sadly, I missed that opportunity.

Chávez was scheduled to fly back the following morning and, since I was there at his house, I decided to ask for a ride on his plane. The thought of returning on the Hercules was nerve-wracking. I told him of my experience flying to Havana and he laughed, having flown on many a Hercules himself during his time as a paratrooper. Of course I could fly back with him to Caracas, he said. There was always room on his plane for me. And so the trip on which I had fulfilled my dream of meeting Fidel Castro came to an end.

11

Between the Devil and an angel

Over the years I was in the eye of Washington's defense and intelligence agencies, as well as the State Department and the US Embassy in Caracas. However, to my knowledge, I was never confronted or approached directly by anyone in the US government. Once, at a meeting on Venezuela hosted by the Department of Defense's US Southern Command (SOUTHCOM) in Miami, General Bantz Craddock, who was the Commander of SOUTHCOM at the time, referred to me as a troublemaker, according to several people present at the event. One time in early 2006 the US Ambassador in Caracas, William Brownfield, told Chávez's communications minister, who was also a close friend of mine, that 'Ms Golinger should watch her back'. The US National Security Advisor on Latin American Affairs, Otto Reich, accused me of being a 'paid Cuban and Venezuelan agent', as did Roger Noriega, Assistant Secretary of State for Western Hemisphere Affairs under George W Bush. I knew they didn't like my work and how it exposed their covert activities in Venezuela aimed at undermining Chávez's government and his Bolivarian Revolution, but I was always acting within the confines of the law. I was not a paid agent of any government, nor was I a spy.

None of their allegations about me were ever true. Nor were those coming from inside the Venezuelan government and Chávez's movement that claimed I was a Mata Hari, a CIA agent and an opportunist.

While I was privileged to be close to Chávez and to enjoy his confidence, I never took advantage of my access to him as many others did. And I never had any real power or authority in the government, contrary to what many people in Venezuela assumed. Some believed I was Chávez's girlfriend, others saw me as one of his closest advisors and almost everyone was sure that I was getting rich and gaining power. When I gave talks in public forums and events, or presented my book to different audiences, in addition to asking for my autograph, people would beg me to help them get a house, a job, a television, a car, a loan, anything that the government might provide. I received hundreds of letters over the years, some addressed to me, others addressed to Chávez, begging for help. A lot of them wanted housing and jobs, but many just wanted handouts from the government, and they believed I was capable of giving it all to them. Nothing could have been further from the truth.

The only time I ever asked Chávez to help with anything I was directly involved in was the thinktank, and I genuinely believed it was a project that would greatly benefit Venezuela – and Latin America as a whole. Even this never actually happened: I never got a dime for the project or any help from anyone in his government or elsewhere in moving it forward. Unlike many inside Venezuela, I never profited from my proximity to Chávez. The idea that I became a millionaire working for Chávez is a complete myth that it suited my opponents to create. The closest I ever came to formally working with the government was briefly as editor-in-chief of the English Edition of *Correo del Orinoco*, a publicly funded newspaper that started in 2010. My salary was so minuscule it barely covered my monthly bills.

At this point, it's even laughable to think about how worthless my salary and my savings were, since the Venezuelan currency has since been so severely devalued. What I earned each month back then couldn't even buy a bottle of water today. The savings I left behind in the bank that I struggled for years to build up are now worth less than one dollar. Where I did make some money in Venezuela was from selling my own book. In fact, I sold so many copies of *The Chávez Code* at book events that I was able to save up for a down payment on an apartment. Most of the sales I made personally, carting my books around in boxes from event to event, to the detriment of my back. A few times I sold hundreds of books to Venezuelan state companies, but most of those never paid me. In fact, the state oil company PDVSA still owes me for 1,000 copies of *The Chávez Code* that I sold them back in 2005, though the sum today would be worth less than one cent because of the massive inflation and currency devaluation. The entire price I paid for my apartment in Caracas back then wouldn't even buy a single roll of toilet paper today in Venezuela. That is what the world's worst inflation looks like.

Putting down roots in Caracas

I had no plans to return to New York: Gustavo and I had finally divorced and I had moved my cat Lola with me to Caracas. I was already working on a second book, so I decided to try my hand at home ownership. I found an amazing apartment in a building where I had visited friends and the price was just right. The owners were also willing to include almost all of their furniture in the purchase price, which was vital for me since I had none of my own. I had just enough money for the downpayment and secured a mortgage from a local bank for the rest. On 31 October 2006 I became the proud owner of a beautiful and spacious apartment in the La Florida neighborhood, a central location in Caracas. The unit had floor-to-ceiling windows with views of the breathtaking Avila Mountain.

Caracas was a chaotic city with no planned urban design, a lack of sidewalks and no traffic laws (at least, none that were enforced). As in Merida, though much worse because Caracas was more than ten times the size, cars zoomed through red lights, motorcycles rode up on sidewalks, in between cars and even traveled in the wrong direction. Accidents were a daily occurrence and the traffic jams were brutal. The metro worked well but didn't reach all parts of the city and was so overcrowded during rush hour that you could barely breathe, if you were even able to squeeze inside in the first place and risk being groped by another passenger.

The absence of sidewalks in Caracas always amazed and frustrated me. The weather in Caracas was perpetually perfect – low 80s in the day and under 60 at night. Even in the rainy season the downpours were generally short and tropical, tapering off enough to allow for walking in the drizzle. But almost no one walked. In part this was because of the outrageously cheap subsidized fuel, but it was also due to the way the city had been designed, or, rather, not designed at all. The historic quarter of Caracas was a basic grid with streets and avenues crisscrossing as in most cities. There, it was preferable to walk because it was too congested to drive through, though many did. But that was just a very small part of the city, a mainly commercial area with little or no nightlife. The rest of the city, including where I lived in La Florida, had sporadic sidewalks that were generally not maintained and therefore were broken and unsafe. You would be walking along the sidewalk and it would end, just like that, with no other sidewalk in sight. So you would be forced into the road, where it was extremely unsafe because, if cars didn't stop for red lights, they definitely did not stop for pedestrians. It's a miracle that I survived walking in Caracas, because I did a lot of it, everywhere.

I had decided early on that I would only use my bodyguards for work-related events, but otherwise I would walk the streets, take the metro, do my own shopping, wait in lines like everyone else to do my errands and go out at night on my own with friends. As much as I appreciated the support of the government and work of the bodyguards to protect me, it was not a lifestyle I felt comfortable with. If I didn't walk the streets myself and experience things like any regular person in the city, how could I understand what it was really like to live there?

I had enough privileges already by having Chávez's ear, and I didn't want to isolate myself from the realities and difficulties people faced every day. I watched too many of Chávez's aides, advisors and assistants withdraw into isolated, protected lifestyles, completely detached from the reality of daily life in the country, and I strongly believe that was a major factor in the increasing dysfunction and misplaced policies of the government over the years. How could any government official understand the difficulties people faced if they never experienced these themselves and instead spent years being carted around in luxury cars, having assistants do their shopping and errands and never interacting with ordinary people in a setting that wasn't staged?

While throughout 2004 and 2005 I was mainly traveling across Venezuela to promote my book, 2006 was my first major year of international touring. By then *The Chávez Code* had been published in English, German and Italian, and I was invited to book tours and political events in the US and Europe. Most of my hosts were local activists or academics with modest homes where I stayed during my visits. There was no pretension or extravagance involved, despite what some people have claimed. The trips involved long hours of traveling, speaking and interacting with local audiences and groups interested in Venezuela. I survived on little sleep and lots of adrenaline.

A nightmare journey to Cuba

When I returned to Caracas, Lola, my kitty, was always meowing and happy to have me home. One day, as I settled back in to my Caracas home after a lengthy European trip, I received an urgent message from Cuba. My presence was requested at an event against international terrorism, which to the Cubans meant Washington's policies against them, and I was slated to speak with none other than Fidel Castro. That was definitely an offer I couldn't refuse.

I wasn't the only one from Venezuela invited to speak on stage with Fidel. Venezuelan Vice President Jose Vicente Rangel, whom I'd known from the time he presented *The Chávez Code* the year before, and National Assembly President Nicolas Maduro were also scheduled to be there. Ideally I wanted to avoid taking a commercial airliner or charter flight to Havana, or another Hercules, so I asked the Vice-President if I could go with him on his plane. Sure, he said, and referred me to his assistant to make arrangements. I was getting used to private air travel and appreciated the ease with which you could come and go without the usual hassles, security checkpoints and airport restrictions. I knew this was a privilege and I hated asking for favors but decided that I would this time – though afterwards I was to wish that I hadn't.

The Vice-President's small jet was an eight-seater, with two sets of seats in groups of four. When I boarded the plane I saw Jose Vicente Rangel, his son, who at the time was the mayor of the Sucre municipality in greater Caracas, and Nicolas Maduro. I took the fourth seat next to them, thanking the Vice-President for allowing me on his flight.

Most of the trip was unmemorable, or maybe that was because of what happened near the end. We were preparing to land when the flight started to get bumpy. At first we didn't think much of it and kept talking, until gradually we each grew silent and started staring out the windows. The sky was heavy and grey, covered in a thick cloud base that looked impenetrable. One of José Vicente's assistants kept going up into the small cockpit to speak with the two pilots and, when he came out, he left the door open. The cockpit was tiny with just enough space for the two pilots. The plane was so small that from our seats we could see right out the front window of the plane when the door was left open. It looked like we were flying into a dark tunnel with no visibility on any side, including whatever was ahead.

José Vicente, his son, Nicolas and I all looked nervously at each other and at the front of the plane. We looked out the windows and back at each other. José Vicente yelled up to the pilots in the cockpit asking if we'd be able to make the landing. They yelled back, informing us that we had already passed Havana and were circling back. A heavy storm had set in and there was zero visibility in the air or on the ground. It wasn't safe to land yet. If you've ever been on a regular airplane during turbulence then you know how terrifying it feels. You have no control over what's happening and are forced to confront the frightening imminence of death by plane crash. On a small aircraft, this fear is a thousand times more intense. And when extreme turbulence causes a small plane to shake, you feel like everything is going to break into pieces. The metal casing around you seems as vulnerable as an eggshell and you appear to be staring death in the face.

We circled for over 30 minutes, all of us remaining silent as we alternated between staring with horror out the window and anxiously glancing at each other. Our minds were all spinning with our lives passing before us and I'm sure the others were turning to prayer. I was just hoping that whatever rules guided the universe would spare us this time. The pilots broke into our silent misery with an alarming affirmation. We were running out of fuel and had to land soon. They would have to make the landing through the wall of clouds and the passage would get even rougher, they said. But running out of fuel and crashing to our deaths was not an option, so we all nodded our agreement to try the route that would at least offer a chance of survival.

Nicolas Maduro broke the tension amongst the four of us, nervously laughing as he pointed out that no one would ever believe our deaths in a plane crash to be an accident. With Chávez's Vice-President and the President of the National Assembly on board, as well as me, notorious denouncer of CIA covert actions, our collective deaths were sure to be seen as a massive conspiracy to assassinate us and undermine Chávez. Just as we were joking over how the media would spin our deaths, the nose of the plane broke through the cloud cover and we saw the runway what seemed like a matter of inches before the windshield. We braced ourselves. It was fast and rough and we were flung forward as the pilots slammed on the brakes. We didn't crash. We landed. We breathed. We sighed. We laughed. We hugged each other and the pilots. And then we all had a shot of Cuban rum when we got off the plane and went into the VIP area of the airport.

Fidel again

After the harrowing trip there, I was wary of being separated from my Venezuelan counterparts, so I asked the Vice-President if I could stay with them. I knew they had been provided with one of those big protocol mansions that always had too many rooms to fill. I had been offered a room in a hotel nearby, but we had just had a near-death experience and I felt compelled to be close to the people who knew what we had been through. He of course was amenable to the idea and adjustments were made at the house so that I had a room. Our first order of business was to sit down with a glass of Cuban rum and a cigar and calm our nerves, then we discussed how the event would go the following day. José Vicente was the keynote speaker and both Nicolas and I were panelists. Fidel would speak at the end of the event and I had no idea how the whole thing would play out. I was used to Venezuelan events with Chávez, where everything was always up in the air until the last minute. But this wasn't Venezuela, it was Cuba. And the Cubans were precise, punctual and orderly, at least by comparison.

We were escorted to the Karl Marx Theater the following morning after a leisurely breakfast over which we had co-ordinated our remarks for the event so that we wouldn't overlap. Nevertheless, José Vicente ended up covering most of my prepared comments in his opening speech, so I was left scrambling to rework my text and find something new to say. I was a bit nervous to be on stage with Fidel. He had arrived shortly after we were seated on stage. The venue was packed, as with any event involving Fidel, but a fair amount of the audience had also come to see us.

Venezuela had become extremely important for Cubans as an economic lifeline and as an ideological ally that was reviving and validating the survival of the Cuban Revolution. Beyond Fidel and Chávez's growing friendship, the Cuban and Venezuelan people were involved in dozens of different exchange programs that crossed cultural, commercial and political lines. There were tens of thousands of Cubans in Venezuela, working as doctors, technicians, scientists, farmers, engineers, security experts and intelligence advisors. Thousands of Venezuelans were also in Cuba being trained in Cuban institutions, working at the newly formed oil company and building refineries throughout the island.

The Venezuelan flag was seen everywhere, banded together with the blue, white and red Cuban flag on posters, banners and billboards, as though the two countries were one trans-Caribbean homeland. The opposition in Venezuela complained about the close ties between the two countries, claiming that Cuba was trying to take over Venezuela to steal its oil wealth and turn it into a communist hub that would expand throughout the region. 'Cubazuela,' they called it, fear-mongering about the destruction of their country under a regime brainwashed by the evils of communism.

In reality, the relationship was mutually beneficial for both countries. Venezuela was getting an enormous amount of quality, skilled services from Cuba that it was severely lacking, while Cuba was receiving a much-needed injection of oil and cash with little or no burden of debt. The difference the relationship had made in Cuba in just a few years was striking. It was as though a tsunami of modernization had overtaken Havana. Construction projects were under way throughout the city and the rehabilitation of Old Havana was advancing, restoring many of the decrepit and deteriorating colonial buildings. Roadways were smooth and newly asphalted and efficient digital electronic timers had been installed at red lights and intersections to facilitate orderly pedestrian crossing and transit. Havana still retained its charm, but it was obviously thriving as a result of the close ties with its South American neighbor.

During José Vicente's keynote speech, I kept hearing a muted thump, thump on the table. I didn't think too much about it until Nicolas Maduro leaned over and whispered in my ear. 'You hear that knocking? That's Fidel,' he told me, adding that 'Fidel always thumps his hands under the table when he's intensely concentrating on something.' Then I really heard it, thump, thump, almost as though he was keeping rhythm as José Vicente spoke, like a background drum to spoken word poetry.

Fidel almost seemed in a trance as he focused on José Vicente, thumping his fingers under the table and occasionally nodding his head in approval. He later praised José Vicente's speech as one of the most astute political speeches he had ever heard – quite a compliment from one of the greatest orators in history. My speech was not in the same league, but Fidel acknowledged the importance of my work, and I was honored to participate on stage with a historically important political figure of his caliber.

Talk-show TV

Back in Caracas, my life was far from normal. I was heavily into writing my second book, but was constantly distracted by television and radio interviews, speaking engagements and meetings. I had become a regular on a late-night political talk show, *La Hojilla* (The Razor Blade), which was despised by the opposition and loved by Chávez's supporters. The host, Mario Silva, was a hardcore admirer of Chávez and Fidel and he viciously attacked the opposition every night for the entire length of his two-hour show. Mario shared a close relationship with the government's military and civilian intelligence agencies, and they frequently provided him with recordings and video of private opposition meetings and conversations that he then used to discredit and expose his enemies. It always made me feel a little uncomfortable because it was clear that most of those recordings were obtained illegally, without a judicial warrant. But in Venezuela, the rules were different, and no one could successfully challenge that type of illegal wiretapping and win in court. The courts were controlled by, or at least strongly allied with, the government. And the recordings were always revealing and immensely popular with the audience, since they exposed the often dirty dealing and underhanded plotting of key opposition figures against the government. For a journalist to share this information publicly was not in itself unethical, but the fact that it was done on a public, state-funded television station and was clearly aimed at harming anti-government figures was distinctly dodgy.

Mario loved having me on the show as often as possible because my investigative work had also exposed the relationship between the opposition and the US government, as well as their ongoing efforts to overthrow and undermine Chávez and his Bolivarian Revolution. I was also the *gringa chavista*, equally loved and despised. Since Mario was also an extremely polarizing public figure, having me on added more spice, and interest, to the show. *La Hojilla* was also Chávez's favorite show and he often called in to speak with us live on air, which made the show even more popular and almost obligatory watching for *chavistas*. In fact, an unusual culture developed where everyone wanted to be on television so that Chávez would see them and listen to what they had to say.

It became common for Chávez to select his new cabinet members after seeing them on TV talk shows or news interviews – a rather impulsive way to make decisions about high-level members of his government who would go on to control billion-dollar budgets and major policy issues. Often those chosen lacked the experience and knowledge to be successful in those positions, which is one reason why there was so much inefficiency and incompetence in his administration. Just because someone appears knowledgeable during a 10- or 15-minute television interview, it doesn't mean they have the skills needed to oversee a massive government bureaucracy affecting the lives of millions of people and the future of the country.

Reflecting on all of this now, as Venezuela spirals downward into chaos and what seems to be never-ending instability, is a very strange experience. It's as though I'm remembering a distant dream or fantasy, a world in another dimension that may or may not have once existed. Did *chavismo* (the movement supporting Chávez and his ideas) really ever become a reality in the way we understood and believed in it or were we all blind followers, seduced by a utopian idea of a better, more just world? There was so much good in what Chávez stood for that it was hard to see, or accept, his failings. They were always apparent and all around us, but it was easier to look beyond the defects towards the bigger picture.

Chávez, in the end, was no superman: he had remarkable gifts but also very human failings. He dreamt from early in his life of one day leading his country in the same fashion as his idol, Simón Bolívar, and he had the leadership skills and magnetism to attract millions of followers. He was a brilliant strategist and a poet, an avid reader of history with a photographic memory that enabled him to recite entire passages from books he had read years before. If he could have transformed Venezuela all alone, that would have been his choice for sure, but clearly that was impossible. Fidel Castro once told him that he couldn't be the mayor of Venezuela and he had to delegate, that he needed a team to rely on, a circle of trusted advisors around him who could carry through his vision into action. I honestly believe Chávez tried to do that, but he had poor judgment and was often too naive about politics, which is why many of the people he brought into his inner circle eventually betrayed him or used their influence to enrich themselves. José 'Pepe' Mujica, former president of Uruguay, wisely said to me in 2014 that there was 'no school or university for becoming a president' – it was all about learning on the job. Some people are more prepared than others to run a country, but most never know what it entails until they are actually president.

The 'devil speech' at the UN

That September, in 2006, I was off to New York again with Chávez for his annual address before the United Nations General Assembly. I had gone ahead as part of an advance team since this time arrangements had been made for him to speak before a local audience at Cooper Union, a prestigious small university in Greenwich Village. I had also helped to arrange several interviews for him with US media, including an appearance on *Nightline* with Ted Koppel, on the veteran news journalist's last show before his retirement. Even though the actual interview with Chávez was balanced and informative, *Nightline* added a collage of reports to the segment that essentially tried to discredit and butcher every point Chávez made. But it wasn't this interview that splashed his face all over US media, it was rather an unexpected, spontaneous, very Chávez-like outburst during his speech before the UN General Assembly that made him a household name in the US and around the world.

Chávez had prepared remarks to read before the General Assembly, honoring the time restraints imposed by the UN on the addresses of heads of state. Chávez normally abhorred following protocol but, since it had gone quite well for him the previous year, when he had given a speech focused on reforming and democratizing the UN that had been well received by member states and the general public, he had reluctantly agreed to stick to scripted remarks that had been prepared by his team. On the plane ride to New York from Caracas, however, Chávez had a change of heart. He was flying in the night before his scheduled address and had intentionally missed the opening of the General Assembly that morning. After the UN Secretary General had introduced the new session there had been a speech by the US president, George W Bush. Chávez despised Bush. He often referred to him as 'Mr Danger', treating him as a boorish, warmongering buffoon. The two heads of state had never had an official meet and greet, despite the extremely close commercial relationship Venezuela and the US had shared for decades. Not only was Venezuela one of the top three suppliers of oil to the United States, it also owned a US company, Citgo, which had over 14,000 gas stations throughout the country and seven oil refineries in US territory.

One of the only times both presidents had been seated at the same table was at a Summit of the Americas in Mar del Plata, Argentina, in spring of 2005. At the previous Summit in Quebec four years earlier, Chávez had been the only outright leftist president and the only voice in opposition to Bush's proposal to expand the

North American Free Trade Agreement (NAFTA) throughout the Americas. The plan, known as the Free Trade of the Americas Agreement (FTAA) was widely opposed by workers' unions, social organizations and leftist parties throughout the region. Bush had pledged the FTAA would become a reality by 2005, but the Washington establishment had underestimated the changes taking place in Latin America. Chávez might have been the sole dissenting voice in 2001, but by 2005 he was accompanied by Presidents Lula da Silva and Nestor Kirchner of Brazil and Argentina, Latin America's two largest economies. Leftists were also rising up in Bolivia, Ecuador and elsewhere. The times were changing – and not in Washington's favor. At that meeting in 2005, Bush's FTAA was buried forever, defeated by a resurgent Latin American left that had surprised Washington by its popularity, power and tenacity.

George W Bush refused to mention Chávez by name in public, always deflecting questions that would push him to comment on his Latin American rival, but other members of his government were not so cautious or restrained. Bush's National Security Advisor Condoleezza Rice labeled Chávez a 'negative force in the region' and 'authoritarian'. Secretary of Defense Donald Rumsfeld once compared Chávez to Hitler and Bush's CIA Director, Porter Goss, labeled Venezuela under Chávez as a 'top 5 hot spot' for the US intelligence community, claiming the South American country had links to terrorism and organized crime.

Chávez, on the other hand, referred to Bush in derogatory ways as often as possible. One particularly notable episode was on live television during his Sunday program, *Aló Presidente*, when Chávez railed at Bush, calling him a drunk, a clown and a donkey. 'Bush, you are a donkey,' said Chávez, looking right into the camera as though he were speaking directly to the American president. Something about George W Bush really seemed to get under his skin. Which is why, when Chávez landed in New York City for the UN General Assembly in September 2006 and found out that Bush had spoken for nearly 30 uninterrupted minutes, despite the strict five-minute rule that applied to all other speakers, he decided to change his plans.

The next morning we all awaited the motorcade to accompany Chávez to his UN address. He had spent the night in an elegant, multi-million-dollar townhouse on East 81st Street and Fifth Avenue, owned by the Venezuelan state for decades and used by the Venezuelan ambassador to the UN as a residence. The area outside the townhouse had been cordoned off by secret-service agents, but those of us who were official members of the presidential delegation were allowed inside. Every September the UN General Assembly turned Manhattan upside down. Entire lanes in major avenues and streets were blocked off for use solely by foreign dignitaries and their caravans. You couldn't even walk past Second Avenue in midtown without a UN identification card authorizing entry into the area.

It was thrilling to ride in a police-escorted motorcade through midtown Manhattan, speeding through intersections and traffic lights with no obstructions. But it made me realize how so many people caught up in this world of power and celebrity became desensitized to the everyday lifestyles and trials of 99.9 per cent of society. They just whizzed through traffic with no impediments, everything was brought to them or prepared for them, and they rarely had to do anything for themselves.

When we arrived at the UN building, Chávez went in first, smartly dressed in a stylish black suit with a wide, shiny red tie. His hair was neatly trimmed and he looked very presidential, far from the image international media normally projected of him wearing military fatigues and a red army beret, shaking his fist at the 'evil empire'. He was carrying with him a folder with his prepared remarks, while his aide held a briefcase full of papers and books, which Chávez often used as props during his public addresses. The presidents are asked to arrive to the holding area at the General Assembly just minutes before their scheduled speaking time, and for once Chávez was right on time.

The General Assembly hall was packed. Hugo Chávez had become an internationally renowned leader, adored or reviled by millions around the world, and everyone was curious as to what he would say. His succinct speech the previous year had become a reference for his harsh criticism of the United States and his demands for democratic reform within the United Nations Security Council. No one, however, expected what was coming.

When his name was announced by the President of the General

Assembly, Chávez was already seated in the speaker's chair next to the podium. He approached the podium, set his folder down and opened it up so he could read his prepared remarks, beginning his address with the standard greetings to UN officials, heads of state, ambassadors and others present in the audience. All of a sudden, he took a deep breath and began shaking his head, moving the papers in his folder around until finally he closed it and rested his hand on top.

'The devil was here yesterday,' he said, pointing at the podium where he was standing. And then, in a rather dramatic motion, he made the sign of the cross and pressed his hands together as though he were praying, looking up towards the ceiling. 'The devil was here in this very same place,' he repeated as he began sniffing, 'and it still smells like sulfur.' The audience erupted in a mix of loud laughter and heavy applause, some even rising to give a standing ovation until they realized that others were watching and thought better of it. Hugo Chávez had just called President George W Bush the devil from the world stage of the United Nations. It was unprecedented, bold, and oh-so-typically Chávez. At that moment, Chávez became a household name across the United States and around the world. If you hadn't heard of Hugo Chávez before, you sure had now.

The rest of his lengthy speech, which he decided to extend because Bush had been given extra time the day before, was overshadowed by his opening lines. We didn't have Twitter back then or other social media, but his statements were blasted all over the press almost immediately. He made the headlines of every news hour around the world, and US newspapers had him on the front page the following morning, some using less than generous images.

I recall a less-than-glamorous cover of the *New York Post* on which Chávez's face was photoshopped with glaring red eyes and two devil horns, referring to him as the 'real devil'. Even progressive politicians who had been friendly to Chávez in the past were outraged by his remarks on Bush. New York's Democratic congress member Charles Rangel told a news reporter, 'You don't come into my city and call my president the devil.' It was shocking to see these harsh Bush critics doing a 180 to defend him. But for many others, calling George W Bush the devil was spot-on.

He was hated on the left and viewed as a boorish, unintelligent, warmongering president who had lied to justify the mass murder of thousands of Iraqis and Afghans. This was, of course, more than a decade before Donald Trump became president and plumbed depths that left the Bush presidency looking sane by comparison.

In addition to substantially raising his notoriety, Chávez's 'devil' remark had its consequences. Venezuela had been campaigning for nearly a year to win a seat on the UN Security Council. The elections were set for October, just a few weeks after Chávez's UN address. Washington had been lobbying against Venezuela earning a seat on the Security Council, but one seat was guaranteed to a Latin American nation that year and so far none were opposing Venezuela. In the wake of the 'devil' speech, however, Washington pushed Guatemala to run.

A brutal, dirty campaign ensued, with the US using scare tactics against member states, threatening to strip them of economic funding if they voted for Venezuela. When the vote came up, neither country was able to garner the two-thirds majority necessary to win the two-year rotating seat. There were an unprecedented 47 rounds of votes that day in the General Assembly with no winner. Finally the Group of Latin American and Caribbean states agreed to settle on a third candidate, Panama, which was also endorsed by Washington. Venezuela reluctantly accepted defeat. The lesson was clear: call the US president the devil and you pay the price.

Calling me an angel

The evening after the 'devil speech', Chávez addressed a different crowd at Cooper Union in downtown Manhattan. It was more of an intellectual, academic and activist audience, with fewer critics and more fans. Chávez was becoming a legend amongst progressives and leftists in the US, and the line to attend his event stretched right around the block of the university's East Village location. The presidential security team was also on high alert, thoroughly searching all guests as they entered the building. His threat-level assessment had escalated after his UN address and the negative coverage he was receiving in the mainstream media. I later learned from Chávez's presidential guard counter-intelligence team that they had discovered a potential threat against the president's life during the pre-event security inspections. According to a high-level member of his security detail with whom I was friendly, they had allegedly found a potentially life-threatening substance near the Cooper Union auditorium stage. It was unclear where it had originated from or who had placed it there, but the counter-intelligence officials said they had discovered its presence after routine inspection. Years later, when Chávez developed an abnormally aggressive cancer, some close to him suspected that his deadly illness may have been induced by one of his many powerful enemies, though such a theory was not proven. I'm not sure how much truth there is to that whole story, but I was privy to internal security information that documented the incident at Cooper Union, and those who were there attested it was true.

After the threat was neutralized and the event was cleared for the president to attend, we arrived in the presidential motorcade, fashionably late. As part of his official delegation, I had a seat towards the front of the auditorium, right in Chávez's line of vision. After he came on stage to wild applause, he began his typical greetings to all the special guests present at the event. When he got to my name he paused. 'Eva Golinger, attorney and author from North America.' He looked up at me. 'Eva, to us you are a Venezuelan,' he said, adding, 'Eva is the author of *The Chávez Code*, about the CIA's coup in Venezuela and she's writing another book called, what's it called Eva? – I don't know what it's called.'

I stood up and said, 'It's called *Bush Vs Chávez: Washington's War on Venezuela*.' The audience erupted into applause. And then Chávez said: 'Eva, look at her, focus the camera on her. Look at the tender, angelic face she has, but Eva, she's more brave and valiant than anyone else.' I turned red in embarrassment as everyone clapped and Chávez moved on to his next greeting.

It had been quite a day. Chávez had called George W Bush the devil in the morning and had then referred to me as angelic in his evening address. I was definitely pleased to be on the other side of the spectrum from Bush, though I'm not sure I would consider myself an angel.

12

Upside-down world

Chávez was up for re-election that December in 2006 and the campaign was well on its way when we returned from New York. He had a clear lead in the polls over the opposition candidate, Manuel Rosales, who represented the old, corrupt parties of the past. By then the Bolivarian Revolution had regained its strength and popularity after several years of intense destabilization and fierce opposition. The opposition, comprising over 30 different political parties ranging from the left to the far right, had reluctantly agreed on Rosales as a unity candidate, but behind the scenes there were serious power struggles and disagreements. This gave Chávez the upper hand since on his side there were no other contenders.

The campaign was lavish and extravagant. The government spent tens of millions of dollars on Chávez's campaign, printing thousands of red shirts and hats and large billboards with his smiling, imposing face that were posted throughout the nation. Songs were composed, videos were produced and commercials were aired nationwide. The opposition led a multi-million-dollar campaign as well, hiring one of the top US political consulting firms: Greenberg Quinlan Rosner, known for handling some of the most important presidential campaigns in the US and around the world. Washington also poured in millions of dollars into Rosales' campaign, despite the unlikelihood of his winning. Venezuela was enjoying an oil boom and the country was flush with wealth, which Chávez was generously using to fund social programs and a vast array of special new missions and efforts aimed at reducing poverty and economic inequality in the country.

By then the government-sponsored social programs had gone

beyond the initial healthcare and education missions, Barrio Adentro and Mission Robinson, both set up and run with the help of the Cuban government and thousands of Cuban doctors, health workers and educators. Chávez had expanded the missions to include job training, athletics, housing subsidies, agricultural initiatives, subsidized food markets, mining, homelessness prevention, drug-addiction therapy, music, art and cultural programs and credits for small businesses. He had shifted focus from the top-down government approach to create community councils that would directly govern their neighborhoods, with resources provided from the national government, bypassing regional authorities. It was the manifestation of Chávez's concept of 'participatory democracy': putting real power in the hands of the people, real resources in the hands of communities, to determine how best to allocate them and prioritize their needs.

In theory it was a groundbreaking, pioneering policy that sought to revolutionize government and traditional power structures. In practice, it was a lengthy, messy process often co-opted by greed and corruption. But it was still effective and empowering, and evolved to become one of the most sustaining aspects of the Bolivarian Revolution.[1] The missions, on the other hand, were a mixed bag. While extremely effective and profound in their transformational impact on Venezuelan society, substantially reducing poverty, providing free and universal healthcare and education and access to jobs, housing and subsidized food, they also became a hotbed of corruption and party politics. The missions became a vast enterprise of state-sponsored employment, unsustainable in the long term because of the heavy economic burden on the government and public funds, but they were very popular nationwide, including with anti-government sectors that benefited from the free healthcare and subsidized food markets.

Chávez was essentially setting up a parallel state while his Bolivarian Revolution dismantled the traditional government

---

1 For more detailed analysis and informative research on Venezuela's community councils I recommend *Building The Commune: Radical Democracy in Venezuela* by George Ciccariello-Maher (Verso, 2016) and *Communes and Workers' Control in Venezuela: Building 21st Century Socialism from Below* by Dario Azzellini (Haymarket Books, 2018).

institutions that were thoroughly corrupted and rotting from within. The problem, he soon discovered, was that the decay within the state had in large part come from the people running the country, and, while his leadership was new, the bureaucrats were not. It was a near-impossible task to transform a rotten system into something functional, which is why Chávez tried to set up an alternative system through the missions. But by not transforming the mentality of those running the system first, the decay kept spreading, even into the new structures he was creating. The corruption in Venezuela was internal, cultural, socialized and was passed on through generations. That blighted the chances of the new system evolving into something functional.

Hated but guarded

I discovered the intense animosity of the opposition towards me on the day of the presidential elections that December, when raw eggs were thrown out of apartment windows as I walked out of my building to go and exercise my right to vote. '*Muere Chávez*' (Die Chávez) they yelled at me as they hurled their eggs like baseballs at my head, luckily missing me entirely, though some of the slimy yolk splashed on my pants. People might have hated me, but they also appreciated the additional security I brought to the building, since I frequently had my bodyguards stationed in the parking garage or out front on the street, which served as a deterrent to any criminals casing the area. Crime was starting to spike upwards in middle-class neighborhoods in Caracas and there had been several carjackings in my building as residents arrived home at night.

We had three security guards 24/7, but they were unarmed and susceptible to bribes. One of my anti-Chávez neighbors approached me pleading for my help after her husband had been victim of an 'express kidnapping' at the entrance to our parking garage. The kidnappers had bound and gagged the security guards working that night and as my neighbor's husband approached the garage and opened the door with his remote control, the criminals popped out of the shadows with large nine-millimeter guns pointing right at him. They got in the car and told him to drive, holding him hostage while forcing him to empty his bank accounts at different

ATM machines. They finally released him on the side of the road after more than eight hours of terror. Of course they stole his car too. I reported the incident to my bodyguards but there was not much they could do. The state security forces were not going to provide protection to my neighbors and the whole building, the chief told me; I was their only responsibility, which made my neighbors hate me even more. I asked him for a gun to keep in my apartment, for when the bodyguards were off duty, just in case someone, neighbors included, tried to attack me in my home.

I was loaned a Beretta handgun and several boxes of bullets. I had previously practiced shooting nine-millimeter semi-automatics back in college when I was on my women's self-defense kick, so I knew how to handle a gun. Still, I was required to practice with the gun they gave me at the shooting range. I was also given a license to carry the gun that authorized my possession of a firearm in general. At first I would carry it with me when I went out in public without my bodyguards, but it was big and bulky and wouldn't fit comfortably under my clothes, so I ended up putting it in my purse, which rendered the rapid-response concept useless, since unzipping my bag to pull it out would have cost precious, lifesaving seconds. Carrying the gun also made me feel less safe, almost as though I were drawing the danger to me. That might have been only in my head, but it was enough to make me leave the gun at home, hidden in one of my closets.

Chávez on a high

Chávez easily won the election that December, with nearly 63 per cent of the vote, a landslide victory. He was riding on a high, having defeated his opposition once again, after years of their trying to undermine and overthrow him through coups, strikes, protests, recall votes and now a presidential election. The opposition was weak, divided and demoralized, with no leadership and no clear agenda. Chávez took advantage of the moment to press forward with what he now proclaimed as a socialist revolution and to deepen his social and economic policies. He viewed his huge electoral victory as a mandate to radicalize the Bolivarian Revolution and move Venezuela further away from capitalism, with the overall goal of redistributing power and wealth and eradicating poverty in every corner of the country. It was an inspiring and bold vision that rallied his supporters and terrified his detractors. How exactly he would accomplish this grandiose idea was less than clear, since Venezuela continued to be entirely dependent on its oil resources and Chávez was stretching these thin through co-operative trade agreements with poorer Caribbean and Central American nations that were basically receiving Venezuelan oil at low or no cost.

The United States was still Venezuela's largest oil customer, despite the contentious relationship between Bush and Chávez. Ironically, that relationship became ever more important, and even life sustaining, as Venezuela entered into oil agreements that provided little or no cash income for the country, but rather 'in kind' trade, such as services, food and consumer products and credits for infrastructure development. The Chávez government made huge multi-billion-dollar deals with China that involved providing millions of barrels of oil daily in exchange for loans and credits to build mass housing projects, bridges, railways and other infrastructural developments. While this fostered the country's growth, it didn't help the national budget – the government was fast spending money that it didn't actually have.

As the opposition licked its wounds and Chávez prepared his next moves, I took the opportunity to spend the Christmas holidays with my mother, who was living in the Miami area at the time. She had visited me shortly after I moved into my new apartment in Caracas to help me settle in and also to pursue a longtime dream of finding her familial roots in Venezuela. She had done as much genealogical research as possible in the US, but most of her family had long passed away or disappeared. While she was in Caracas we spent our days searching through the microfilm records at the local Mormon Temple, which contained an expansive and thorough catalogue of every birth, death and marriage certificate for all people in Venezuela. The records we found on the man my mother believed to be her father, Antonio Calderon, included the certificate for his birth in Caracas, the births of his sisters and brothers, the death of his father and his burial in a particular cemetery, their address in downtown historical Caracas and other relevant facts that gave us glimpses into the lives of relatives neither

I nor my mother had ever known but with whom we began to feel a connection. I was living in their homeland, their city, walking the streets they had roamed a hundred years before. Often after these discoveries, when I would walk in the old city center of Caracas, I would pass by the house they had lived in at the turn of the 20th century and try to imagine them there, in the very same place I now considered my home. It gave me chills to think that the many paths of my life had brought me there, to a location that was in my blood. Or so I thought.

When I returned to Caracas after spending the Christmas and New Year holidays with my mother in Florida, Venezuela was heating up again, and not just from the fireworks. Chávez was making new plans and announcements to consolidate his political project and these were stirring up the opposition. He had announced at the very end of the year that the government would not renew the broadcasting license of RCTV, one of the country's main television stations which had openly aligned with the opposition. Actually, RCTV had gone beyond just aligning with the opposition: the privately owned station had directly participated in the 2002 attempted coup against Chávez by broadcasting manipulated images and calling on anti-government activists to oust the President. After the coup was defeated and Chávez returned to power, RCTV continued to broadcast open calls for insurrection against the government during its news and opinion programming. Nevertheless, the channel was hugely popular nationwide because it primarily aired *telenovelas*, Latin American soap operas that dramatize daily events and personal relationships. It was also the station with the widest reach into households in Venezuela, even in the most remote areas.

When people began returning from holiday in January 2007, the street protests against the non-renewal of RCTV's license began. Whatever brief respite Venezuela had enjoyed from the turmoil of the previous years was over almost as soon as it had begun. Chávez might have been emboldened by his crushing electoral victory, but his move against a beloved television station rallied opposition forces once again – and this time with a facelift.

As though out of nowhere, a group of previously unknown university students began creative public protests against Chávez's decision to revoke the RCTV broadcast license. Of course they received widespread, uninterrupted coverage in the corporate-owned media. Internationally, the student movement, as it came to be known in the private press, was the new face of anti-Chávez protest: young people rising up against a tyrant who now wanted to shut down their favorite television station, cutting off their unbridled access to *telenovelas*. I had never seen a vanguard youth movement before demanding their right to watch soap operas and cheesy television shows. It wasn't exactly the kind of protest one imagined would rally the masses, but the movement began to grow and traditional opposition politicians seized the moment. They thrust a select group of student leaders into the center of battle as the new face of the opposition, the leaders of the future. It was no longer the old guard trying to retake power, it was the future as youthful activists defended their freedom to watch soap operas.

The movement gained a lot of traction because of the massive media attention it received, and because of the savvy tactics the protestors employed. They called themselves the *Manos Blancas* (White Hands) movement, painting their hands white and wearing white shirts during their protests. It made for great television, especially with their youthful, innocent faces and post-adolescent passion. It was definitely like watching the world upside-down to see all these young, mainly white middle- and upper-class students protesting against a socially progressive government because they wanted their soap operas and bad sitcoms back on air. They didn't appear to be fighting to save democracy or human rights in the traditional sense, or battling a real brutal, repressive dictatorship. They were angry because the government had flexed its muscles and taken their favorite shows away.

Of course no one wants a state to decide what we can or cannot watch on television, but the reality is that there is no 'right' to watch certain shows on the open airwaves. The public airwaves, publicly owned broadcast channels, radio and television, are owned by the state and licensed to private companies through concessions, contracts of limited duration with regulation. In the case of RCTV, the Venezuelan government felt as though it was within its rights to decide not to renew the concession, despite the extreme unpopularity of that decision. In legal terms, the government did not 'shut down' RCTV. It denied the renewal of its broadcast license on the public airwaves, though the station was free to broadcast on cable, satellite and digital television.

Chávez had underestimated the reaction to his hardline move against RCTV and it became a *cause célèbre* for the opposition within Venezuela and for freedom of press and human rights defenders worldwide. It might not actually have been an issue of press freedom, since there is no 'right' for a corporation to possess a public broadcast license beyond its contract term, and even less a human rights issue, since there is no fundamental 'right' to watch certain television shows on public airwaves, but because of the sophisticated help the opposition had in crafting and projecting their anti-government message, it worked. Chávez was made to look more like an authoritarian leader with each passing day, despite his consistent electoral victories and his policies favoring people over profits.

Back in the spotlight

The government tried to push back against the growing student movement by selecting a group of youth leaders from within the newly created state party, the United Socialist Party of Venezuela. Chávez embraced the youth movement, believing those on the opposition side were being manipulated by the traditional elites and their allies in Washington, who, as I soon discovered through my freedom-of-information investigations, were funding the White Hands and closely advising them on their protest tactics. Through the National Endowment for Democracy and USAID, the US government was pouring hundreds of thousands of dollars into the anti-government student movement in Venezuela, providing strategic and communication training in addition to hard cash. Dozens of anti-Chávez youth leaders were hand-selected by the US Embassy in Caracas and sent up for training sessions at several US government-funded institutions and organizations, including the Albert Einstein Institute and the Non-Violent Action Coordinating Committee, later known as CANVAS.

My exposure of the US funding sources behind the anti-Chávez student movement made headlines in Venezuela and once again I was thrust into the spotlight. Since I once again had evidence of foreign meddling, I became a primary target for the opposition, and a useful propaganda tool for the government. The information that I uncovered demonstrated how youth leaders were selected for their potential leadership skills and ideological affinity with US interests. The chosen few were enticed by grants and stipends in US dollars to participate in different programs and workshops in the US aimed at providing them with the skills and tools to build a 'grassroots' anti-government youth movement in Venezuela. They succeeded in their initial goals, but because I discovered their direct ties to US agencies who were pulling the strings, they were largely discredited for not being genuine Venezuelan movements working in the best interests of the people.

Ironically, the United States strictly forbids any foreign funding or influence of political or media activities in US territory, and there is an uproar in Washington and in public opinion if it occurs. Just look at the 2016 US presidential election and the swirling accusations that Russia sought to influence public opinion through media, document leaks and promoting both anti- and pro-government protests. Washington rightly denounces this kind of interventionism when it happens at home, yet engages in the same interference abroad if it is thought to advance US interests. It was precisely this sort of hypocrisy that offended my own values, which were rooted in justice, freedom and self-determination.

At the same time as I was exposing US funding of anti-government youth movements in Venezuela, I also received a batch of documents from the State Department providing evidence of direct funding to dozens of well-known Venezuelan journalists. While most of these journalists worked with private media outlets and took up distinctly anti-Chávez positions, some of them did not. A few actually worked in public media and several even held positions in the Chávez administration. I decided not to withhold that information, but instead to release all the documents in order to demonstrate how the US intelligence agencies target certain individuals for recruitment, and often lure them in through attractive educational and professional programs that appear apolitical. Once recruited to participate in a Washington-sponsored program, the US agencies then evaluate the potential of the individuals, either to become a valuable US informant or to influence public opinion in ways favorable to US interests.

There was a massive response to this information and I quickly garnered even more enemies than I had before, especially on the pro-Chávez side. My face was plastered on the front pages of newspapers and magazines that labeled me as a 'tattle tail' and a '*sapo*' (toad) for exposing other journalists and their financial ties to the US government. Again I was accused of being a CIA agent, an agent of the Cuban government or simply a traitor. Most of those insults never made much sense but were just attempts to smear my name and reputation, and to intimidate me. I was constantly under attack from all sides and grew distrustful of almost everyone – with the exception of Chávez, who seemed to be my only genuine protector.

After I had made several appearances on Mario Silva's show *La Hojilla* talking about the documents revealing both the student movement and Venezuelan journalists' ties to the US government, both Mario and I were summoned to appear before a special investigative committee at the National Assembly, Venezuela's legislature. They wanted to see the evidence I possessed about alleged foreign funding of media and political activities in their country. I did what I always did in the confines of my modest work space, usually a room in my home somewhere, which was to draw out a map of connections by hand, using different colors in marker to show the various groups, political parties, agencies and individuals involved. I prepared it on a piece of poster board to use as a reference for the written testimony I would read before the committee. Since I wasn't particularly adept with graphic design, it never occurred to me to do an intricate, sleek modern digital design of my hand-drawn map that I could project in a PowerPoint presentation or screen show. Like Chávez, I preferred using props in my presentations – tangible items that I could hold in my hand to illustrate my point. I didn't expect my dingy map to make headlines, but it did.

Mario spoke first at the hearing, which was held in a smallish conference room inside the administrative offices of the National Assembly. There were about a dozen members of parliament there and a handful of journalists authorized to cover our testimony.

Mario talked about the overall political ties and implications of the anti-government group's relationships to foreign agencies and hard-right opposition elites who had been actively pushing for the overthrow of the Chávez administration. He didn't have prepared remarks like I did, but he was lively and provocative, holding the attention of the legislators who most likely watched him on television every night. He was brief in his statement and then turned the microphone over to me.

I had a lengthy speech prepared that was about 20 pages long, with my quirky graphic map to illustrate the evidence I was presenting. The connections were complicated and intertwined and my basic school-style map made them easier to comprehend. Mario held the map up while I spoke and often pointed to different areas on it as I read from my written testimony. When I was finished with my remarks, some of the legislators asked questions which I did my best to reply to, and then they closed the session. They asked for a copy of my statement and the map to keep as part of their investigation. My hand-drawn map? Really? I didn't have a problem leaving it there, it just seemed silly to me that they would want to keep it as an official document of their serious investigation.

The press had a field day with my silly map, mocking its lack of design sophistication. While I wasn't surprised, I also knew that they were more interested in discrediting the assertions presented in the map, which got a little too close for comfort in Venezuelan media circles. Not only were journalists, editors and executives from all the major private media in Venezuela named at one time or another in the State Department documents, but so were some of the more prominent members of the pro-Chávez public media. The ties shown on the map linked media and key journalists in Venezuela to US intelligence agencies, which was a pretty damning charge. It is not as though the CIA has not used journalists in the past to push their agenda abroad. The notorious links between the primary newspaper in Chile, *El Mercurio*, and the CIA during the time of the coup against Salvador Allende in 1973 were exposed in declassified US government documents. In the 1980s, US intelligence agencies set up a special propaganda office to execute a covert media warfare program against the Sandinistas in

Nicaragua. The Office of Public Diplomacy was overseen by Otto Reich, who later became a Special Advisor for Latin American Affairs to President George W Bush and was directly involved in the 2002 coup against Chávez.

Even more astonishingly, my handmade map somehow made its way into the newly created counter-espionage division of Venezuela's intelligence agency, SEBIN, as a point of reference. I was astounded that their level of sophistication and knowledge did not exceed that of my map. However, as I soon reluctantly discovered, while they may not have been very advanced in their intelligence collection and analysis, they were very good at dirty tactics and deception.

How I was scammed

Shortly after I made the explosive revelations about youth movements and journalists on Washington's payroll, a curious document landed in my hands that seemed to perfectly detail the plans of the Bush administration against Venezuela. 'Operation Pliers' it was titled, and it appeared to be an internal secret memo written by a high-level official inside the US Embassy in Caracas. Instead of doing my research and pursuing proper authentication of the document, which I had not obtained via freedom-of-information requests but rather through suddenly surfacing in local media, I jumped on the opportunity to analyze and expose it.

I felt like I was the declassified document expert and queen of the show, and I wanted to be the one to show the world the new hard evidence that Washington was up to its usual exploits against the Chávez government. I was again plastered all over the print and television media in Venezuela, and even garnered some international coverage. 'Another US government plot against Venezuela revealed.' I relished the spotlight and the satisfaction of documentation that proved my theories. I should have scrutinized the document more. I should have fact checked. I should have verified the sources and the authenticity of the document. This was all well before Wikileaks and Julian Assange had flooded the media with tens of thousands of unfiltered, unredacted classified US government documents. Up until then, we either had evidence gained by freedom-of-information requests or random leaks. Both were time-consuming and required meticulous and often tedious research.

But I couldn't wait. And I paid the price. The document was a fake. Some 'analyst' had conjured it up in the SEBIN laboratories and made sure it got to me, the perfect patsy to execute their plan. They figured I had the credibility to make the document believable to the *chavistas*, but they didn't do me the courtesy of telling me I was being set up. It was my old investigative partner back in Washington, Jeremy Bigwood, who called me out. He pointed out that the document had grammatical errors uncommon to a native English speaker, and that the way it was drafted was inconsistent with the thousands of US government documents he had seen over his decades of research. Plus, it revealed too many details in too explicit a way, untypical of such memos. I had taken the bait and paid a price in terms of my credibility. My reputation in Venezuela was not affected at all, since Chávez supporters didn't seem to care if the document was real or fake, given that such things were happening in reality. But internationally, more reputable media began to label me as a 'Chávez propagandist', and as someone too close to the government to be an independent voice.

Almost unbelievably, years later I repeated the same error by opening a document sent to me by someone I knew and generally trusted in terms of information. I immediately publicized the document, which laid out a plan of aggression and interference in Venezuela coming from Colombian entities working closely with US agencies and related groups. I again jumped on the opportunity to get the document circulating in the media, believing it was a detailed plot of intervention worthy of full exposure, but I failed to verify the sources. It was another fake, probably prepared by a different intelligence agency because this time, it contained spyware. My computer was hacked into and some of my email communications were distributed to various journalists who used them to try and discredit me and others.

The break-in

Sometimes threats against me were more tangible and direct, often the result of my own vulnerabilities and indiscretions. Shortly after my testimony in the National Assembly about the US funding of journalists in Venezuela, my apartment was broken into and ransacked. I had gone out for a run one Saturday morning, as I did most days, on my usual route up through the hills at the base of the Avila mountain. I had a regular run time of about 50 minutes and it was no different that day. When I arrived back at my apartment I noticed my door was wide open. This didn't completely freak me out since the night before a university student from the US had arrived at my apartment to stay for a few days until she could find another place in Caracas. I got really angry when I saw the open door, thinking she had been incredibly irresponsible, not least because my cat Lola could get out and lost in the building. But when I went to shut the door I realized that the entire handle and lock had been removed. My heart started pounding and I broke out in a cold sweat. I called to Lola, frightened that she might have been hurt. Thankfully, she came running out to me from under the couch, seemingly scared as well.

I headed towards my room, noticing that the door to the guest room was still closed, as it had been when I left for my run. Before I could open it to see if my guest was inside, I noticed that my own room was a complete mess. Drawers had been emptied on my bed, closet doors were wide open and there was stuff all over the floor. What the hell was going on? I thought. I immediately opened the guest door and the young woman was still in bed, looking at her phone as though nothing had happened. 'What the hell happened?' I asked her angrily. 'What are you talking about?' she responded, dumbfounded. 'Didn't you hear anything or notice anyone here?' She said she had heard someone moving around and opening closet doors and drawers but had thought it was just me, so she hadn't got up. She said her phone alarm had only gone off a few minutes ago and that she was just waking up.

At first I found it hard to believe, but then I realized what must have happened. Whoever had done this had been watching me for days, or even weeks. They knew I would go for a run and how long I'd be gone. Since I rarely had overnight guests and the woman had arrived around 1.00am the night before, they had had no idea anyone else was in my apartment. When her phone alarm had gone off, they had realized someone else was there and run out, just before I got back home.

I immediately called my bodyguard and told him what had happened. Within minutes an entire forensic team of SEBIN detectives was in my apartment, dusting for fingerprints and taking pictures. Both my guest and I were taken in for questioning at the SEBIN headquarters. I was so rattled that I hadn't even checked to see what was missing, beyond the obvious.

My new digital camera that had been on top of my dresser was gone, as well as my old Swiss Army watch my father had given me years ago. Some inexpensive jewelry was taken, but no documents or files, and thankfully not my laptop, which was out in the office area of my apartment off the living room. It seemed to me that whoever had done this had left in a rush before making it into my office area, because they realized someone was in the apartment in the guest room. It wasn't until I was back home after the initial report was taken that I realized what else had been taken. In my closet, hidden under folds of clothes on different shelves, I had placed little envelopes of cash, dollars. It was my entire life savings at the time, and I had kept it there as an emergency fund. They had also taken my nine-millimeter Beretta handgun and two boxes of bullets.

The incident made the nightly news. I had been ransacked right after exposing financial ties between the US government and Venezuelan media, so the conclusion seemed obvious. It was an intimidation tactic. They could get to me anywhere, even in my bedroom. My bodyguard stayed in my apartment with me for the next week, sleeping in the extra room off the kitchen, originally designed for 'service people' (many apartments were built to include a 'maid's room').

SEBIN came and installed an extra security door at the entrance to my apartment, creating a 'cage' before you could actually access the apartment. A large mirror was also installed high above in the cage, so I could see it from the inside of the apartment through the peep hole and know who was there before opening the door. Plus, the security door had six steel rods that extended two into the floor, two into the upper bar of the cage and two horizontally. I was told that the only way to open it without a key would be with dynamite. As it turned out, the major suspect in the break-in was a crazy guy I had dated and broken up with a few weeks earlier. He worked as the bouncer at a local club popular amongst *chavistas*. I let him into my home and actually allowed him to stay with me for nearly a month before I came to my senses and realized he was a completely crazy drug addict who had spent several years in prison. He became the main person of interest in the break-in, but he was never caught. He disappeared off the grid and even Venezuela's new intelligence force was incapable of tracking down a common criminal. I'll never know if he acted on his own accord or if he was put up to it by my many detractors. But it was definitely a wake-up call to me to get my act together and not behave so recklessly.

13

A defeat for socialism
(or the return of toilet paper)

After his resounding electoral victory in December 2006 won him another six-year term as president, Chávez had decided it was time to deepen the Bolivarian Revolution, which he had now declared as socialist. So far most of the 'socialist' aspects of Chávez's policies were centered on free and universal healthcare and education, as well as the prioritizing of people over profits. As oil prices began to bound upward, pouring millions upon millions of dollars into the country, Chávez was investing around 60 per cent of the national budget in social programs. And the investment was paying off, not just in votes, but in concrete economic and social advances. Poverty was decreasing, UNESCO had declared Venezuela a territory free of illiteracy, and infant mortality rates were dropping. In human terms, Venezuela was on a rapid path to development with a healthier, more educated society. Politically, meanwhile, Chávez had been counseled by both the Cubans and the Chinese to build a new political party that would bridge together all parties on the left and create a new grassroots structure in government. At least, that was the idea.

I had never declared loyalty to any political party, in the US or elsewhere, and was skeptical about the idea now, but I decided to give it the benefit of the doubt. By then, the Bolivarian Revolution had been through several attempts at formalizing grassroots organizing, first through the short-lived Bolivarian Circles, and subsequently through Community Councils, which had a rough start but became a staple of Venezuelan political power beyond elected officials. Now the new United Socialist Party of Venezuela (PSUV) was to be launched, which purported to be completely horizontal in its power structure, with no party 'benefits' to members or hierarchies. I attended the first few local meetings in my neighborhood as the new party was taking shape. Assemblies were held every weekend in every neighborhood nationwide, and we were allegedly discussing our ideas for the party structure and internal functioning, as well as the party's strategic objectives. Each assembly was supposed to put forward a slate of candidates that would be voted on by all members nationwide as party representatives. The candidates were supposed to be nominated by a grassroots, democratic selection. Unsurprisingly, it didn't end up working that way.

While some candidates were selected at a community level, the entire leadership of the party was hand selected by Chávez and his closest advisors, rendering the horizontal approach completely null and void. I stopped going to the assemblies once reading material was distributed that you were obliged to read and discuss if you wanted to be in the party. Most of this was written by a few hand-selected figures from within the party leadership. I just didn't want to be told what to read. Nor was I prepared to be duped by the claims about the horizontal party structure. It was top-down with an elite leadership, just like all political parties have been traditionally in Venezuela and elsewhere. In general, political parties, especially those in power, don't like to share decision-making powers with the common folk or with those beyond the circle of proven loyalty.

I still supported the idea of the PSUV and agreed that it was necessary to formalize a new party for the *chavista* movement. I interpreted my own reaction to the party process as my typical rejection of all authority and conventional structures. It was important for Venezuelans to come together and build a solid political party that could achieve, maintain and sustain the overall objectives of the Bolivarian Revolution. I just preferred to be an observer instead of a direct participant.

My gut instinct proved right later on as PSUV became an increasingly closed, loyalist party with Stalinist tendencies. Anyone who tried to criticize or challenge decisions made by the hand-selected party leadership was branded a traitor and expelled. Candidates for elections were all exclusively chosen by party elites, with little or no input from constituents. This type of dangerously authoritarian behavior worsened after Chávez's death when internal divisions ruptured party unity and the circle of loyalists was dramatically reduced.

Ramping up public ownership

Around the same time as the PSUV was being created, Chávez also decided that it was time to radicalize Venezuela's sovereign control of its natural resources. While oil had been nationalized in 1976 by the government of Carlos Andrés Pérez, not all hydrocarbons had been included in that decree. In the Orinoco River Basin, in the southeast region of Venezuela, huge deposits of 'bitumen' had been found over the years. According to Chávez, it was the United States that had labeled those deposits bitumen (a very heavy type of practically unrefinable crude oil), in order to prevent them from being encompassed by the nationalization decree. That way, major US oil giants like Exxon, ConocoPhilips and Chevron would be able to control those vast reserves and exploit them for the sole benefit of the United States. When Chávez suspected what was going on and had the deposits tested again, it turned out they actually constituted over 300 billion barrels of heavy crude, making Venezuela the country with the largest oil reserves on the planet.

Chávez acted quickly, decreeing the nationalization of all reserves in the Orinoco River Basin on 1 May 2007. Along with those nationalizations, he also decreed state control over all strategic resources, including electricity and landline telephone service, two utilities that at that time were owned by US corporations. It was Carlos Andrés Pérez, during his second term of president before he was forced to resign, who had privatized those utilities and sold them to US companies. Chávez, fearful of sabotage against the electrical grid and determined to protect Venezuela's sovereignty against foreign intervention or manipulation of its internet and telephone services, brought these utilities back into public ownership, creating new state entities to oversee them that had significant worker control.

In Chávez's vision, all nationalized companies would eventually become worker-controlled, under a modern version of Marxism that would create workplace equality. The idea was grandiose, but it required more than just theory. In practice, without the proper training, internal structure, regulations and oversight, many of the expropriated and nationalized companies became more corrupt, dysfunctional and exploitative than they were before, leading to the severe economic and development problems Venezuela would face years later.

But back in 2007, Chávez was riding high on the tide of nationalization, much to the disapproval of the United States. Both Exxon and ConocoPhilips refused to accept state control of the deposits in the Orinoco River Basin and sued Venezuela for billions of dollars in lost profits. Chávez refused to pay. The only US company that stayed was Chevron, which eventually became Venezuela's largest oil trading partner. With US companies withdrawing, Chávez opened up foreign investment to other regions, making deals with China, Russia, Iran, India, Malaysia and other nations in Europe, Asia, the Middle East and Africa. Washington was quickly losing economic control over its own backyard and some of its most ardent adversaries were picking up the slack.

Just months earlier, the US government had discreetly imposed sanctions on Venezuela for allegedly not fully co-operating with the war on terrorism. This was essentially Washington's way of ramping up the pressure on the Chávez administration to do its bidding. But Chávez would have none of it. When those sanctions prohibited the sale of military and arms equipment to Venezuela, Chávez turned to Russia, making multi-million-dollar arms deals, reviving fears from the Cold War era when the Soviet Union had an amped-up presence in Latin America. As Washington tried to squeeze Chávez, the idea was that he would expand into other areas, his messages and vision becoming more influential in Latin America and around the world.

Referendum on the constitution

At home, beyond the nationalizations and the closure of RCTV, Chávez decided it was time to deepen his revolution in legal terms.

He proposed a radical reform of the very same constitution he had brought to life not even a decade earlier and had then lauded as the 'best constitution in the world'. Now he wanted to make it a 'socialist constitution', incorporating the term 'socialism' into the government structure and economic regulations. He proposed to constitutionalize the community councils, providing them with a power equal to the other five branches of government enshrined in the little blue book he carried around in his pocket. The constitution would become Bolivarian and socialist, the country would move away from a capitalist-based economy to a full-fledged socialist economy with a 21st-century vision. Again, in theory these ideas were big and bold, rallying under the banners of equality, fairness, justice. But in reality, it was an impossible and impractical dream for an oil-based economy dependent on the global market – especially one with an embedded culture of corruption.

A referendum was to be held on the constitutional reform, and, as the campaigning on this geared up, the opposition mobilized, benefiting from the momentum they had built up during the student protests against the closure of RCTV. It wasn't too hard to arouse opposition to the proposed constitutional reform. Most of the country was not on board for an abrupt transformation to socialism. Chávez had mistaken his landslide re-election victory as a mandate to do whatever he believed was best for the nation, rather than what the majority of people really wanted. Once again, private enterprises joined in the mass anti-government protests by hoarding basic goods and products as a form of economic sabotage. Toilet paper became scarce, as did milk, sugar, cornflour and other major lifestyle necessities. The government tried to cover the shortages by created state-subsidized markets in which basic goods were sold at a third of the price, a policy that filled the void at that time but eventually created an unsustainable dependency on severely subsidized products that contributed to the partial bankruptcy of the government and resulted in a mass corruption ring inside the state.

I was asked to be a part of a group working inside the presidential palace to provide real-time strategic analysis to Chávez during the constitutional reform campaign. Our data was showing there was no way to win the referendum, but the Chávez loyalists charged with running the campaign refused to listen or accept our conclusions. Our group was the only one with the guts to inform Chávez that his proposal would lose, which it did, albeit by a slim 51-49 per cent margin. While the reform had proposed some widely accepted changes to the constitution, such as reducing the working day from eight hours to six hours, banning discrimination based on sexual orientation and lowering the voting age to 16, other more controversial proposals like abolishing term limits to the presidency, incorporating the term socialism into the constitution and authorizing the President to impose indefinite national emergencies were widely opposed.

It took several hours for Chávez to publicly recognize his loss, and much of our data helped him understand what had gone wrong and where he had overestimated his support base. At first his campaign team didn't want him to accept the results so they could save their own asses. They had deceived him throughout the campaign by only providing positive data and polls showing the reform proposal would win. They didn't want to be responsible for the first major loss of *chavismo*, since surely someone's head would roll. Finally, Chávez accepted the results, calling them a 'shitty victory for the opposition' since they had won through a dirty campaign and by a super-slim margin. His acceptance of electoral defeat was at least a necessary sign of democracy in Venezuela.

Toilet paper wins the argument

As soon as the referendum was over in early December and the opposition had won, supermarket shelves returned to their normal robust state, just in time for the Christmas holidays. Once again, it was apparent how much influence private companies had over Venezuelan society and politics, and how they manipulated votes through people's stomachs. Beyond the stress of being in the presidential palace throughout the losing campaign and of knowing Chávez was going to lose but not being told so by his advisors, I had been freaking out because of the potential lack of toilet paper and other essential goods.

For the first time since I had lived in Venezuela, my entire immediate family – mom, dad and brother – were coming to spend the Christmas holidays with me in my apartment. The thought of not having enough regular food for their visit was nerve-wracking. But the toilet paper was what worried me most. We could eat whatever was available and didn't need typical Venezuelan Christmas foods. But how can you not have enough toilet paper in your home? How could I possibly explain to my parents that there was no toilet paper because the opposition didn't want socialism? Should I ask each of them to bring several rolls of toilet paper in their suitcases? Such a request would certainly give them pause before getting on the plane to come and visit me in my alleged South American paradise. The thought of hosting my family without toilet paper caused me many sleepless nights and, frankly, I was relieved when Chávez's proposal lost and we got our toilet paper back.

Also, like magic, bountiful holiday foods suddenly appeared everywhere, with their colorful displays and Christmassy designs. One of the things that always amazed me about Venezuela was that all public employees, and many private employees as well, received lavish Christmas baskets and bonuses each year. Bonuses for public employees could equate to an entire three months of annual salary, which was a lot of money for most people and a significant source of income. While some incorporated these funds into their annual budgets, others blew it all as soon as December came around, on loads of alcohol, luxury vacations, imported clothes and electronics. It was common in December to see lines outside stores that sold the newest television sets or whatever was hot that year in electronics. Venezuelans bought a lot and saved little. Many were probably traumatized by the banking scandal in the early 1990s under Carlos Andrés Pérez's government when hundreds of thousands of regular customers lost all their savings to corrupt bankers who stole everything and moved to Miami. Why save if someone can steal it all tomorrow? Better to spend it all today.

In addition to the cash bonuses, public and private employees alike would receive plentiful Christmas baskets from their employers. On the public-sector side this amazed me, because these goods were funded out of the public purse. And I'm not talking about just a ham or a basket of fruit. These baskets were traditionally filled to the brim with imported hams, cheeses, chocolates, cakes, and alcohol galore: imported whiskies and wines, rums and liquors. They all contained Frangelica, which I personally was repulsed by, having drunk it in my early teens at a neighbor's house and thrown up everywhere. The mere sight of it made me nauseous. Over the years I must have acquired about a dozen bottles of Frangelica from these Christmas baskets, and they were impossible to give away. None of my friends wanted to drink the stuff or take it home, either. That 2007, I received my first Christmas basket – and I didn't just get one, but two. I had been invited to a holiday lunch by the presidential palace guard, and the head of the regiment at the time was a colonel of whom I was briefly fond. He gave me a large basket with a big ham and lots of cured meats and sweets. I can truthfully say that, despite my being a vegetarian, that basket was by far the meatiest thing I ever got from him.

I received a second, unexpected Christmas basket from the new Minister of Defense, Gustavo Rangel Briceño, who had summoned me to his office in mid-December for a meet and greet. He had just been named to his new role and was an old friend of Chávez's. I had become a more prominent public fixture of *chavismo*, especially in the international arena, and a confidante of Chávez, so he wanted to become better acquainted. The basket was a total surprise, since I had already received one, but luckily that year I had holiday guests who would surely make good use of all the goodies inside. In a period of days, I had gone from being stressed out by the scarcities, to being overwhelmed by the abundance of food and other products I now had in my home. Once again, the Venezuelan pendulum had swung from extreme to extreme.

The family visit went relatively smoothly, considering my divorced parents and my brother and I were all in one apartment for a week. None of them could venture out without me because they didn't speak Spanish and it just wasn't safe. Despite all the risks I took with my own life, I was unwilling to risk their lives. So we were all bound together the whole time, or had to leave in pairs.

Once my dad and I went to the local pharmacy and he got a glimpse of my real life there. As we were buying some Diet Coke for him and more toilet paper (just in case!), a middle-aged woman approached us and started cursing me, yelling that I had no right to be in that pharmacy buying anything. She said I should be in a government-subsidized pharmacy, not in 'her' pharmacy. As though I should have been banned from any store not owned by the state because I supported Chávez. She was aggressive and relentless, as the opposition always was with me. I knew they would kill me if they had the chance and this was no joke. Dad was horrified to see me treated this way, but was so shocked by it that his response was delayed. He also had no clue what the woman was saying since he didn't speak Spanish, but he could tell by her menacing tone that it wasn't anything nice.

My mom also experienced these threats with me numerous times over the years, some in Venezuela during her visits, and at other times when she'd pick me up at the airport on my way back to the US, in Miami or New York. I would get screamed at by old ladies with stretched-out faces and puffy lips wearing designer clothes. They would call me a 'thief' and a 'killer', sometimes bizarrely accusing me of being 'corrupt' as well, even though I was never a public official and never had any access to public funds. I would get spat on, pulled and hit with purses, bags and elbows, and sometimes even threatened with knives.

Once, when a group of lawyers from the US National Lawyers' Guild was visiting Caracas, I took them out to dinner at one of my favorite restaurants in the downtown area, La Huerta. It was a Spanish-style *tasca* that was only walking distance from my apartment, with incredibly succulent grilled seafood and delicious homemade garlic bread, complete with a wine cellar downstairs. It was my go-to joint for the years I lived there, a place where I would often bring friends and visitors to conspire about new ideas and theories over delicious meals and bottles of wine. It was a Sunday evening and we were sitting at a large table in the middle of the restaurant. I knew all the waiters and the manager, and they attended to us well. There were just a few other full tables in the place, since on Sunday evenings it was less frequented and it was close to closing time.

We were having a discussion in English about the latest events in Venezuela, when all of a sudden a woman at one of the other tables started yelling. 'I know you,' she screamed. '*Chavista de mierda*' (shitty chavista), she wailed, followed by a stream of epithets. My guests were a bit taken aback, but I quickly shrugged it off as just part of regular life in polarized Caracas. People were passionate and unbridled about their beliefs and unafraid to express themselves in public. This lady, however, kept at it, escalating her tone of voice, volume and threat level. I ignored her, but a man at a nearby table took up our defense.

Things got pretty crazy and a steak knife was waved around, followed by a tackle to the floor and the woman being literally dragged out the back door by the restaurant workers and forced to leave. It turned out that she was a public prosecutor working for the Chávez government, even though she opposed it. She was clearly drunk and had lost her temper, but it was an experience those US lawyers would probably never forget.

Other than the few public incidents of harassment and an excess of cured ham, my family's Christmas holiday in Caracas was uneventful, thankfully. There were a few jolting moments from cherry bomb blasts and overbearing merengue music blaring out of passing cars, but thankfully none of us were harmed or traumatized. I did, however, have to creatively explain my new security cage to my parents, who were alarmed at the excessive security I now had at the entrance to my apartment. I kept quiet about the recent break-in and just said the government wanted me to be more protected since I had become increasingly visible as a public figure and advocate. That was one way of putting it.

A Christmas tragedy

I spent a fair amount of 2008 traveling back and forth between Caracas and Europe for varied book and work-related events, most of which I tried to focus in Paris, a city I loved. After an all-too-brief month-long stint at a glorious Parisian apartment on Rue du Bac, it was time to go back home to Venezuela. Shortly after returning home, I received an invitation from the Office of the President in Ecuador to visit that country and discuss my investigative work.

Ecuador was undergoing a radical transformation with Rafael Correa newly elected to the presidency, a leftist-leaning US-educated economist with a broad vision for rebuilding his small nation after nearly a decade of political turmoil and economic devastation. While Correa had been slow to join forces publicly with Chávez, Cuba and the growing alliance of leftist governments in Latin America, just as had happened with Chávez, the further he delved into the depths of his government's bureaucratic structure, the more decisive he became about the need for a revolution. His was the 'Citizens' Revolution', not as radical as Venezuela's Bolivarian Revolution or the Cuban Revolution, but a clear break from the neoliberal regimes that had led his country on a path to destruction and near ungovernability. The further Correa moved to the left, the more aggressive the opposition against him became. Many of the same tactics being deployed in Venezuela began appearing in Ecuador. All of a sudden, newly formed rightwing, anti-government student movements were taking to the streets in protest, creating similar disruptions and media-savvy demonstrations to those in Venezuela a year earlier. Media coverage of Correa and his policies grew increasingly distorted and one-sided against him, and US-funded NGOs started popping up all over the country, interfering in local and national politics under the guise of promoting democracy. It was the kind of stuff that was right up my alley and I could recognize US meddling anywhere.

I traveled to Ecuador in early December for a brief three-day trip. Quito is a beautiful city, set high in the Andean mountains. Surrounded by snowy peaks and volcanoes in the distance, and similar to Merida, its vegetation is tropical mixed with desert from the high altitude. Palm trees and cactuses blend together in the arid soil and humid air. When the sun hits, the warmth spreads as quickly as the chill once clouds or night set in. Ecuador is an incredibly diverse country with a tropical western coastline on the Pacific, where the famous Galapagos Islands and their giant tortoises reside, and Amazonian rainforests filled with monkeys, colorful birds and magical fauna covering the eastern part of the country. Quito, perched in the Andes mountains, was right in the middle, with its meticulously preserved colonial downtown, which is a UNESCO world heritage site.

Cradled in the city center was the presidential palace, an exquisite colonial building with a large courtyard full of gardens and wraparound staircases and walkways allowing the fresh breeze to reach even the hidden nooks where the country's decision-makers sat tucked away. The Palacio Carondolet was a place I would return to over and over again during the following years, as I grew closer to President Correa and his team and counseled them on several highly sensitive matters of international importance. But back then, on my first trip to Ecuador, I was merely taking in the scenery, speaking at local universities and being interviewed on the local news media and opinion shows. It was the type of trip I had become used to – a quick meet and greet, a speech or two and a few interviews, then off on a plane home to Venezuela.

But this time, just as I was wrapping up the trip, having established the groundwork for a future working relationship with President Correa, I received terrible news from home. Being away from home is the worst time to receive bad news. Well, any time is bad, but when you are so far away there is literally nothing you can do about it except despair. My trip was so short that I hadn't even brought my laptop with me and I only had one working international phone line, a Blackberry issued by the Venezuelan government. It was my lifeline to Chávez and other high-level officials with whom I frequently interacted. I was checking my email before going to bed when a cryptic message appeared from my mother that merely said something had happened and to call her when I got home. Seriously, when you get a message like that the last thing you want to do is wait nearly 24 hours to find out what is going on. It was nearly 1.00am but her message had only just come in, so I knew something terrible had happened.

Just as I was about to call her, another message came in on my email with an urgent heading. It was from my ex-husband's father, which I found both strange and scary. Why on earth would he be sending me an urgent message in the middle of the night? I should have called my mother before opening his message, because what it said is not something you should ever find out about from an email. But, I opened it and read it several times to make sure I understood what it said. My ex-husband's son, my stepson whom I had raised for nearly six years, had been hit by a car and killed just hours earlier. I called my mom. 'Is it true?' I asked her, in a shaky voice. 'How did you find out?' she wanted to know. I told her Gustavo's father had sent me an email. 'What a horrible way to find out!' she said, as though it mattered at that point. She hadn't wanted to tell me until I was home, she said. I appreciated her thoughtfulness, but I wanted to know what had happened.

It was a tragedy. By then my ex-husband had sent his son back to live in Merida with his birth mother – he couldn't afford to keep him in New York and refused to accept my financial help. I had seen my stepson over the years when he would visit me in Caracas, and spoke with him several times a year on the telephone, on holidays and his birthday, when I'd always send a gift. Those were difficult years when he lived with Gustavo and me but I had tried my best to be a good parent to him, even though I knew I wasn't the best. Still, I felt he was better off with us in a safe, healthy environment rather than with his birth mother, who had drug problems and frequently changed boyfriends. The roads in Merida had always terrified me, from the first time I ever went there. And they were living up in the Valley, on winding roads with no sidewalks or shoulders; cars would zoom by with no regard for pedestrians. My stepson had been driving a home-made go-kart, a custom in Merida during the December holidays. He had been going down the side of the road when a car, presumably a drunk driver, had run over him and killed him instantly. He was only 12 years old.

I flew home in sadness the next morning and as I arrived in Caracas I switched on my local cellphone, which started beeping like crazy. The messages were pouring in from Gustavo's family telling me of what had happened. Part of me felt anger at them for bombarding me with text messages and emails about such a horrific accident. Couldn't they call me on the telephone? Was texting really an appropriate way to inform someone of a tragic event? I called them all to express my sympathies and told them I had been out of the country and was just getting back. I also called Gustavo. He was, of course, destroyed. There are just no words, and really no comfort, when you lose a child. Somehow you have to move forward, grief shadowing your soul forever.

Those were dark days. I soon left Venezuela again to spend the holidays with my family back in the US. When you lose someone close to you, you realize there is nothing more important than the moments you share with your loved ones.

14

From Caracas to New York to Moscow

The year 2009 brought more political turmoil in Venezuela. Even though Chávez had accepted the defeat of his proposed constitutional reform to bring the country closer to a socialist model, he was finding ways to make changes by using his executive authority and seeking other avenues. One of the more contentious issues proposed under the constitutional reform had been the elimination of term limits for any elected official, including the president. The opposition had seen this as a way for Chávez to become president for life, but it wasn't as if the abolition of term limits would simply have allowed him to remain in office forever. He, like any other elected official, would still have had to be re-elected through a majority vote.

There were no term limits in the United States until Franklin Delano Roosevelt won the presidency four times in a row on a populist, left-leaning political platform. FDR was a president of the people: he pushed for social security, public healthcare and other social-welfare services that remain in place today as integral parts of US society. But conservatives were terrified that he would keep getting elected and the country would move further and further to the left, and so launched a campaign to guard against that possibility. Roosevelt died in 1945 but the Twenty-Second Amendment of the US Constitution was still ratified in 1951, limiting a president to just two four-year terms. Of course, there are no term limits on senators or members of the House of Representatives. Many European nations don't have term limits either.

But when Chávez proposed abolishing term limits, not just for the president but for all elected officials, he was deemed a dictator by foreign media and international rights organizations, and denounced by Washington as authoritarian. So Chávez decided to give the people a say via another national referendum, this time on the single issue of abolishing term limits for elected officials. Despite a brutally manipulative campaign by the opposition and fear-mongering out of Washington, the amendment passed on 15 February 2009 with 54 per cent of the vote. Over 70 per cent of registered voters voted on that day, way more than vote in most elections in the US and other Western countries. It was a victory for Chávez, but one that could come back to haunt the Venezuelan people some day since now any politician can be elected to office for multiple terms with no limitations.

Things remained in constant flux in Venezuela, and I tried to keep up with things by writing, making television appearances and traveling to promote my books and investigations. I had settled in to my Caracas lifestyle and felt more secure in my surroundings. I decided to dismiss my bodyguard while keeping the car and gun for myself. It was too stressful for me to always have an armed guard following me around and aware of my every move. Despite my very public lifestyle, I still valued my privacy and resented being constantly under surveillance. I did appreciate the service provided to me by all the various bodyguards I had, who risked their lives and spent time away from their families to protect me but, after all I had gone through, I thought I would be able to protect myself as well as anyone else. I had some close calls over the years, but in the end, none of those were situations that could have been prevented by my bodyguards. Plus, having a big guy with a gun following you around makes it really hard to have a boyfriend. Don't get me wrong, I wasn't deprived on that front – I had my share of flings over the years. I knew I never wanted to get married again, but I didn't want to have only secretive affairs forever. So I said goodbye to the bodyguards, took the keys to the car and tucked my gun away in a discreet place, hoping never to have to take it out again.

I was constantly traveling to Europe, Cuba, Bolivia, Ecuador and other countries to continue my investigations, network and participate in events. I went to the book fair in Buenos Aires,

Argentina, to present yet another edition of *The Chávez Code*. I published new books that I promoted throughout the Latin American region. I was a guest of Bolivia's charismatic new president, Evo Morales, and toured the country giving speeches about US-Latin American relations. I became close to one of Evo's highest-level cabinet members who oversaw presidential affairs and counseled him on foreign policy and other matters of international law.

I was riding a professional high and relished my celebrity, even though I craved private moments and seclusion. I could sign hundreds of autographs and pose for dozens of pictures with readers and fans, but then I would need hours or even days of down time on my own to recover. Fame was in that sense something of a bitter pill to swallow. People make all kinds of assumptions about you when you're in the public eye. They love you, they hate you; they comment on your hair, your face, your body, your clothes; they think you are brilliant or stupid. But no one really knows you, and probably none of them really want to. People prefer to hold up a semi-fictionalized idol or demon, instead of accepting both the greatness and the flaws that we all possess.

For me, the prices of fame were: the lack of a social life, an overwhelming number of superficial relationships, being unable to trust people, and living with constant paranoia and threats. On the flip side, when someone stopped me in the street to tell me that my work had transformed them as a person or how grateful they were for my defending the Venezuelan people, that made it all seem worthwhile. That and hanging out with Hugo Chávez.

Returning to the UN

That August of 2009, palace rumors suggested that Chávez would finally return to New York to address the United Nations General Assembly, having not done so since the infamous 'devil speech' in 2006. Chávez dreaded going to the United States, even though he had had kind words for its newly elected president, Barack Obama, and actually believed at that point that the relationship between the two countries would now change for the better. The invitation to the White House never came, nor did the phone call, and Chávez doubled down and asserted Latin America's sovereignty in the face of Obama's renewed calls to recover US influence in the region.

Things had not changed at all, and were arguably getting worse. In late June, Washington had tacitly supported a coup d'état against Manuel Zelaya, president of Honduras, who had become increasingly allied with Venezuela, Cuba and other leftist governments in the region. The US-trained Honduran military forces swept in and literally removed Zelaya from the country at gunpoint, in his pajamas. A dictatorship approved by the Obama administration was installed and the region reacted in protest and disgust. Despite the friendly rhetoric coming out of Washington, it was the same old attitude to what the US considered to be its 'backyard'. Regimes were plucked out and replaced at the whim of a US president and there was nothing anyone could do except scream and yell.

I wanted to accompany Chávez on his trip to New York and started gently suggesting this early on, even before he announced he was definitely going. But, as always, I knew that doing things through the regular channels would get you nowhere and that I would have to ask Chávez in person if I could go with him. I didn't have constant, unabridged access to Chávez – it was something that would happen every now and then. Over the years, I would get a call every once in a while from Nicolas Maduro, or one of his assistants, either asking me to prepare a report or document, or to meet Chávez at the palace. At other times I would be invited to presidential events, where Chávez would greet me with a big hug and kiss and maybe make some comment about me and my work in his speech.

But most of the time, I lived my life, I did my work and I simply watched him on television. When I wanted to tell him something important, or to show him some interesting documents I had unearthed, I had to fight tooth and nail to get near him. His guards changed often, so that many didn't know who I was and wouldn't let me near him. Some of his high-level security personnel also never trusted me, suspecting I was a CIA agent or infiltrator and so keeping me at arm's length. And others just didn't want Chávez to be distracted by anything or anyone, which I understood since he was so susceptible to influence by anyone in need.

Finally, I got my chance. I received an invitation from the Cultural Ministry to attend the inaugural event for a newly launched arts university and thought this would be a good opportunity to persuade him that I should go with him to New York. I had ideas for his speech to world leaders as well as several contacts for media interviews that might allow Chávez to debunk some of the major falsehoods about his government and the changes taking place in Venezuela.

Normally I would arrive two to three hours before a presidential event in order to go through all the security revisions and snag a seat right in Chávez's line of vision. But I had grown tired of the long waits, of just sitting around unable to do anything until Chávez appeared. So this time I got there late – so late that Chávez was already there and the event had begun. Just my luck that the one time I tried to play it the Venezuelan way, I was left out.

Still, I had an official invitation so I passed by the first set of security guards and then the next, flashing my paper card with the ministry's seal on it as the young officers waved me through. But then I hit a barrier. The security ring protecting the VIP seating area refused to let me through. I protested. I was invited. I'm a friend of the President. Let me through. They refused, and I persisted, becoming more agitated as they became more forceful. I asked to speak with the presidential guard officer in charge of security for the event, but I was ignored. I knew that someone amongst them had given an order not to let me in, not to let me near the President. This kind of crap always drove me crazy, not least because I knew that if Chávez found out what they were doing to me, he would be furious. Finally, I caught the attention of Chávez's nurse, who was also a military officer and member of the presidential guard. I waved to her to come over.

'What's going on, Eva, why aren't you coming in?' She grabbed my arm to bring me in but one of the guards stopped her.

'She's not authorized,' he said.

'What are you talking about?' said the nurse, angrily. 'Do you know who she is? She's a friend of the Comandante's and she's coming in and I'm putting my job on the line if you don't let her pass.'

The nurse had the rank of colonel so she was the guard's

superior officer; he stepped aside and she pulled me through, bringing me to a seat near the front of the event and apologizing for the mistreatment.

After the event was over, I approached Chávez, and this time none of the guards tried to stop me. 'Eva,' he exclaimed with delight, 'How are you?' Chávez loved to practice his broken English whenever he had the chance. I decided not to tell him what had happened and to use the precious moments to make my pitch to go to New York.

'Can I come to the UN with you?' I asked directly. 'I can help with some of the strategy.'

'I'm not completely decided that I'm going,' he told me, 'but, if I do, I want you to come. Prepare some materials for me. And now, please excuse me because I have to go urinate.' Chávez spent hours sitting or standing at events and giving lengthy, improvised speeches. He never took a bathroom break. His longest stretch was once a nine-hour speech before the National Assembly for a State of the Union address. It was pretty amazing that he could hold it for that long, but not exactly good for his health.

I've spent a lot of time around presidents throughout the years and one of the most remarkable moments is the bathroom break. Being president means you are on all the time, always in the spotlight, always surrounded by people, even if they are just bodyguards or close advisors. Everyone sees a president as superhuman, but they also need to eat, sleep and go to the bathroom. I once watched a swarm of people follow Bolivian president Evo Morales to the bathroom when he tried to take a quick potty break after an event. His guards had to physically restrain the people from entering the bathroom and plead with them to give the President a moment of privacy. Imagine not even being able to go to the bathroom without people swarming all around, trying to follow you and talk about god knows what, having no respect for your privacy or your basic human necessities.

I waited for Chávez outside the bathroom, which was awkward, but I felt like I wasn't done ensuring I'd be on the New York trip. I think he expected me to be gone when he came out because he looked surprised: 'Eva, you're still here!'

'Yes, Presidente, I just want to make sure I'll be on the trip with you.' I was concerned his inner circle would not include me on the travel roster and I wouldn't get to go. They'd tell the President that for some reason or other I couldn't make it because of my own schedule. It wouldn't be the first time that had happened. Often over the years I found out that Chávez had asked for me and his aides would lie and say I wasn't available. On this particular day, I found out later, the security officer in charge of the event had ordered the guards to keep me out, spreading a vicious rumor that I was an infiltrator there to harm Chávez. His superior subsequently apologized to me and promised it wouldn't happen again. 'A lot of people on the inside are envious of your access to the Comandante,' he explained. 'So they try to keep you away. But many of us appreciate and admire you for your courage,' he assured me.

Once an acquaintance came to me with some disturbing information. One of his family members worked at a gallery that had received a check for several thousands of dollars. The check was from an entrepreneur known for his close ties to the government, and who had multi-million-dollar contracts with the government for food supply and distribution. The check had been written to purchase several pieces of expensive artwork as a gift for one of Chávez's closest aides, who had just married a *telenovela* superstar – a wedding which in itself had raised eyebrows among some of the more hardcore government supporters. The aide and his new wife had gone together to pick out the art pieces, which had then been paid for by the entrepreneur. The gallery owner was suspicious of corruption or bribery. A well-positioned business owner with lucrative government contracts was buying expensive artwork for the President's closest aide. I agreed that it didn't look good and passed the information on to Chávez. He was outraged and immediately fired the aide, calling for an inquiry into possible corruption. Once the aide figured out that I was the one who had given Chávez the information, well, you can imagine that it didn't bode well for me. Chávez eventually forgave the aide and returned him to a similarly powerful position, but the corruption never stopped. In fact, it grew.

New York – and Courtney Love

The trip happened. Chávez decided to go to New York and made sure I was coming. We were initially supposed to fly together on his airplane, but at the last minute plans changed. He had a personal issue going on with his ex-wife and daughter and wanted to fly to Barquisimeto to see them before heading off to New York. So we were sent on two different Falcon jets, just a handful of us on board. Only one minister was on the trip, his Communications minister at the time. Other than that there were a few of his presidential guard members and assistants, one of his older daughters, Maria Gabriela, and me. We flew out in a pair, our plane following the President's, and arrived together in New York at JFK airport. It was by far the most low-key and smallest delegation I had ever seen with Chávez – usually he had well over 100 people on his trips, between aides, ministers, press and special guests.

We stayed at the Grand Hyatt Hotel on 42nd Street in Manhattan, right above Grand Central Station. In previous years, Chávez had stayed in the townhouse owned by Venezuela on East 81st Street and Fifth Avenue, where generally the Venezuelan ambassador to the United Nations resided. But this time he chose the hotel instead for convenience and privacy, or at least the guise of privacy. The Grand Hyatt was the hotel of choice for dozens of heads of states and official delegations during the UN General Assembly. President Evo Morales also stayed there on almost all his trips to New York to participate in UN events. It was a nice hotel, with the normal level of discretion to be expected during a presidential visit, except of course when I and others in our delegation returned to our rooms the first evening and found men inside looking very much like secret-service personnel going through our stuff. They ran out when they saw us but left us with the certainty that we were being watched. I shrugged it off as routine – it came with the territory. Everything Chávez and anyone close to him did was under close watch and vigilance by the intelligence agencies of the US and probably those of other countries too.

In addition to his speech before the UN, there were several other events and interviews we had arranged for his visit, some more controversial than others. I had come along as an advisor and special guest of Chávez's to counsel him during his visit, and I didn't take my responsibilities lightly. I had huge arguments with one of Venezuela's diplomats in the US who wanted to sign away all Chávez's rights to CNN so as to guarantee an interview with Larry King. I said no way. We fought over it in Chávez's room until he became disgusted with both of us. 'Work it out,' he told us, 'or I won't do it at all.' And then there was the issue of Oliver Stone's new feature documentary starring Chávez, *South of the Border*. One of Chávez's advisors had convinced him to attend a special 'red carpet' screening of the film at Lincoln Center, claiming it would be attended by prominent actors and influential members of the New York City arts and political community. We'd already had the film screened in Venezuela, with Chávez and Oliver Stone. It was cool to do it again in New York City, but it seemed to me that it wasn't actually a huge event or one that could have a significant impact. Chávez's time in New York was extremely limited and doing that event meant sacrificing other potentially more important events.

Fame and celebrity won out and we went to Lincoln Center. There was a red carpet, but at a back door, and it wasn't in a major cinema in Lincoln Center, but rather one of the smaller ones. Evo Morales had come along too, since he was in town and was also featured in the film. After the movie was screened and Oliver Stone, Chávez and Evo made a few remarks, there was an invitation-only cocktail reception in a separate room. Chávez didn't really drink alcohol and wasn't one for cocktails and small talk. The whole thing seemed like a waste of time. That is, until Courtney Love, the infamous punk rock star, came over to Chávez and planted a big sloppy kiss right on his lips, calling him a 'sexy dawg'. He invited her to Venezuela to visit him. He wasn't one to resist a blue-eyed blonde freely giving him kisses.

Unsurprisingly, that was the image on the front pages of newspapers and tabloids the next day, instead of anything about the UN speech, the film or other events: Chávez being smooched by a raunchy Courtney Love with bright red lipstick smeared all over his face. Chávez's New York trips weren't doing much to improve his international image. It made me think it maybe wasn't a good idea for him to come back any time soon. In any case, that ended up being his last-ever trip to the United States.

Trumpian luxury in Moscow

I had two other intriguing trips that year. First, I received a very insistent invitation from the President of Nicaragua, Daniel Ortega, to visit him in Managua and speak at several universities in the country. Then, just days later, I was invited to Moscow to speak at the People's Friendship University of Russia and oversee the Russian translation and publication of *The Chávez Code*.

The Venezuelan Embassy in Russia put me up at the fanciest hotel I've ever stayed at in my life. The Ritz Carlton Red Square is right out of a movie, with a doorman wearing a foot-high top hat, dressed in a black tuxedo velvet-lined coat with tails, a grand piano in the middle of the marble-floored lobby and a grandiose wraparound staircase covered in a red carpet ascending to the upper floors. The front doors were so tall and wide that, when they opened, it seemed as though I were entering an elegant ballroom, filled with the finest-dressed members of high society – that is, except for me.

I was so jetlagged and exhausted when I got in, and in a state of shock having come from the intense tropical heat of Nicaragua, where even wearing sandals made me break out in a sweat. The frigid blast of cold air of Moscow in December was like a slap in the face I wasn't prepared for. I needed rest before I could actually realize where I was and why I was there. It was hard to see straight when I entered my room and my eyes were immediately blinded by the gold-covered and excessively ornate window hangings, bedspreads, pillow cases and furniture. Everything looked like it belonged in a museum of 18th-century cheesy, opulent, overdone design.

An unverified report by a former British intelligence agent, Christopher Steele, revealed after the 2016 US presidential election that Donald Trump had stayed in the same hotel and it is easy to imagine him there, relishing in the golden luxury. The hotel was Trump on steroids.

The minibar was actually an ultra-maxibar overflowing with

caviar and the finest champagne and truffles. The bathroom had three rooms and was larger than my apartment in Caracas, all covered in floor-to-ceiling marble and mirrors. The windows in the front of the room opened right onto Red Square, with the Kremlin just a footstep away. And yet I was in the smallest, most inexpensive room, which, according to the hotel's website, cost a little over $1,000 a night.

For a brief moment, I indulged myself, taking a hot bath in the oversized marble tub while sipping champagne and gorging on truffles. But then I felt gross and out of place, unable to enjoy a luxury I didn't want or deserve, and I certainly didn't want the Venezuelan people to pay for this excess. I'm always grateful for a nice place to stay, but not at the cost of taking public funds from necessary programs that help people in need. What was clear to me was that, even though it was 2009 and Chávez had been in power for a decade, little had changed in the Venezuelan mentality. Those who had access to the public wealth still abused it for their own benefit, enjoying luxuries at the expense of the millions who could barely afford to eat and maintain a tin shack. The culture of corruption that had brought previous governments down in Venezuela, and was so thoroughly berated by Chávez and his followers, was also destroying the Bolivarian Revolution, from the highest levels downward.

There are all kinds of problems in the United States, of course, but one thing I always cherished about going home was the generalized respect for the basic tenets of society and a functioning system of law and order. People stop at red lights. Public funds aren't regularly – and routinely – plundered or misused for personal gain. You don't have to bribe people to receive public services. There is corruption in the US, but it hasn't reached the level and depth of penetration that it has in Venezuela, where it's a way of life. Venezuela under Chávez had so much potential to overcome that dysfunctional, destructive syndrome, but ultimately his failure to excise the corrupt circle around him contributed to the unraveling of his movement and the erosion of democracy – along with the nepotism and the cult of personality that he allowed.

15

Freeing Americans in Iran (a woman's work is never known)

My first and only official job offer in Venezuela came in early January of 2010. Vanessa Davies, then director of the national newspaper *Correo del Orinoco*, called me down to her office to discuss an exciting new opportunity. She asked me to oversee and edit the English language edition of the newspaper, which was funded through a public foundation. Finally, after all these years, they appeared to understand the importance of international public opinion. I accepted on the condition that I would have full editorial control over the content of the newspaper and be able to select a team of writers and contributors without any interference from the government. She fully agreed: she said they trusted me and had confidence that I would be ethical and as objective as possible. The pay was nothing life-changing and would barely help cover my monthly mortgage payment, condo fee and utilities, but I was pleased finally to have a structured role in a movement I cared about and believed in deeply. Information was vital to understanding the changes in Venezuela and the complexities of the political situation, especially in international public opinion where there was a real scarcity of balanced reporting on the country.

I committed to my new role and put a team together. Contrary to false media reports, I never received 'millions of dollars' from the Venezuelan government to run the newspaper. It was a fairly barebones operation, with a rather small staff that overlapped with the Spanish-language paper's team. Our tabloid was to be published as a weekly supplement to the daily Spanish edition. Our first mock-up was ready by February, just as Chávez convened an international press conference, inviting foreign correspondents in Venezuela to the presidential palace. I was invited and proudly brought along the mock copy to show to Chávez. We had featured a column by Cindy Sheehan, the famous anti-war activist who had set up a tent in front of George W Bush's Texas ranch after her son had been killed in the war in Iraq. I had met Cindy several years earlier, during her first visit to Venezuela, and we had remained in contact since then. She had reached out to me about interviewing Chávez for a documentary film she was making about the Bolivarian Revolution and I helped set this up for the first days of March. On the day of the press conference, Cindy was arriving in Caracas to prepare for the interview.

To my surprise, when Chávez entered the Ayacucho Salon in the presidential palace where a packed room of journalists and most of his cabinet members were waiting for him, he came right over to me and gave me a big hug. He told me he had just been with Fidel in Cuba and they had been talking about me. He said he was very jealous because Fidel had a copy of my newest book, *La Agresion Permanente* (The Permanent Aggression) signed and dedicated by me. 'Eva, how is it possible that Fidel has a signed copy of your book and I don't have one? I am very jealous,' he said. 'I told Fidel you were my friend first, so it's not fair,' he added, jokingly.

I was flattered that Chávez and Fidel were fighting over me, but also a bit taken aback. 'Of course I sent you a copy,' I told him. 'I sent it to your office the day it was published, signed and dedicated to you.' His aides started fumbling around trying to figure out why they hadn't got the book to him. And Chávez was pissed off. He told his assistant to find that book, as in yesterday.

I knew why he didn't have it – they hadn't given it to him so that he wouldn't be reminded of me. That was the type of thing they did to try to keep me away from him. It was truly bizarre that Chávez found out about my new book while in Cuba with Fidel, when I had sent him a copy months earlier and it had probably been thrown into the trash bin by one of his aides.

I took advantage of the moment to show Chávez the new English-language edition of *Correo del Orinoco* and told him it featured a column by Cindy Sheehan, who was about to interview him. 'Yes,' he said, 'she'll have to come with me on my trip to Uruguay for Pepe Mujica's inauguration tomorrow.' And then he added, 'You come too, Eva.'

I didn't hide my surprise. What? Really? Yup, that's how it usually happened. Chávez would just spontaneously invite me on an international trip the night before, often for no apparent reason except that he wanted to talk to me about something and he used his trips out of the country and away from his usual staff to hold meetings he was prevented from holding at home. That was that. I was now going with him to Uruguay the following day for the inauguration of newly elected President José Pepe Mujica, an old leftist political leader who had spent 13 years in prison for his political activism and had been shot six times in his abdomen by the dictatorship of the time.

Cindy Sheehan was glad Chávez had invited me on the trip because she didn't speak Spanish and there was no translator on board. I ended up being the translator, a role I often had to assume for him on international trips when his official translator wasn't around. I had been his last-minute translator before during spontaneous encounters with Jesse Jackson, Larry King, Noam Chomsky, Danny Glover and journalists ranging from *Forbes* to the progressive *Democracy Now!*

As usual, everything about the trip happened at the last minute and we didn't even know what time we would be leaving or if we'd actually be going until a few hours before take-off when Chávez's assistant called to confirm our seats on the presidential plane. This time, since I was accompanying Cindy and her producer, I didn't get one of the extra-plush special seats in the front section of the plane. But I could hardly complain: I was on Chávez's airplane once again, invited by him personally, and going to the inauguration of one of the most admired new Latin American leaders. Plus, I had never been to Uruguay before so I was looking forward to experiencing another South American nation renowned for its intense wines, beautiful coastline and laid-back people. Silly me, thinking that I would actually have time to stroll around Montevideo while on a fast-paced presidential trip with Chávez.

The thing about these presidential trips is that you get to go to all these exotic places and stay in fancy hotels, go to exclusive high-level events and receptions, and mingle with world leaders, but you never actually get to see the country you visit. You go from airplane to car to hotel to car to event to car to airplane and then home. So often, my view and experience of the many places I visited with Chávez around the world was through the window of a hotel room, a car or an airplane, or sometimes a helicopter. It was exciting and intriguing, but definitely not a way to get to know a new country or city. If I were writing a travel guide it would probably be titled *Seeing The World Through Tinted Glass*.

A night-time encounter

We were in Montevideo for less than 36 hours and my glimpse of the city was almost entirely from the tinted windows of the presidential motorcade as we were whisked through the wide streets and shuffled into a well-preserved historic mansion that functioned as an exclusive hotel for foreign dignitaries and other high-profile figures. The members of the delegation were all given envelopes by the presidential protocol team, which contained a hotel key and a letter stating we had to pay a $100 fee for the room. After all these years of witnessing the free flow of *viaticos* on these trips, I was shocked – were Cindy and I going to have to pay for our own rooms in a hotel we were basically forced to stay in? Cindy was happy to pay her own way, but I felt differently. I had no plans to be on that trip. Chávez had personally invited me to come along and, as it turned out, I ended up working as his translator free of charge.

I immediately complained to the President's assistant and told him that it was inappropriate to give guests of the President a bill for their hotel room. Especially because I knew everyone else on the trip wasn't paying for their own stay. We weren't given a per diem like the other members of the delegation so the money would have to come out of our own pockets. A few moments later the head of presidential security for the trip came over to me and apologized profusely. It was a total misunderstanding, he said. Of course we wouldn't have to pay for our rooms since we were guests of the President, he said, and asked me to let Cindy know it had all been a big mistake.

I was given a key to stay in a different hotel with Cindy, her producer and other lower-level members of the delegation. I didn't think too much about it at first, but then realized it would be more difficult to get the interview done with Chávez if we weren't in the same hotel – he hadn't yet confirmed a time to do it and often he would decide at the last minute. If we weren't right there, we could miss the window of opportunity. We had arrived around midnight and were all exhausted. As we were saying good night to Chávez and heading off in a shuttle bus to the other hotel, he asked me where we were going. I told him his team was sending us to a different hotel, and reminded him about the interview with Cindy. 'I'll let you know later what time we'll do the interview,' he said, and he gave me a kiss on the cheek and said good night. Later? I thought, it's already midnight, so he must have meant tomorrow, though with Chávez you just never knew. He was, after all, a night owl.

Just as I was unpacking my overnight bag in the hotel room the phone rang. It was Chávez's assistant. He wanted to apologize for the earlier misunderstanding about payment for the hotel room. 'It's fine,' I told him, 'it's all been cleared up.' And then he asked me if I was in a room by myself. 'Yes,' I said, 'why do you want to know?' He said that the President wanted to meet with me in a little while, that he'd call me back and then he hung up. Seriously? I was already brushing my teeth and putting on my pajamas. It was already past one o'clock in the morning. Now what? I guess Chávez wasn't kidding when he said he'd tell me later about the interview time. A few moments later there was a knock on my door. I opened it slowly, since I wasn't expecting anyone in the middle of the night, but after that phone call I knew I should expect anything.

A plain-clothed presidential guard officer was at my door when I opened it.

'Are you ready to go?' he asked me.

'Ready to go where?' I asked, dumbfounded.

'There's a room at the other hotel for you and the President is waiting.'

'Give me a minute,' I said and closed the door. I quickly gathered up all my clothes and toiletries and shoved them in my red suitcase, brushing my hair with my free hand and swiping on some lipstick to make sure I didn't look half asleep, which I pretty much was.

I tucked an envelope I had been carrying on the whole trip into my purse, ready to give to Chávez if I had the chance. Inside was a letter from Noam Chomsky, the famous US linguist and leftist writer whom Chávez greatly respected. I had come to know Chomsky over the years because of my involvement with Venezuela, and had been one of his hosts during his trip to Venezuela that year. The letter was a plea for Chávez's assistance in helping to free three Americans detained in Iran who had been accused of espionage. They were young, progressive activists from the west coast of the US and were not spies, but rather fearless Americans in the wrong place at the wrong time. A lawyer acquaintance of mine in California had contacted me months earlier after the three of them – Joshua Fattal, Shane Bauer and Sarah Shroud – had been detained in Iran during a hiking trip on the Iran-Iraq border and subsequently imprisoned.

My acquaintance thought I could perhaps ask Chávez to intervene and negotiate the release of the three Americans, since he had a very close relationship with the President of Iran, Mahmoud Ahmadinejad. After months of discussion about the issue, I brought it up with Nicolas Maduro, then Foreign Minister, asking him if he thought we could discuss it with Chávez. He was open to the idea but didn't see it as the opportunity that I did. I thought that if Chávez were able to secure the release of the three Americans from Iran, it could have a very positive effect on his international image as well as possibly save their lives. I provided Maduro with profiles of each of the American prisoners, a detailed analysis and a political and media strategy underlining the impact of Chávez's involvement, but the issue never seemed to gain traction. He was dismissive of the whole thing. I had also mentioned it to two senior foreign policy advisors and, while they thought the idea was entertaining, they were not interested in pushing the matter with their superiors and potentially putting their jobs on the line.

Meanwhile, the situation for the three Americans was getting worse. They were formally tried and convicted of espionage in

Iran, despite the lack of evidence. The US State Department didn't appear to be progressing with efforts to secure their release and it seemed as though Chávez could really have an impact. He was, after all, really close to Ahmadinejad, who was the one with final say over the Americans' fate.

So, we decided to amp up the pressure and take it to another level. A letter from someone like Chomsky could help persuade Chávez to act, and I offered to pass it on at the first opportunity. And now, here I was, in the middle of the night in Montevideo, being escorted to Chávez's hotel room. I was first shown to my new room and given a few minutes to settle in and unpack before I was summoned.

'He's ready for you,' the guard told me, signaling for me to follow him. I clutched the envelope with Chomsky's letter under my arm and ascended the staircase behind him. The young guard opened a door and waved me in, closing it behind me. It was dark except for a light in an adjoining room, and I heard Chávez's deep voice call out.

'Come in here,' he said. I pushed the second door open and saw him sitting there at a small round table, smoking a cigarette. 'What's in the envelope?' he asked. 'Top secret documents?' He laughed, putting me at ease.

Chávez was known for these middle-of-the-night meetings, but it was a first for me, especially in his hotel room. And once again I felt uncomfortable and vulnerable. I knew I had to get right to the point before his mind started wandering, so I launched into the story of the three Americans and how he could help them.

'What do you think, are they spies?' he asked me.

'Honestly,' I told him, 'I can't say for certain, but I don't think so. I think they are just clueless gringos who were in the wrong place at the wrong time and thought they were invincible because they were Americans.' I handed him Chomsky's letter.

We discussed it for a few minutes more and I emphasized how his help could not only save the lives of these young people, but also shed a more favorable light upon his image in the US and abroad. It could be huge, I told him. He said he'd talk to Ahmadinejad about it and see what he could do. Then he dismissed me. '*Buenas noches,*' he said, kissing me on the cheek, and I walked out, feeling excited about the possibility of helping to secure the release of the Americans in Iran. Before I shut the door I remembered the interview. 'What about Cindy?' I asked him. 'What about the interview?'

'Let's do it tomorrow morning,' he said, '11 o'clock.'

'Good night, Mr President,' I said. I shut the door quietly as he flicked his ashes in a tray on the nightstand, and tiptoed down the stairs. It was nearing dawn and everything was eerily quiet but I knew his guards were lurking in the shadows keeping track of my every move.

Why the prisoners in Iran were released

At breakfast that morning Nicolas Maduro's assistant approached me and asked for a copy of everything I had given to Chávez the night before. 'He wants us to take care of it,' he said. Yeah, finally you'll do it, I thought to myself, even though I had already told them all about it months ago. No one did anything on their own initiative, they only acted if Chávez told them to. Luckily, I had a copy of Chomsky's letter on a memory stick and was able to give it to Maduro's assistant right away.

That night in Montevideo was the first time Chávez had heard of the three Americans detained in Iran and the campaign for their release. Months later, Sean Penn, the Oscar-winning actor and friend of Chávez, would also broach the subject with him, asking for his help. I communicated practically daily with Maduro via text messages and often in person about the case throughout the following year up until the moment of their release from prison. Ironically, the same male advisors who had dismissed my pleas for help with the case months earlier had taken credit for the whole affair after the fact. Women are often erased from history, and our ideas are co-opted, while men take credit for our efforts, actions and successes. Our accomplishments are diminished, as though somehow the mere admission of our victories threatens their masculinity. How many times in my life have I been told that I wasn't capable or knowledgeable enough to do what I was doing? I have been written off, undermined and degraded time and time again. But in this case I didn't care: I had achieved my objective.

All that mattered was the freedom of those three young people and I took pride knowing I was one of many who had helped secure their release from prison.

Despite the fact that barely any media mentioned the role Chávez played in the young Americans' release, it was absolutely defining. Chávez personally spoke to Ahmadinejad about the issue and said he supported their release. They discussed it numerous times over a period of months, both in person and on the phone. I was physically present at some of those encounters. In the end, after nearly two years of such conversations, it was Chávez who persuaded Ahmadinejad to release them. The Iranian foreign minister later told his Venezuelan counterpart, Nicolas Maduro, that they had done so because Chávez had asked.

Back in Montevideo, Cindy got her interview done with Chávez, with me as impromptu translator, just before we were all whisked off to Pepe Mujica's inauguration in the middle of downtown Montevideo. It was a historic event, witnessing an admired and internationally respected former political prisoner being sworn in as president, bringing Uruguay closer to the growing leftist alliance in the region. After Pepe's ceremony our delegation was swept off to a Venezuelan naval ship that had docked in Montevideo for training exercises. We were saluted and serenaded by the young naval cadets, while Chávez, their commander-in-chief, posed for selfies with them and sang traditional military songs as though he were that youthful, daydreaming soldier back in the barracks and not a leader with the weight of the world on his shoulders.

16

Touring the 'Axis of Evil'

Traveling with Chávez was like a drug – or an extreme sport. It was a constant rush of adrenaline to be around him and the frenzied activity of his entourage. It felt exhilarating and exhausting: exciting but also chock full of anxiety, risk taking, highs and lows, spontaneity and surprising humility. It was a constant behind-the-scenes look at the highest echelons of power and a glimpse of powerful leaders and politicians in their most basic human state. We ate together, exercised together, saw each other's exhaustion, irritability, stress and moments of humor, fun and rare relaxation.

As with the trips to Uruguay and Peru, almost every time I traveled with Chávez it was the result of a spur-of-the-moment invitation from him. I was by no means the only person to experience this: most of his travel companions who were not government officials were invited spontaneously, after Chávez saw them and something just sparked. It always amazed me how anything he said would set into motion a massive chain of events involving dozens, if not hundreds of people. And then, just like that, he could change his mind and move on to the next idea or decision, leaving a significant train wreck behind him that he probably never even noticed.

Things were at an all-time high in Venezuela and Latin America in 2010. By then the majority of governments in the region were led by leftist-leaning popular leaders. There was Luiz Inácio 'Lula' da Silva in Brazil, Evo Morales in Bolivia, Rafael Correa in Ecuador, Pepe Mujica in Uruguay, Cristina Fernandez de Kirchner in Argentina, Raul Castro in Cuba, Ollanta Humala in Peru, Fernando Lugo in Paraguay, Daniel Ortega and the Sandinistas back in power in Nicaragua, Mauricio Funes in El Salvador,

Alvaro Colom in Guatemala and others throughout the Caribbean. Chávez had led the region towards sovereignty and unity with the creation of the Union of South American Nations (UNASUR), the Bolivarian Alliance for the Peoples of Our America (ALBA) and the soon-to-be-ratified Community of Latin American and Caribbean States (CELAC), which would bring together all 33 countries in the region, excluding the US and Canada.

The Bolivarian Revolution was in full swing and marching onward, deepening the communal councils and grassroots participation in the national economy and political system. The economy was booming from consistently high oil prices and Venezuela was advancing down the path towards progressive human development. The free healthcare system was servicing millions of patients nationwide, illiteracy had been officially eradicated, infant mortality rates were down, people were eating better and more often, they had jobs and roofs over their heads, often courtesy of the government's housing mission that built hundreds of thousands of subsidized, low-cost homes for middle- and lower-income Venezuelans. There were state-subsidized car companies offering affordable automobiles to the public, cheap Chinese television and electronics available in most parts of the country and even nationally produced cellphones and a version of the Blackberry, which Chávez had comically named *'el vergatario'*, a colloquial Venezuelan word that is often translated to mean 'large penis'. The 'penis' phone of course grabbed international headlines as just another one of Chávez's gaffes.

That September, I had received news from Moscow that my book, *The Chávez Code*, would soon go to print there just in time for Chávez's imminent trip to the Russian Federation. His leadership and influence were growing internationally, although, despite his early hopes for the Barack Obama White House, relations with Washington continued to go downhill. Chávez was determined to transform Venezuela into a potent force on the world stage, using oil diplomacy and discourse focused on building a multi-polar, balanced global community. Reform at the United Nations was not happening, so Chávez decided to build new alliances, first between Latin American and Caribbean nations and then with the rest of the world.

Since Washington didn't seem interested in a respectful relationship with its southern neighbors, Chávez felt he had no choice but to bridge those gaps with US adversaries in the so-called 'Axis of Evil'. Venezuela already had long-term relationships with oil-producing countries from OPEC, some of which had become staunch enemies of Washington, including Iran and Libya. Other nations, including Russia, China, Belarus, Ukraine and Syria, had strong strategic and technological resources to offer developing Latin American countries, and the thought of irking Washington by bringing some of its major adversaries into the hemisphere was an added bonus for Chávez.

In the days before his trip to Moscow, Chávez held a press conference with international media. I attended as director of the international edition of the *Correo del Orinoco* and looked forward to telling him that *The Chávez Code* would be released in Russian as part of his visit there. The Venezuelan Embassy in Moscow had informed me they were planning to 'baptize' the book in Russian during one of Chávez's events at a Russian university, though they hadn't invited me to be there and I wasn't inviting myself. It was far away and cold, and I had already made a disastrous trip to Europe earlier that year during which I had been stuck for nearly two weeks due to the ash from a volcanic eruption in Iceland. So I wasn't anxious to return.

At the press conference, Chávez announced that the trip still wasn't finalized, but that he would most likely go on from Moscow to other countries in the region, potentially Belarus and Ukraine, and then maybe swing by Iran on the way home. He talked about his vision of multilateralism and of forging a forceful alliance with anti-imperialist nations which had stronger technological and strategic capacities that could foster Latin American development. This time around, I hadn't had the chance to ask a formal question as part of the journalist pool, so after the session ended I approached Chávez on the stage to tell him about the launch of my book in Russian during his visit. 'Hello, Eva!' he said, giving me a big hug and kiss, and practicing his English with a 'how are you today?' I told him that *The Chávez Code* would be released when he was in Moscow and jokingly asked him to bring me a copy when he came back.

'Your book is coming out in Russian?' He seemed impressed.

'Then you're coming with me to Moscow – you must be there for its release.' He looked at his newly appointed personal secretary, a very young woman known as 'La China' who I knew completely despised me, and told her to make the arrangements for my inclusion on the trip. Then he said goodbye and exited through the secret tunnel that connected the events room to the main presidential palace. A thousand thoughts raced through my head. When were we leaving? Where exactly were we going? Would I be on the whole trip or only the part to Moscow? Would La China try to prevent me from going by leaving me off the seating chart for the airplane? How long would I be gone? What should I pack? I was freaking out a little bit, though excited about practicing the extreme sport of Chávez travel again.

To say I was anxious in the days leading up to the big trip would be an understatement. I was on edge every day wondering when we would be leaving, for how long and to where. I was also convinced that Chávez's staff was conspiring to leave me behind, so I made sure to text some of my allies in the presidential palace several times a day, probably driving all of them crazy. Finally, a matter of hours before departure time I got word that I had a seat on the plane. Since no one could tell me how long the trip would be or if I would be on it beyond Moscow, I packed my usual red carry-on bag with a few assorted changes of clothes, running shoes and my laptop. I brought a jean jacket and a not-so-winter black Betsey Johnson coat with hanging pom poms. I had bought it nearly a decade earlier in Manhattan and it was rather stylish. I had a few cotton dresses folded up in my bag in case of any fancier events, but suffice it to say I was extremely unprepared for what was ahead.

As it turned out, La China had done her best to keep me off the flight roster, but one of Chávez's lead presidential guards, who was in charge of security for the trip and knew the President wanted me along, made sure that I was included. Because of the large number of people in the delegation, we didn't all fit on the official presidential plane. An extra plane carrying members of the press was arranged, along with a companion luxury falcon jet for key members of Chávez's security team and high-level assistants to the Foreign Minister. I was given a seat on that plane. It was known as the 'backup presidential plane', which followed the presidential jet everywhere it went and was used by Chávez if for some reason his official plane was grounded or otherwise unable to fly. It was also essentially the cargo plane for presidential gifts and assorted items acquired during the trip, but I didn't find that out until we were deep into our world travel.

We flew to Moscow, stopping for a few hours of refueling in Lisbon, Portugal, where we briefly deplaned to stretch our legs on the tarmac. Since I wasn't on the plane with Chávez this time, I made a point of seeing him at the stopover and reminding him I was there. I was still uncertain as to whether I would be on the trip beyond Moscow, so I took advantage of the stop in Lisbon to ask Morales, Chávez's assistant, if I would be on the whole trip. Part of me wanted to go, but since I didn't really know where we were going I wasn't entirely sure. I was a little hesitant since I knew Chávez was calling the trip his tour of the 'Axis of Evil', and there was talk of going to Iran, Syria and Libya, as well as Belarus and Ukraine. Some of those were countries where US citizens were forbidden to travel, and even though I was traveling under a Venezuelan official service passport as a Venezuelan citizen and member of the presidential delegation, I still had my concerns.

Before I could even ask Morales, he saw me and said that he had a ticket for my return to Caracas from Moscow. When he said it I felt disappointed and shunned, and unaware if that was Chávez's decision or his. His dislike of me was never hidden, especially after I had informed Chávez of his suspected corrupt acts. He was the one who had accepted expensive artwork from an entrepreneur with lucrative financial ties to the Chávez government. I decided to ask the Foreign Minister, Nicolas Maduro, if he knew whether I was supposed to be on the whole trip or to depart after Moscow. He was adamant. You're in for the long haul, the whole thing, he said: Chávez wouldn't have it otherwise. I told Morales what Maduro had said and he grudgingly shrugged in acknowledgement. He wasn't getting rid of me yet.

Russia

It was only October, but it was already freezing in Moscow, and gloomy. The motorcade from the airport swept around the massive city, escorting us to a hotel once owned by the KGB but now used by the state for foreign visitors and delegations. Its name was appropriate: Hotel President. The lobby was expansive but nowhere near as luxurious and opulent as the Ritz Carlton Red Square I had stayed in a year earlier. This was a Soviet hotel, dully and blandly designed and rather blockish. It had lovely views of the river, but the rooms were simple. I had no real complaints though: after being cooped up on a small aircraft for nearly 14 hours, I was just glad to have a private room with a bed and a bathroom.

I have to confess that the Moscow portion of this trip was actually the least exciting part. Yeah, we hung out in the Kremlin, saw Vladimir Putin and Dmitry Medvedev and got a pretty cool serenade by Russian soldiers at the entrance to the Kremlin. But overall, it was less intriguing because only a very limited portion of the delegation were allowed to participate in the high-level events. The rest of us were left wandering the halls of the Kremlin and eventually shuffled out by the security guards into the drippy, dreary Moscow weather, too far from the hotel to walk back but with nowhere else to go given that none of us spoke Russian, and we had no roubles. Plus, I had learned early on when traveling with Chávez that you should never stray from the delegation or you could be left stranded. So we waited, and waited, and waited. I had gone jogging earlier that morning down to Red Square with a colleague on the delegation. We had gone out around 5am in the dark, damp city streets, just as the Muscovites were getting up to go to work. Moscow has some of the worst traffic in the world. Traffic jams can take hours just to go a few blocks, and the metro system is overcrowded and outdated. It's a sprawling city with a mix of ornate, colorful and elaborate structures and dull Soviet box-like buildings. The Kremlin is, of course, the biggest attraction with its imposing walls, gold-trimmed buildings and cake-like orthodox churches.

Chávez had a private dinner with Putin that evening at the Russian leader's private residence. At that time, to get around the problem of term limits, Putin had switched roles and become prime minister while Dmitry Medvedev was president. But everyone knew it was Putin who was in charge. Chávez and Putin had become good friends over the previous years, bonding together on their anti-imperialist, multilateral view of the world. Both were major adversaries of Washington and both wanted a more prominent role on the international stage.

I had met Vladimir Putin the first time during his trip to Venezuela just months earlier, in April. His short stature contrasted with a stern, tight-lipped face that gave him a fiercely intimidating air. Despite his hardened appearance in public, with Chávez he was always jovial and relaxed. He would even crack a full-toothed smile in Chávez's presence, a rarity for the feared and secretive Russian leader.

The two countries were deepening their ties in defense and technology, and, to the horror of the US government, Russia had offered to help Venezuela build a nuclear power plant and its own space industry. Putin's visit to Caracas had also coincided with the docking of a Russian nuclear warship in Venezuelan territory, on a routine tour of the Southern Hemisphere. Along with the two presidents, I had been given the opportunity to visit this nuclear warship during its stay off the Venezuelan coast. The ship was known as 'Peter the Great', a very fitting name for a Russian warship. I took in its alarming power and capacity, as well as the more than 200 young Russian sailors wearing very short, striped red shorts and no shirts who had been traveling for months on that ship with no women. I jumped back onto the Venezuelan military boat that had brought us out to the warship as fast as I could – there's nothing quite like being on a nuclear-armed Russian warship with hundreds of horny, barely clad sailors.

What surprised me most about Putin when I first met him was his size. He's not much taller than I am, and I'm only five foot two, but he exudes a confident, masculine energy and has a 'don't mess with me' look in his eyes. While he's a bit of a showman who often bares his muscular chest in public and loves to wrangle tigers and bears, he also has a wicked (and very Russian) sense of humor, cracking jokes and making sarcastic comments with a completely straight face. I once got him to smile, which meant a barely noticeable raising of one corner of his upper lip. It was five years later in Moscow at a dinner which unexpectedly became a focal point of US politics after the election of Donald Trump. Trump's first National Security Advisor, Michael Flynn, was also there, sitting at Putin's table. I wasn't at Putin's table, but I was a few tables back, near Mikhail Gorbachev. It was the 10th anniversary of RT, the publicly funded international Russian television station, and since I had later become one of the leading faces on RT Spanish with my show *Detras de la Noticia* (Behind the News), I was one of the honorees at the dinner.

During the course of the event, I took the opportunity to greet Putin and ask him if he'd come on a special show I hosted with presidents, where I'd spend a full day with them and show their human side. I had done the show with the presidents of Bolivia, Ecuador, Uruguay and Venezuela, and also with the five Cuban spies who were released in a historic deal between Castro and Obama in December 2014 after nearly 16 years in US prisons. I suggested to Putin that he do the show, and joked that we could spar together since I knew he was a black belt in martial arts and I had a green belt in Taekwondo. He looked me in the eyes with that slight smirk and said in English, 'I am very afraid of you.' We never did the show together, but that dinner became a historic and intriguing moment in world politics, and I was there.

Back in Moscow in 2010, the launch of the Russian version of *The Chávez Code* ended up being quite anti-climactic. Considering that this was the only reason I was on the trip, it was a bit disappointing when Chávez almost forgot to present the book at the university event where it was set to be launched. I was sitting in the audience in the front row and had to wave my arms wildly and catch his attention, mouthing to him not to forget and holding up a copy of the book. He finally mentioned it at the end of his talk and recommended that it be read by Russians. That was it. Yet again, I was left wondering why I was along for this long trip if my main event had been an afterthought. But I wasn't going to pass up the opportunity to witness these powerful and highly controversial world leaders behind the scenes, so I decided my purpose was actually to observe everything and then write about the experience.

Belarus

We left Moscow 48 hours later, heading south to Minsk, a city I had visited briefly the previous year to give a talk at a Belarusian university. I had also seen Aleksander Lukashenko, the imposing Belarusian president since 1994, during his previous visits to Caracas. In contrast to Putin, Lukashenko was a very large man, big boned and tall, with a hardened face and stiff posture. He was often referred to in Western media as the 'last dictator of Europe' due to his authoritarian style and his lengthy time in the presidency, albeit elected for new terms every five years. He was a holdover from the Soviet Union and still believed in that overall model, with massive state ownership and control over the means of production.

Minsk is a beautiful city: tranquil and clean, properly laid out and preserved. The low crime rate and pristine look of the city were attributed to Lukashenko's style of governance – heavy handed, yet steadfast and patriotic. He rebuilt Belarus after its break from the Soviet Union and fought to retain centralized control while paying lipservice to democracy. His approach to dissenting views was questionable, to say the least. He once suggested in private that Chávez consider following his model of crime control: rounding up criminals and shooting them. Chávez made it clear that wasn't his style. Despite how the media portrayed him, Chávez was a humanist and way too compassionate ever to sanction the murder of other human beings. He had spent his entire time in government trying to figure out how to make people's lives better, not to take them away in haste.

Nevertheless, in many ways Lukashenko found a partner in Chávez, an ally and an ideological brother. After years of being isolated and shunned by Western nations, Lukashenko was thrilled when Chávez was elected and began building ties with non-traditional partners, such as Russia and China, and he sensed an opportunity for Belarus as well. The former Soviet republic had a lot to offer Venezuela, especially as Washington became more adversarial and began limiting sales of military and defense equipment. Like Russia, Belarus had a substantial arms-production program and began selling military equipment to Venezuela, along with agricultural products and vehicles. In return, Venezuela pledged a near-eternal supply of oil or, as Chávez put it during our visit, 'enough oil to last Belarus for the next 200 years'.

We stayed in a private, wooded compound on the outskirts of

Minsk in a highly guarded area reserved for special guests of the Belarusian president. It was a group of four or five large residences, each with multiple bedrooms. Only high-level members of the delegation and special guests, me included, were housed there. The rest stayed at hotels outside the compound and were supplied with a bus to transport them back and forth as necessary. I had to share a room with the Cuban agricultural minister, who had been invited on the trip by Chávez. Unlike me with my small carry-on bag, she had three large suitcases filled with varying outfits, shoes and accessories. I may not have been dressed in the fanciest of clothes or shoes, but I had no problem keeping up with Chávez and his entourage. The Minister, Barbara, on the other hand, was always trailing behind, teetering on high heels and struggling to keep pace with the rest of us. She was obviously not trained in the extreme sport of Chávez travel.

Sharing a room was not ideal, as nice as she was. She had a bad cough, all night long, which made it impossible for me to sleep. I moved to the couch outside the bedroom area, but was only able to get an hour or so of rest before I had to get up. If I wanted to go for a run, eat breakfast, shower and be ready so as not to be at risk of being left behind by Chávez's entourage, it meant waking up by 6am. Mind you, Chávez rarely began his day before 9am, and it was usually later if it were up to him. But on these trips, the schedules were out of whack because they depended on other presidents and their agendas as well. It was better to sleep less and not risk being stranded in an unfamiliar country with no local currency and no one to call.

The Belarus portion of the 'Axis of Evil' tour was tightly packed with activities. We spent several hours the next day at the presidential palace while Chávez and Lukashenko held high-level talks. The rest of us spent most of the time quietly waiting in the outer room near the presidents, in between uniformed soldiers with very high burgundy military hats who stood guard. There was a bowl of wrapped chocolates we snacked on without realizing that it constituted our lunch. Afterwards, we accompanied the presidents to the Minsk library, where an entire exhibit dedicated to Chávez, Bolivar and Venezuela had been erected. I took advantage of the opportunity to give Lukashenko a copy of *The*

Chávez Code in Russian, which he then grabbed out of my hands as though I were a courier and not the author, and then sternly instructed his assistant to place it on the library shelves. Yes, Mr President. I hung back. A chorus of Belarusian youth performed a version in Spanish of one of Chávez's favorite songs, 'Venezuela', in beautifully harmonized voices. It was a teary moment, seeing those blond-haired blue-eyed pale-faced young Belarusians singing angelically and perfectly in Spanish, serenading the two leaders in a true sign of solidarity. Really, I'm not kidding. It was beautiful.

And then we went from that feel-good, serene moment to a more ferocious one outside the library, where Lukashenko had a monster truck parked so as to show off to Chávez. The two of them climbed inside and drove it around the library parking lot. It was surreal. Chávez was obsessed with the massive truck, vowing right there and then to build a joint Venezuelan-Belarusian truck factory in his home state of Barinas to manufacture these trucks for agricultural purposes. He was so fascinated with the monstrously large vehicles that when it was time to leave the country, on our way to the airport he made the motorcade take a detour to the truck factory so he could drive them around again. I know he really wanted to bring those trucks to Venezuela and build Latin America's first large modern truck factory, but like so many of his projects and plans, it never got off the ground. The agreements were signed, and surely money was paid, but the work was never done to make it happen. Chávez had great ambitions, but without a competent team to implement his ideas and plans, many were left by the wayside.

That evening, Lukashenko hosted a presidential dinner and this time I was invited. Between Moscow and Minsk, the main sources of food had been either at receptions or cocktails put on by the host governments. As a vegetarian and occasional fish eater, I was always limited in my options, though thankfully Eastern Europeans ate a lot of vegetables and smoked fish. The food layouts were almost identical in Moscow and Minsk. Large platters with smoked salmon and sturgeon, assorted caviars and lots of pickled vegetables: tomatoes, cucumbers, peppers and onions. It was pickle heaven. Chávez was not a drinker, but I had decided to take advantage of the free alcohol whenever it was available. I definitely did not overdo it, since we always had to be on and ready to engage with Chávez and other presidents, but a glass of chilled wine with some smoked salmon and pickled cucumber was hard to pass up.

That evening at the dinner, there was a small round table for the presidents, foreign ministers and a few other select guests. The rest of us were left standing around in an adjacent room, listening in on their conversations while we devoured the pickled goods and other delicacies that were circulating. I may have had more than a glass or two of wine at that dinner, because somehow I ended up with a full, unopened bottle of wine in my purse as we exited the premises. I can't exactly remember, but I must have swindled it out of one of the servers, as a consolation prize for not getting a seat at the table. We had all left together, presidents included, and were walking to the line of cars parked nearby that would take us back to the compound for the night. I wasn't expecting to talk to either of them when all of a sudden I was face to face with Chávez and Lukashenko and Chávez was mouthing off to him flatteringly about my investigations, books and my work, without mentioning my US citizenship. At that moment, standing next to Alexander Lukashenko with a bottle of possibly stolen wine in my bag from his dinner, which I was desperately trying to disguise under my elbow while I discussed my work with him, I was grateful not to be outed as an American.

Chávez was busy asking me to tell Lukashenko about my amazing investigations, explaining the similarity to what had nearly happened in Belarus years earlier when Washington had backed an opposition movement against him through NGOs and anti-government media. Meanwhile I was doing my best to be coherent and not slur from all the wine in my blood. This is no big deal, I thought, I'm just hanging out in Minsk with the 'last dictator of Europe' and a laughing Hugo Chávez, with a stolen bottle of wine under my arm.

That bottle of wine was consumed later that evening in the room of Nicolas Maduro, though he didn't drink a drop. I shared it with his boy band of advisors and assistants, all young, good-looking guys who, as it turned out, all had musical talent. Nicolas smoked a fat Cuban cigar while I drank a glass of red wine and we listened to these guys, highly strung foreign-policy advisors by day and rock and rollers by night, play guitar and sing songs in astonishingly smooth, good singing voices. It was a much-needed few hours of relaxation before the heavy-duty phase of the trip.

Lukashenko insisted that we did not fly out immediately to Kiev, where Chávez was scheduled to meet with then President Viktor Yanukovych, so we ended up spending an extra night in Minsk at the compound. Ukraine was too unsafe and unstable for Chávez to spend more than a few hours there, according to the Belarusian president. In the end, he was proved right given that Yanukovych was overthrown just a few years later and the country was consumed by civil war. It meant I had to put up with another night of coughing Barbara, but by then I was so exhausted I could sleep through the hacking. We had spent the final day at a state-owned farm named Agragorodok Dziarzhynski.

The farm produced over 30,000 tons of chicken and a variety of other foods, including beef, grains, seeds, fish and dairy products, nearly half of which was distributed and sold by a state-owned food company. Chávez was so taken with the model that he later tried to implement similar versions in Venezuela, though none enjoyed the same level of success as in Belarus. We were greeted at the farm by workers in coveralls and women in traditional Belarusian peasant outfits. It was very provincial and quaint, and rather propagandistic. We were shown around the farm in trolleys and fully equipped with sanitary uniforms to enter the dairy production areas. Chávez milked a cow or two and sifted through seeds in the mill. We were later treated to a lavish lunch with fresh food from the farm that seemed in endless supply. Chávez was impressed, imagining all the ways in which Venezuela could prosper if it had similar agricultural enterprises across the nation. It had always been his dream to revive Venezuela's long-abandoned agricultural industry and he seemed inspired by this showpiece model farm, reasoning that if Belarus could do it, why couldn't Venezuela?

On the way to the airport the next morning, the presidential motorcade took a detour. In my car, no one had a clue what was happening or where we were going. Chávez, as it turned out, had decided he simply wanted to drive for a while out on a country road. The farmlands reminded him of his homeland, Barinas – a vast, wide-open plain with grazing cows and grassy fields filled with wildflowers. Granted it was Belarus in October and not exactly the dry, hot stretch of land he was used to, but he still had the motorcade pull over to the side of the road so he could get out and drive the car. As it turned out, this unexpected detour wasn't that spontaneous after all. He had connived secretly with Lukashenko to make it happen, and the Belarusian leader had mapped out a route that would allow him to drive safely and discreetly on that brisk fall morning. Lukashenko couldn't resist arranging for a dozen supporters to appear out of nowhere on a back country road with Venezuelan flags and signs welcoming Chávez to their country. Chávez appreciated the hospitality and graciously slowed the car. With a cheek-to-cheek smile he waved to all the people cheering him as he passed by.

He then continued on his way, our trail of black cars and vans following behind until he reached another planned stopover. A massive tractor was parked on the side of the road, its enormous tires towering over our cars. It was from the same Belarusian factory that made the monster trucks Chávez wanted to manufacture in Venezuela. Lukashenko had told him about the tractors so he wanted to see these too before we left. The winds were picking up and the cold breeze was bringing in the crisp October air, but Chávez didn't seem to mind. He wanted to test that tractor out on the field. He climbed right up inside it and headed off through the muddy fields, the rest of us running to take cover in case he lost control or went too fast. Chávez loved stuff like that. He wasn't the kind of president who wore stuffy suits and sat in closed, formal meetings, isolated and protected from the world. He liked to get dirty. He liked to do stuff, get his hands in the mud. He hugged strangers, talked to them and shared meals, he went for drives in the countryside, and sometimes in the city, often in disguise so he'd be unrecognizable.

I have to say that, after spending years at his side and being around numerous other presidents and heads of state, it's a pretty crappy job. Your life is not your own. Millions of people will hate you, others will believe you are a god who will make them rich and happy. Almost all of them will be disappointed in you. No president can ever fulfill all their promises – or even half of them. Most are lucky if they can get anything significant done for their country and their people that is sustainable and recognized as part of their legacy, which itself will be constantly under attack and threatened with total destruction or re-interpretation. If you are lucky enough to leave a respectable legacy, millions will work to destroy it and tarnish it forever. Some presidents will make incredible gains, only for these to be completely rolled back by their successors and by changing circumstances in the country and the world.

On the flip side, being president is an unbelievable opportunity to improve and transform the lives of millions of people in your country and around the world, and contribute to peace, stability, development, progress and overall happiness. Few are up to the task, but those who choose to try for noble reasons deserve respect, even when they fail. Those who do it to masturbate their own egos or to oppress others are deserving of the bitter consequences of their inevitable unraveling and defeat.

I firmly believe, after years at his side, that Hugo Chávez had noble intentions. He wanted to make the world better. I never witnessed him personally take advantage of his power for his own benefit, nor enrich himself. He never personally fell prey to corruption. But he was human, and he did make mistakes. The more powerful he became, the more isolated he was, distanced and detached from the reality of Venezuelans. Those around him took advantage of his faith and his unwavering belief in humanity and exploited their positions to enrich themselves and their families. A giant, intricate web of corruption and power struggles grew all around him, entrapping him in the middle. He did turn a blind eye to some of this, to his discredit, allowing it to continue because he believed it was the only way to move forward. He hated corruption and criminality, but he wasn't willing to turn his back on those closest to him who were involved in illegal acts, those who ultimately betrayed him. His guiding light was always the dream he had for his homeland and his people, that Venezuela could be a fully developed nation of great potential, sovereign and prosperous. And that economic progress could be balanced with social justice. He believed that another world was possible and he tried to make it happen.Chávez liked what he saw in Belarus, notwithstanding Lukashenko's reputation for brutality. The thriving and productive agricultural industry, the clean and orderly streets, the low crime rate, the high education level of the people, employment, housing, food supply, healthcare: nothing seemed lacking, except perhaps respect for human rights. The basic necessities were satisfied, the country held its ground and defended its sovereignty against foreign aggression. It was a model he wanted to emulate in many ways. So he was able to look past Lukashenko's authoritarianism. Maybe that was evidence of the poor judgment that would eventually result in the undermining of much of his own legacy. Strong leaders make productive, healthy nations. Chávez believed that to be true, but was it really?

Ukraine

The flight to Kiev took under an hour. Chávez had heeded Lukashenko's warnings so we were only going to be in Ukraine for a few hours. Even though at that time Ukraine was relatively peaceful, the electoral victory of Yanukovych a few months earlier had been highly contentious and riddled with allegations of fraud and corruption. He had narrowly defeated the Western-backed candidate Yulia Tymoshenko in a second round run-off election, and he would go on to lose legitimacy as his presidency progressed, culminating in the bloody coup against him four years later. Yanukovych had also been the target of the 'Orange Revolution' in 2004, when he had won the presidential elections but been accused of widespread fraud, leading to a US-backed uprising. While Belarus President Alexander Lukashenko was moving further away from Russia, despite their long-term strategic and ideological relationship, Yanukovych was distancing Ukraine from the European Union and strengthening ties with Russia and Putin. Obviously that didn't sit well with Washington and its European allies.

It seemed that this three-way feud had influenced our trip and Chávez did his best to tread lightly amongst the competing heads of state. Russia was re-establishing its influence and potency in the world and especially in its immediate vicinity. Belarus was more stringent ideologically, a stickler to a traditional communist model, and didn't want to be a mere underling of Russia, which had rapidly evolved into a consumer-capitalist society with few remnants of its communist past. Meanwhile Ukraine, under Yanukovych's leadership, seemed to revel in its new-found alliance with Russia, in clear defiance of the West.

Chávez hadn't met Yanukovych yet and was eager to expand Venezuela's relations with the former Soviet bloc, with Putin's blessings, of course. On the agenda during the quick trip to Kiev was a bilateral meeting with Yanukovych and then a visit to Antonov State Company, a former top-secret Soviet military aircraft manufacturer: you know, the usual.

One of Europe's oldest cities, Kiev was beautiful, a classical European city with ornately decorated limestone buildings, wide avenues and medieval details. Sadly I only got to see it from the windows of our motorcade as we raced from the airport through the city to a curious neighborhood in the historic Lypky quarter. We didn't go to the opulent presidential palace that Yanukovych had taken as his residence, with its famously expensive decorations, gold-laced curtains and lavish furnishings. We went to a much more peculiar place known as the Horodecki House, or the House with Chimaeras. It was one of the most incredible structures I'd ever seen, a concrete building so architecturally exotic and Art Nouveau, decorated with ornate sculptures of animals, mythological creatures and artistically designed hunters hanging off the top and sides of the exterior. It was located in the middle of an enclosed, brick-lined street, protected by uniformed soldiers.

The Presidential Administration Building was also on the grounds, as was the National Defense Council of Ukraine. The area was highly guarded and inaccessible to outsiders, despite its location near the city center. The House with Chimaeras was used by presidents for official receptions and ceremonies with foreign leaders. Yanukovych treated Chávez to a bountiful Ukrainian lunch on one of the upper floors inside the remarkable building. A traditional Ukrainian cultural group serenaded the two presidents as they feasted, while the rest of us milled about on the lower level, chomping down pickled vegetables and smoked fishes (again). The interior of the house was equally striking, with grandiose wide stairways and imposing, yet eclectic, chandeliers.

We hadn't seen Yanukovych upon arrival and Chávez had been quickly ushered upstairs before I could even enter the building. But after the leaders finished their meeting and made their way down the winding staircase to bid farewell, I caught Chávez's eye and he called me over to introduce me to Yanukovych on the stone steps outside. 'Viktor,' he said, 'this is Eva, my friend and defender. She wrote a book you should read about how the CIA was behind the coup against me. Tell him, Eva.' He pushed me towards the Ukrainian leader whom I had only before seen in pictures. I happened to have a copy of *The Chávez Code* in Russian, which I knew he could understand, and I presented it to him, adding that many of the same strategies the US had employed against Venezuela had also been used during the 2004 Orange Revolution.

We talked a bit about the foreign funding of opposition groups and the 'colored revolutions', Washington-backed uprisings against Russian-aligned former Soviet bloc countries the West wanted to control. I kept talking until finally Chávez nudged me, indicating it was time to go. 'Wait, Eva,' he said. 'You didn't sign the book for Viktor.' He looked at the Ukrainian president and told him he had to have me sign the book before we could leave. Yanukovych reached in his pocket and handed me his pen, which I took with my nervously shaking hand, trying to absorb another most unusual moment. Here I was, standing in front of this marvelously historical and exotic building in one of the oldest cities of Europe, in between two incredibly controversial heads of state who were insisting I autograph a copy of my book. 'Dear President Viktor Yanukovych,' I wrote. 'Read this book so this doesn't happen to you again,' I scribbled, signing my name at the bottom. Yeah, a lot of good that advice did him.

We bade them farewell and were shuffled back into the motorcade. Off we went to the famous Antonov aircraft company headquarters, which remained under Ukrainian control after the fall of the Soviet Union. Antonov makes some of the largest military transport planes in the world and Chávez was in the market since Washington had not sold military supplies to Venezuela since 2006. Venezuela's main defense supplier had historically been the US, but without access to replacement parts and new equipment, Chávez was forced to look elsewhere, especially given the threat of foreign intervention. We poked around a few giant aircraft, exploring the insides and outsides of the imposing machines. We had a guided tour by the factory's manager and Chávez called me to his side to be sure I could hear the explanations of each different aircraft and its potential uses. Occasionally he'd ask me what I thought of this one or that one, as though my opinion mattered. I told him about my flight to Havana on the rickety old Hercules with his advance team and how long and awful it had been. I agreed it was a good idea to acquire some new military transport planes with more modern attributes, though I hoped I wouldn't have to travel in any of them, ever. He laughed and exclaimed that he'd love to be a paratrooper again and jump off one of those aircraft, soaring above the clouds. There he was, the head of the country with the largest oil reserves on the planet on the verge of making a multi-million-dollar purchase of military equipment to defend his nation, and he was busy daydreaming about parachuting through the thin air, uninhibited, light and free.

Iran

It was happening. We were going to Iran. Not only this, but I now had confirmation that after Iran we were going to Syria, and then Libya. There was talk of going to Algeria as well, but this seemed unlikely since relations had been affected by pressure from Washington for the Algerians not to deepen their ties with Chávez. Still, Iran, Syria, Libya: man, what was I in for? I had no choice, I had to go – I was on the trip and couldn't just ditch out now. I would be protected by Chávez and the presidential delegation, so it was not as though my life or liberty were at risk; it was rather just the idea of going to three places that were notoriously major enemies of my own country. It was October 2010 and the wars had not yet begun in Syria or Libya, but the Arab Spring was in full swing in Tunisia and Egypt, and there were signs that it might expand throughout the region.

We left the European airspace of Kiev and flew south towards the deserts of the Arab world, straight into the 'Axis of Evil'. Maduro's assistants had a good time joking with me about leaving me in Iran, but it didn't seem like much of a joke to me. The three US hikers were still imprisoned there despite Chávez's gentle nudging of Ahmadinejad to release them. I planned to remind

Chávez of the case when we arrived in Tehran, though I didn't want to give anyone any ideas about leaving me there to negotiate their release. I looked out the window in nervous anticipation as we entered Iranian airspace. The pilots on our small Falcon jet were in on the jokes, announcing over the intercom as we progressed further into the 'Axis of Evil' – or 'point of no return', as they called it. They kidded around about being on a mission to drop off an American spy while I tried hard to mask the uncertainty I felt as we came in to land. All right, I thought to myself, this is it, we're here. I took out my scarf and wrapped it around my head, trying my best to conceal my hair, and I put my jacket on over my dress. I was wearing a dress that hit at about knee level, but I had black leggings on underneath and they were pretty thick. I had high leather boots that came up to just below the knee, leaving a couple of inches of leg showing that were covered in black fabric so I thought that would be okay.

It was late at night when we arrived, close to midnight. The air was humid and warm, and I was grateful for the darkness so no one could see my legs or look too closely at my face in case a strand or two of hair had fallen out from the scarf. We descended onto the runway and quickly caught up with Chávez and the rest of the delegation as they entered the VIP area of the airport in Tehran. The large delegation was clustered in a room, everyone looking a little disoriented as we passed yet again into a new cultural dimension with different codes and rules, a new language, new smells. We were finally out of the Eastern European vibe: even though Moscow, Minsk and Kiev were in different countries with different politics and presidents, they all shared a similar history and culture, their foods were almost the same and the language was just slightly varied, though Russian was a common thread throughout that region. But Iran? Iran was a whole new ballgame.

A young Iranian woman approached me in the holding room and asked if I was Chávez's daughter. His oldest daughter, Rosa Virginia, was accompanying him on the trip as well, but she had told me back in Minsk that she wasn't planning on deplaning in Iran. There was no way she'd wear a headscarf or cover herself up. I totally respected her choice, though I tried to help her see the merits of doing it so she could be a part of the visit and experience. I had to justify it to myself as well, since I wasn't crazy about covering myself up from head to toe and could recite every feminist argument there is against such treatment of women. But I had come to understand through my experiences over the years that sometimes putting up with something uncomfortable and strange for a short time can be worth it in order to experience a different culture and see things in a different way. I can't say I would have done it if I hadn't been with Chávez, and I did turn down every offer I received after that to return to Iran and lecture at universities or participate in events. I even turned down an offer to star in my own television show on Iranian television, on the state-owned channel Press TV and its Spanish language version, Hispan TV. They said they would require me to wear a headscarf on the show and that was just not acceptable to me.

Rosa Virginia refused to get off the plane and I informed the young Iranian woman, who probably was from the Iranian presidential protocol office, that I was not the President's daughter but rather a friend. His daughter had remained on the airplane as far as I knew. That sent her scurrying off to huddle with the other members of the protocol team to figure out what exactly they could do to lure poor Rosa off the airplane and assure her that she would be all right in Tehran, even with her hair flowing freely. Meanwhile, the amount of eyes on the two inches of visible leggings between my boots and my dress felt like burning embers. Obviously I had made a mistake. No leggings, none – not even two inches of them. I didn't want to be noticed, I didn't want to be stared at. For the first time in my life, I wanted to be completely nondescript and blend in like just another boring face in the crowd. Unfortunately, the silhouette of my ass was also visible through my dress – damn you, stretchy material! We had just arrived in Tehran and I was already well on my way to violating the rules and potentially jeopardizing my freedom. I wanted to help free those three US hikers, not hang out with them in prison.

Thankfully I was rescued by Chávez's head of security, a towering, dark-skinned army colonel with a disarming smile, before any of the locals could close in on me. Churio, as he was called by Chávez, came over and asked me how I was doing, if I needed anything. I asked about the hotel. Would I have a room to myself? I needed to evaluate every piece of clothing I had in my suitcase and figure out what exactly I could wear over the next 48 hours during our stay in Iran. He handed me a room key and said yes, I'd definitely have it to myself. He also said Chávez wanted to talk to me privately at some point during our stay in Iran. I should be available and prepared at a moment's notice. Of course, I told him, thinking to myself, what else would I be doing? It's not like I was going to wander off like a tourist for a stroll in the streets of Tehran. At that point all I wanted to do was take a hot shower and get a good night's rest in a quiet room with no coughing roommate or any other disruption. I had no plans to leave my room unless it was with Chávez and the rest of the delegation.

A most curious thing happened when we arrived at our hotel in Tehran. Despite the late hour, a large gathering of dozens of Iranians was waiting to greet Chávez as he entered the lobby. The hotel was surprisingly modern and upscale and seemed bustling and alive with the cheering Chávez fans waving small Venezuelan flags and calling out his name. I was trailing close behind him as he entered the main lobby and we walked through the people like it was a victory parade, smiling and saluting everyone, some stopping to grab Chávez's hand or embrace him. Everywhere I traveled with Chávez around the world there were crowds of people of all cultures, who received him with an outpouring of love, admiration and hope. They would wait for hours just to see him in person and have the chance to touch him, shake his hand, hug him or exchange a few words.

Amongst the crowd of admirers in the hotel lobby was a slender man waving a book in the air trying to get Chávez's attention. He kept shouting out 'Chávez, Chávez', but I could tell the President was getting tired and was trying to move through the crowd as quickly as possible to go up to his private room. He always tried to be attentive and gracious with his supporters, doing his best to give them all a few seconds of his undivided attention, but it wasn't always easy. I never saw him snap at anyone or brush them off. In fact it was amazing how patient and tolerant he was with the hordes of people constantly wanting a piece of him. I got crushed, pulled at, trampled and pushed countless times when I was with him in public, by people who would do anything for the mere opportunity to touch him. I saw grown men tremble and cry when given the opportunity to shake his hand or embrace him. As Chávez was making his way through the lobby towards the elevators, I got a closer look at the man waving the book. It had a white cover and a picture of Chávez that seemed very familiar to me. In fact, it was more than familiar – it looked exactly like the US version of my book, *The Chávez Code*, except the writing was all in Farsi.

'What book is that?' I asked the man in English.

He looked at me strangely and said, 'It's *The Chávez Code* by Eva Golinger.'

'I'm Eva Golinger,' I said, 'and that's my book, but I didn't know there was a version in Farsi. Who published it?'

'Eva, it's you!' he exclaimed, extending his hand to mine. 'We are so happy you're here.'

I shook his hand but persisted with my inquiry as to who had published my book and why I hadn't been consulted.

'Oh,' he said, 'our institute published it. You must know the former Iranian Ambassador to Venezuela – he authorized the whole thing.'

'Huh, I had no idea. Can I at least have a copy?' I asked him.

He wouldn't give me his copy because he wanted to give it to Chávez. I mean, for real? It was my book and I never authorized the publication in Iran or even knew about it, and they couldn't even give me a copy? I was flattered and happy that my book had been published in Farsi, I just wish I had been involved with the process. The guy actually came back the next morning and gave me two copies of the book. After the trip, I ended up with no copies, because I had given one to Chávez to give to Ahmadinejad not knowing I'd be having dinner with them that evening, and then I gave him the other one personally and he told me he loved me. But that's another story.

My welcome to Iran basically blew to hell all my preconceived stereotypes and fears. Yes, I still had to cover myself up, but I was a celebrity! They weren't waiting for me to lock me up, they wanted my autograph. Not only was my book published in Farsi, but the next morning a group of 'fans' waiting for me in the lobby presented me with an entire compilation of my writings translated into Farsi with my picture on the cover – photoshopped with a headscarf, of course. Several local media outlets interviewed me and, overall, I was received with open arms, not closed minds. The hotel room also ended up being the nicest and most upscale of all the places we stayed in on the entire trip, and it had a mini bar stocked with Iranian chocolates and nuts. I ate everything in it that first night, took a hot shower in what seemed like a luxurious bathroom with marble-tiled walls, and I snoozed in a plush bed all to myself.

I had seen Chávez briefly after we had escaped the welcome crew in the lobby and ascended in the elevator. I accompanied him to his presidential suite before heading back down two floors to my own room. We discussed the case of the hikers and he agreed to bring it up again with Ahmadinejad when he had the opportunity. He was smoking like a chimney, one cigarette after the other. It seemed more than usual, and I wondered what was really going on that was causing him so much anxiety, beyond, you know, being president of a country constantly under siege by Washington, and now forging closer ties with its main enemies. The only other place we needed to visit on this tour to top it all off was North Korea. It was enough to drive anyone to chain smoking.

I was giddy the next morning with nervous excitement about the day's events. I knew we were going to the Iranian presidential palace, a place where few American women had been in recent times. I had the headscarf thing down and had fully covered myself, putting pants under my dress this time so no part of my shape would be visible. The streets of Tehran were wild: it was like Caracas on steroids. The driving was insane, cars weaving in and out, speeding, honking, completely ignoring basic traffic rules, though I didn't really know what the rules were in Iran. We were in a procession of cars and minivans on the route to the presidential palace and I had taken the shotgun seat in the front next to the driver. He wasn't quite sure what to think about me, but I wasn't going to miss this experience now that I was there. I was going full in, front seat action. It was harrowing and exhilarating. There was no time for photos or calmly taking in the scenes as we were ripping through the city, competing with local drivers who couldn't care less that we were in a presidential motorcade on the way to the palace. We virtually had to smash our way through. A few of the presidential press team had almost been arrested earlier that morning when they had gone out to capture B-roll footage of city life. They learned the hard way that it was prohibited to film or photograph Iranian women, which basically meant you couldn't just take pictures of street scenes. I never even took out my camera in Iran. Frankly, I rarely had the opportunity to whip out a camera during the entire trip.

We were greeted at the palace entrance by a large entourage of Iranian presidential guards. President Mahmoud Ahmadinejad, who was standing on the deep red carpet laid out from the entrance, held his arms out wide to embrace Chávez as he bestowed upon him the official honors and recognitions as a visiting head of state. The rest of us were all hurried along to line up along the red carpet. After the official salutes were over, Chávez introduced Ahmadinejad to his delegation, starting with the high-level ministers and members of cabinet accompanying him, and ending with special guests, me included. It was so fast that I didn't get to say much more than 'hello, nice to meet you', and then we followed the two leaders inside. Set back from the busy streets of Tehran, the presidential palace was elaborate and intricately adorned with Persian art and sculptures. I didn't get to see more than a few rooms on the first level where those of us not included in the private bilateral talks were left to wait, but I did notice some pretty incredible Persian rugs and artifacts.

After a few hours, the two presidents came back downstairs and spoke to a group of journalists who had been invited to the palace for a press conference. The room was packed full of Iranian and international media and it was hot as blazes. It must have been around 90 degrees outside and over 100 degrees inside. Chávez and Ahmadinejad had a portable air conditioner blowing on them, but the rest of us were left to sweat it out in the crowded, suffocating room. The women had it worst – we were covered from head to toe. A few of the Venezuelan journalists on the delegation were less prepared than I was for the Iranian portion of our visit and had nothing to cover their arms and chests with other than the winter coats they had worn in Moscow and Minsk. Wearing a puffy jacket in 100-degree heat with a woolen winter scarf wrapped around your head is not ideal, but they had no choice. We were inside the presidential palace of the Islamic Republic of Iran. There were no ifs, ands or buts; women had to be fully covered or leave.

I had a serious dilemma after we returned to the hotel. I had received an official invitation to the state dinner that evening with Ahmadinejad and Chávez and I had nothing to wear. I couldn't exactly wear my shabby pants under a dress with a jean jacket to dinner with presidents, foreign ministers and other dignitaries. Chávez's daughter wasn't going. She stuck to her guns and never showed her face during the entire Iran trip, so I was going to be one of the only women at the dinner from the delegation – possibly the only one, since I was unsure whether the Cuban minister, Barbara, had been invited. Thankfully, my problem was solved by the wife of the Venezuelan Ambassador in Tehran. Well aware that some of us ladies were probably unprepared for the severe dress code in Iran, especially at official state events, she appeared at my door with a selection of full-body Iranian garments that could pass as 'dressy'. I chose a lavender piece with delicate Iranian embroidery, full length with long sleeves and a high neck.

The dinner was held in a state compound in Tehran where several administrative buildings and other government facilities were located, though I didn't have the opportunity to poke around or inquire much. No one in our group knew anything more than I did, as was usually the case on these trips. There was little time to explore or to do anything else beyond the official events and we weren't given maps or information on the places we visited. It was also nearly impossible to think beyond the moment. Chávez was always switching the schedule around, so if you tried to do anything on your own, most likely you'd be left behind without access to your belongings, passport or transportation. His security team held all of our passports for the entire length of the trip since they dealt with our entry and exit out of each country. So we were literally stuck together the entire time. I mean, after all, it was a presidential trip – that's what we had signed up for. It wasn't a vacation or tourist outing. It was work, and it was a highly privileged experience that I'll never regret.

We made our way up a winding staircase to the dining hall. There were about two dozen round tables in a large room, fully set and embellished with ornate centerpieces. At the front was a long rectangular table for the heads of state set out like a king's banquet overlooking the entire salon. The Iranian guests had already arrived and taken seats at the tables on the left side of the room, so the Venezuelans occupied the right side. There were no assigned seats so I took one of the open seats with a direct view of the presidents. I had a pack of documents and books with me, including my only copy of *The Chávez Code* in Farsi and the second copy of my articles translated into Farsi that I had been given that morning by my Iranian fan club. Both Chávez and Maduro had suggested that I bring these to the dinner to give to Ahmadinejad personally. I knew how these things worked, and that there was only a 50-50 chance that this would happen.

We were served traditional Iranian food, including fragrant, fresh salads, eggplant dips and sheep cheeses, which I gobbled up happily. It was nice to have something other than pickled vegetables and smoked fish. I passed on the main course, lamb and herbed rice. Chávez and Ahmadinejad chatted throughout the meal, occasionally smiling and laughing, enjoying a lighter moment. At one point Chávez caught my eye and signaled with his index finger for me to approach. I did a double take to make sure he was talking to me and when I pointed at myself mouthing 'me?' as a question, Maduro, who was next to Chávez, nodded his head and waved me up to their table.

I don't know what I was thinking, but I scooped up the book and binder of my articles and hurried up to the king's table without checking my headscarf, which was falling further backward off my head, exposing about the front third of my hair. Instead of going straight to the front of the table like I should have, across from Chávez and Ahmadinejad and appropriately distanced, I went around the back, provoking the Iranian president's security team to move towards me. It was seen as an aggressive move by a foreign woman in a country where women are expected to be submissive, and not touch men in public. As I was nearing the presidents, Maduro was loudly whispering to me, 'don't touch him, don't try to touch him or shake his hand'. Both Chávez and Ahmadinejad stood up and I realized my mistake. I should have greeted them from the front while they sat, with the large table in between us as a buffer zone.

I was never one to conform or behave appropriately, even when it wasn't intentional. It was just habit, just who I was. They both took it in their stride. Ahmadinejad told his guards to back down, I wasn't a threat. Chávez introduced me to him as his defender. Ahmadinejad told me that if I was Chávez's 'defender', then 'he loved me'. 'We love you, we love you,' he said in a soft voice. I couldn't quite absorb the oddity of that statement while it was happening and Chávez was gently touching my arm, trying to get me to go back to my seat, so I quickly offered my book and texts to Ahmadinejad, explaining their content, and he gratefully accepted them, almost surprised. 'These are for me?' He took them and thanked me, seemingly interested in my work and welcoming me to his country. Chávez gave me a very kind but telling look that meant 'that's enough, Eva', so I nodded my head down in an awkward bow, since I couldn't shake his hand, and I returned to my seat. It was only afterwards that I realized all eyes in the room were on me thinking, 'who the hell is that woman who approached our president and nearly caused an uproar?'

I made it out of Iran unscathed with my freedom and with the very weird sensation of yet another demonized figure and proclaimed enemy of the United States expressing his love for me. You can imagine my mixed feelings.

Syria

The trip to Damascus was smooth and uneventful. We stayed at a modern hotel near the city center next to a very large billboard with changing images of President Bashar al-Assad. The vibe was way different in Syria from that in Iran. There was no strict dress code for women, it was not an Islamic republic and headscarves were optional. Alcohol was freely available (in Iran it was prohibited) and there was a bustling nightlife. Even my hotel minibar was stocked with a half bottle of red wine and some small bottles of assorted liquors. The wine was Syrian, and I immediately stuffed it into my suitcase as a souvenir and forgot about it. We had arrived late in the afternoon and been given the evening off. No events with Chávez, just a free night in Damascus, one of the oldest cities in the world. I was excited to be there and check out the city and especially the food. I love Middle Eastern food – all those fresh salads, herbs, spices, eggplant dishes, pita bread, goat and sheep cheeses, yum! The food in Iran wasn't bad, but I was really looking forward to trying Syrian food at its source.

One of my friends, who at the time was a senior advisor to the Foreign Minister, had been to Damascus countless times and suggested a few of us go to a restaurant in the old historic city center and then check out a Syrian night club. The scene in Damascus was modern, young and progressive. Women were dressed stylishly and elegantly, some with and some without headscarves. There was no evidence of repression or the heavy hand of the state, as Syria had been portrayed in Western media. The city was vibrant and alive, the mix of the old historic buildings and streets with modern infrastructures and venues. The food was delicious, by far the best Middle Eastern food I'd ever had in my life. The flavors were rich and authentic. I had a glass of wine. I wore a dress that showed cleavage, though nothing too provocative. It felt good there, relaxing and free. Later we went to a night club that could have been in the middle of Paris or Caracas. It was just normal people of all ages, men and women, dancing, drinking and listening to music. It was far from the Syria I had been told about in the United States.

The civil war had not begun yet and there were loads of tourists in the streets and restaurants. There was no apparent military presence or scary government forces ready to pounce on anyone who got out of line. It seemed like a relatively normal place, similar to any European or Latin American city I'd been to before, with abundant and colorful marketplaces and lots of traffic. There were no unusual or even noticeable restrictions on freedoms. I'm just relaying what my personal, on-the-ground experience was and what I perceived during a very brief stay in Syria. In no way does my impression discount or dismiss the undoubted violations of rights or other abuses of power in the country. I was just surprised that during a completely unscheduled visit to the city center, I glimpsed a country and culture that seemed quite different from how it had been portrayed in the US media.

The next morning we went to the presidential palace, an oasis in a breathtakingly beautiful setting. I had seen the Syrian president before in Caracas with Chávez and knew he was tall, slender and softly spoken. He also spoke perfect English. Bashar al-Assad had resided in Britain for several years and pursued graduate studies in London, where he had met his wife, Asma. Even though his father had reigned over Syria for decades, Bashar claimed never to have aspired to lead his country. He was a doctor, who gave the impression of being cultured and progressive, despite his convoluted background and autocratic position. His wife Asma was born in London to Syrian parents and raised in Britain. She seemed like a regular British woman, except she was the First Lady of a major US nemesis that was accused of being a state sponsor of terrorism. They married in 2000 when Assad was first elected president of Syria (he was re-elected with an overwhelming majority in 2007, though the opposition claimed the process was a sham). Washington considered Assad to be a brutal dictator and after the civil war began in 2011, just a few months after we had been there, Assad became a world pariah and has since ruthlessly prosecuted a conflict that has caused the deaths of hundreds of thousands of his own people.

I experienced a different side of Assad and Asma during our days in Syria. We shared meals and went for walks in the Damascus countryside. I met their three beautiful children. We ate in a local restaurant in the open air, amidst regular patrons having their lunch. It wasn't just me and them – Chávez was there, as were other members of our delegation. But it felt intimate because they were accessible, down to earth and apparently humble. Asma and I conversed in English as we strolled to the ancient town of Ma'loula, a UNESCO World Heritage site set in the rugged mountains less than an hour from Damascus. Assad wanted to take Chávez there to see one of the last places where Aramaic, the language of Jesus Christ, was still spoken by the local Christian community. We had driven as far as we could from Damascus by car and then proceeded on foot. We walked through the village, up the old stone stairs into one of the ancient sanctuaries set back in a cave, a church that was still functional and preserved with relics dating back centuries. A service was held in honor of Chávez's visit by priests speaking Aramaic, and the townsfolk followed and crowded the two leaders as they walked through the stone streets and caverns of the old town. In 2013, Ma'loula was taken by al-Nusra, the local offshoot of al-Qaeda, and turned into a battle scene as part of the violent uprising against the Assad government. The Syrian Army fought ferociously to recover control of the ancient village, desperate to preserve its history, the history of our collective civilization. Sadly, many of the buildings and sanctuaries were severely damaged, valuable relics and religious items were destroyed and plundered by the terrorists and mercenaries. The Syrian government regained control of Ma'loula, but it still remains vulnerable to threats from groups with an utter disregard for the memory and historical evidence of an important part of humanity. In retrospect, it is very strange to have shared such personal moments with Assad, especially considering the barbarities and atrocities that later occurred under his direction during the Syrian war which began just months later in 2011. I saw him in a family setting, with his wife and young children – calm, cultured and approachable, and not as the brutal dictator portrayed in Western media. Now, I am forced to juxtapose that image of him with the brutality that has since occurred: the horrific slaughter of hundreds of thousands of his own people, the bombardment and destruction of his own nation. He had appeared to care about his people and his country, so how could he have ordered such brutal attacks against them? What had happened to the alleged reformist he had proposed to become, leading his country into a new form of progressive system in the 21st century? Faced with war and aggression from abroad – particularly from Washington – and an unwavering desire to remain in power, and believing, as so many authoritarian rulers do, that he and only he could save his country, Assad became the brutal dictator portrayed by the West instead of the reformer he had pledged to be.

What was most striking about meeting all of these vilified men was witnessing the layers of human complexity behind the images of them as tyrants. Were they responsible for monstrosities and grave violations of human rights? Undoubtedly so. But they were still human beings, full of contradictions and vulnerabilities. They believed themselves to be saviors of their people yet too often ended up destroying what they had pledged to protect.

Libya

The trip to Ma'loula had cost us an extra day in Syria, but no one was complaining. No one, that is, except Colonel Muammar Qadafi. We had been scheduled to arrive in Libya by noon, but thanks to our leisurely stroll through the Syrian mountainside, followed by probably the most scrumptious, mouthwatering lunch I've ever had at a roadside restaurant with the Assads, we didn't get to Tripoli until almost midnight. Qadafi was not waiting at the airport to greet Chávez, and the word was that he was displeased with our tardiness. There seemed to be a lot of competition among all these heads of state. When we were in Russia we were told not to discuss our subsequent trip to Belarus, and once in Minsk, Lukashenko warned heavily against going to Ukraine to see Yanukovych. Then when Chávez chose to stay longer with Assad in Syria, Qadafi was offended. There were a lot of big egos involved and Chávez seemed to be the man of the moment whom they all wanted to captivate and woo. Venezuela was a big prize as an ally and oil supplier, not to mention a strategically located partner with the capacity to make Washington really uncomfortable, which is something all these leaders reveled in doing.

Seeing the Mediterranean coast of Tripoli from the airplane window as we were close to landing sent shivers down my spine. I had never been to the African continent and it seemed majestic and profoundly humbling to enter its sphere. Mother Africa. So much history, so much beauty, so much tragedy. I knew I wouldn't get to see much of Libya beyond the hotel and wherever else we went in Chávez's wake, but I was grateful to enter its embrace.

There was some confusion as we piled into the cars, vans and buses. No one was sure where we were going. Apparently Chávez was supposed to meet with Qadafi somewhere, but since we were late it was all up in the air. One of the guards on my bus said we were going to the hotel as we sped through the streets of Tripoli towards the Radisson, right on the coast. I thought it was ironic that we would be staying in a US hotel chain in Libya, a country long considered by Washington as a sponsor of terrorism and an enemy state. Relations had been up and down in recent times and conversations were then taking place between European nations and the Qadafi government. The US had removed Libya from its list of terrorist nations in 2006, after Qadafi had agreed to dismantle its nuclear-weapons program in 2003 and had subsequently 'co-operated' with Washington's efforts in the war on terrorism. A lot of good that did him, given that only a year after my visit, in 2011, the West helped to overthrow Qadafi, bombing Libya, destroying the country's infrastructure and leading to the Libyan president's assassination.

I saw the Radisson as we drove by it, thinking to myself that we must be turning around somewhere up ahead. But we didn't. We kept going. And going. It seemed like we were driving in circles and, as it turned out, we were. Qadafi was deciding whether or not he'd forgive Chávez for the late arrival and meet with him in one of his many secret tents. While the Libyan leader was pondering this difficult decision, we were driving in circles. Just hold on to that for a second. Qadafi was pissed off because Chávez had stayed for lunch with Assad in Syria and, as punishment, he was making us literally drive around in circles in his city while he contemplated our fate. Finally, the motorcade picked up speed and made a beeline in another direction. Qadafi had found it in his heart to forgive Chávez. We were going to his tent.

I was determined. There was no way I was going to miss this event. I was three cars back from Chávez in a minibus and we pulled in to the dirt driveway and halted abruptly just as Chávez was already getting out of his car and heading towards a very large tent that looked more like an outdoor room with moveable walls. Needless to say, I ran as fast as I could to catch up. It was a good thing I did, because I was the last one of our delegation to be allowed into the tent; the rest were shut out. Qadafi's security guards confiscated everything we were carrying – literally everything. They took my purse, my camera, my phone. We weren't allowed to bring anything into the tent, just ourselves. By the time I made it through the checkpoint, Chávez was already greeting Qadafi and a dozen or so people, Libyans and Venezuelans, were seated around the tent on benches with velvet cushions and beautifully embroidered pillows. There were little wooden tables with ornate carvings, almost stool sized, with colorfully decorated teapots brewing and a few matching cups and saucers placed nearby. Not wanting to interrupt, I took the first open spot I saw on a bench next to Chávez's daughter, Rosa Virginia.

Qadafi had the appearance of a performance artist. He wore long layered robes of varying shades of green and deep brown, dark sunglasses and a squarish-shaped black hat on his head with a tassle. His curly black hair jutted out from under his hat. He looked ageless. He and Chávez were talking through a translator and, from where I was sitting, I could only hear mumbling from Qadafi's mouth. His lips barely opened or moved, yet the translator seemed animated and articulate and relayed lengthy statements to Chávez that allegedly were interpreted from Qadafi, but the whole thing seemed like a ventriloquist's act to me. I was leaning in to try to hear more of the conversation when, all of a sudden, one of Chávez's guards came over to me and asked me to leave. 'Me? Why?' I asked him. I was a guest of the President, why did I have to leave? He firmly touched my arm and again asked me to leave, so I got up and followed him towards the opening of the tent, fuming with humiliation. Once again Chávez's people were trying to get rid of me and I hadn't even done anything. I had just been sitting there observing a scene of world politics.

Before I could reach the exit, Nicolas Maduro came running up to me and grabbed my arm. 'Come back and sit down,' he said. He gave the guard a look that said 'back down'. 'The Comandante wants her here, she's our guest,' he scolded the officer and escorted me back to my seat. Just as I was sitting down and trying to take in the moment, Chávez called me over to introduce me to Qadafi. I knew that Qadafi had been a fairly prominent advocate of women's rights and his policies had enabled one of the highest levels of progress and education for women in the Arab world. Libya was still an Islamic nation and women were not treated as equals, but Qadafi was notorious for creating the first high-level security force of women presidential guards, trained military officers whom he liked to showcase as evidence of his fair treatment of women. But, after my experience in Iran, I didn't want to touch him or extend my hand, even if he would have taken it as a gesture of respect. So I awkwardly bowed as Chávez explained that I was a lawyer and investigator who wrote about CIA intervention in Venezuela, joking that surely Qadafi could use my services. The infamous

Colonel, whose name I had heard and whose strange face I had seen since my early adolescence plastered over US media and portrayed as a villainous tyrant, greeted me with a few mumbles and offered me tea.

The meeting did not last more than an hour. It was past midnight when we left for the Radisson. This time, we actually went inside and were able to check into our rooms. The hotel lobby had been set up as a security zone, with metal detectors and an x-ray machine for luggage to be searched for any suspicious items. When my bag went through the machine, I grabbed it and headed upstairs toward my assigned room. There was a small balcony overlooking the Tripoli coastline in the modest, single room. The room was nondescript, neither luxurious nor dingy, but the view was exquisite. I opened my bag to unpack a few pieces of clothes and my toiletries that I would use during our two nights in Libya and realized I had that half bottle of red wine in there I had taken from the hotel minibar in Damascus. Oh crap. I suddenly realized that I was in possession of contraband in Libya that could land me in prison. Alcohol was strictly forbidden in Libya and foreigners who tried to bring it into the country often ended up in prison or paying steep fines. My bag had gone through the x-ray machine in the hotel lobby but thankfully they hadn't seen the wine. What was I going to do? I decided I had no choice but to get rid of the contraband, so I sat on the balcony overlooking the tranquil Mediterranean Sea and drank up.

Our only full day in Libya was literally full from morning until night. Chávez was honored by the Academy of Higher Studies at the University of Tripoli and awarded an Honoris Causa Doctorate for his contribution towards social justice. He praised Qadafi and Libya's progress towards 'direct democracy', fully pledging his allegiance to Libya as a staunch ally. Chávez would later become one of the only world leaders backing Qadafi during the 2011 war. He refused to turn on him and even offered him refuge in Venezuela, which Qadafi refused, saying he would rather fight to the death in his own country. We all know how that ended. Tortured, brutally sodomized and extrajudicially assassinated.

Later in the afternoon, Chávez met members of the Libyan government and state enterprises at our hotel. Those of us who were not part of the bilateral meetings took advantage of the opportunity to have coffee in the lobby bar and stroll around the hotel browsing at the gift shops. After a couple of hours went by and we had no news about when we'd be leaving for one of Qadafi's compounds where the two presidents would have more private talks and then a state dinner, which we had all been invited to attend, I started to get antsy. I realized I had better make my way into the area where Chávez was having his meetings and wait there with his team until it was time to go. I knew from experience that he could just decide to leave at any moment and his entourage could go out a back door, and whoosh, be gone, leaving the rest of us behind. I asked a couple of the other members of the delegation if they wanted to come with me to stake out Chávez, but they were content hanging out in the lobby, drinking coffee and chatting.

I made it upstairs to the mezzanine just in time. Chávez was wrapping up his meetings and wanted to leave immediately. There was no time to notify the other members of the delegation who were not in the room. The cars were brought around to the side of the hotel instead of to the main lobby and we exited out a back door. Whoever wasn't there at that moment was left behind. That's how it was: you snooze, you lose. There was no middle ground. It wasn't like if you missed the motorcade you could take a taxi. This was a presidential trip, a state visit. The areas we went to were highly secured and often secret. There was no access if you weren't with the delegation. In all the years I traveled with Chávez I was never given a contact list by his assistants or security team telling me who to contact if I got lost. You just didn't get lost. You didn't separate, you didn't go off on your own. I did not want to get left behind in Libya or anywhere else on our 'Axis of Evil' tour, so I stuck to Chávez like glue. They weren't getting rid of me yet.

This time the drive to the compound was longer than expected. I knew of Qadafi's extreme security measures, but one would think that he wouldn't make his guests conduct extensive counter-surveillance in order to visit him. We must have driven around for nearly 90 minutes on long arid roads through the desert, often looping around and repeating routes, until finally we entered a nondescript area at the end of long road with nothing nearby except camels – lots of camels. The compound had about a half a dozen tents of varying sizes and camels wandering around everywhere. Did I mention the camels? Chávez entered a tent where Qadafi was waiting for him and the rest of us stayed outside with the camels. Night had fallen and it was dark. There was almost no light except that emanating from the tents. It was one of the only times during the entire trip that I took out my camera and asked someone to take a picture of me. It was with the camels, of course.

Chávez and Qadafi talked nukes, energy and trade. Chávez had pledged to develop Venezuela's nuclear-energy capacity with Libya, Russia and Iran, much to the dismay of Washington, but it seemed more of a rhetorical threat than a real objective. I know there was some research into building a nuclear plant, but nothing in that realm ever materialized, at least not to my knowledge. The two governments signed a lot of agreements, though there was little tangible that flowed from Venezuela's relationship with Libya, beyond the broad anti-imperialist alliance. Unlike the relationships with Russia, Iran and Belarus, from which Venezuela obtained numerous benefits, with Libya it was more about Chávez's admiration of Qadafi as a historical revolutionary figure who had overcome severe aggression from the US.

Chávez praised Qadafi's 'green book' as a reference on direct democracy, which he saw as similar to what the Bolivarian Revolution was trying to build through participatory democracy. Over time, Qadafi had concentrated power in his own hands and created a cult of personality. His government was infested with corruption and there was little resemblance to democracy as traditionally understood in the West. Nevertheless, under Qadafi's rule, Libya achieved the highest level of development in Africa, with advanced women's rights (for an Islamic republic) and a functional infrastructure. All of that was destroyed by the war against Qadafi in 2011 that resulted in his murder. The ravages of war not only resulted in mass deaths but a total destruction of the country's institutions and developed infrastructure.

It was unfathomable at the time of our visit that, just six months later, Libya would be in a state of war, and within a year Qadafi would be dead, his corpse dragged around like an animal by his assassins to show to the world. When I saw him in Tripoli, Qadafi was eccentric, but certainly didn't seem threatening anymore. Not like the tyrant I remembered from my youth. That night we had dinner in one of the bedouin tents. A more modest king's table was set just for Chávez and Qadafi, while the rest of us sat at a handful of round tables. Before dinner was served, there was a cultural show. Men played African rhythms on varying sized drums while women, clad from head to toe in flowing Islamic dress, danced subtly, so as not to appear provocative. It was the first time during our trip to Libya that I had seen women fully covered. Those of us on the delegation were not required to wear headscarves. It was optional. I even wore a dress with short sleeves and an exposed neckline, which didn't seem to draw any unwanted attention. The dancing was so odd because the women barely moved their bodies, which couldn't be seen under their dark, loose coverings. They moved in an almost ghostly fashion around the room, as if they were floating to the deep, droning sounds of the drums.

When dinner was served I stuck with the salad. It had a white cheese on it that I thought was similar to what I had in Iran and Syria, like a goat's or sheep's cheese. It tasted funny: dry and sour. 'That's camel cheese,' said the person next to me, who happened to be Venezuela's Vice Foreign Minister for Africa. So he knew. Eww. After the unbelievably delicious food in Damascus, there was just no contest. Everything from that point was downhill. The main course was served next, a plate with a meat item and rice. 'That's camel,' said the Vice-Minister. I thought of the camels wandering around outside and wondered if it had come from them. I pushed the plate away and looked up at Chávez, who was biting into his camel leg with a big grin.

'Tastes just like chicken,' he said, giggling like a little kid while smacking his lips.

17

The unraveling of a revolution

I had started feeling the itch to leave Venezuela and transition back to New York around midyear in 2010, before the 'Axis of Evil' trip. Even though I finally had my first formal job as the editor-in-chief of the *Correo del Orinoco International*, the pay was nominal and I had no savings. I was ready to move on with my life. I was tired of the unbridled chaos and the unreliability. I had been in Venezuela for over five years and, despite publishing several books and traveling the world with President Chávez, I felt stifled. The projects I tried to achieve seemed unattainable and I was exhausted by the constant attacks on me from inside and outside the *chavista* movement. The October trip with Chávez was unexpected and exhilarating, but it didn't change my mind. I had already set into motion a series of events that would facilitate my return to the US.

I was ready to be close to my family again: my parents were aging and I had been far away for a long time. I wanted to be near them and also to figure out my own future. I was now 37 years old with no desire to remarry, but I did want to have a child. I didn't want to pass up that experience in life and had begun to consider doing it on my own. I wasn't planning to abandon Venezuela, but rather to divide my time between the two countries again – at least that's how I tried to rationalize the change. I never thought I'd sell my Caracas apartment, but I did want a place to live in New York City and an income source that was more stable. The stars aligned just weeks before the 'Axis of Evil' trip.

I had received a call from the television station Russia Today, which had frequently interviewed me on its English-language channel, offering me the opportunity to host my own show. They had just started a new Spanish-language channel, RT Spanish, and wanted me to start hosting my own weekly program within a few months. Why not? I thought. I was already in bed with the Venezuelans and the Cubans, so it seemed logical that the Russians should be next. Over the years I had actually been approached by people I suspected of being intelligence operatives from Canada, Britain, North Korea, Iran and Russia, though I had never taken the bait. The North Koreans had practically begged me to visit their nuclear facilities, but I had politely refused. Their Consul in Havana had called me frequently, inviting me on special trips to Pyongyang. Eventually I had stopped taking his calls. That was not something I wanted to get involved with.

When the RT offer came in, my one non-negotiable issue was that I would have full editorial control over my show – content, topics, everything. They agreed, so I considered it seriously. Originally the plan was to do the show from a New York City studio once a month and from Caracas the remaining three weeks. I wasn't fully committed when I left for the trip with Chávez, but upon my return, coming down off the high from all the excitement, I made my decision. This, of course, was well before RT became a household name in the US for its role in the 2016 presidential election and the accusations of Russian meddling.

I was privileged to take that final trip with Chávez, but I knew that I had always remained an outsider. I yearned to go home where I felt more at ease in the culture, where I could go for a run without getting harassed by passers-by, where law and order were basic, respected tenets of society and where I could feel anonymous once again. In New York City, nobody cared who you were, what you were doing or where you were going. There was a common code of respect, deference and, well, people were just too damn busy to get in your business. All those years being under the spotlight had taken their toll. I was drinking too much wine and not getting enough done. I took the job with RT Spanish and planned to map out the structure of the show over the next few months, with the goal of taping a pilot in January 2011.

I found a tiny, unrenovated apartment in Park Slope, Brooklyn, at a good price and made an offer. It was located on President Street – a rather fitting name. No, I didn't steal money from the Venezuelan people to buy it, as many have wrongly accused me of doing. My mother helped me buy it with money from the house that she had just sold in Miami. I never stole money or corruptly obtained anything from Venezuela. All the years I lived there I barely got by paying my bills. I worked for everything I ever earned. Sometimes I feel like the big fool who was too naive and law-abiding to figure out that everyone around me was dipping their fingers in the honey. I was the only idiot who never took advantage of anything. Not my contacts, not my celebrity, not my access to Chávez. Nothing. The more I began to understand what was happening around me and how deep the corruption really ran, the more I wanted out. Once again, my gut told me it was time to go.

Don't get me wrong, I wasn't disappointed in my professional achievements and accomplishments. I just wanted to do more, I wanted to be more. For nearly a decade I had given myself to the movement in Venezuela. I had dedicated my life to the investigation uncovering US intervention in Venezuela and throughout Latin America. I had put my name and face to it. I had been paraded on television, smeared in newspapers, hounded and hugged in the streets. I believed in what I was doing. I believed I was fighting for social justice, fighting for a better world. I believed in Chávez and believed we were building a people's movement, a grassroots democracy where people were valued above profits. It was a constant struggle, but there were real, tangible results. People's lives seemed better. The country appeared to be advancing and the whole region was blossoming. It was a fascinating time to live in Latin America, but something deep inside me urged me to go.

Unexpected pregnancy

In February 2011, I turned 38 and had something of a mid-life crisis. I started dating younger men. Much younger – in their twenties. They were energetic and cute. It was fun. I dated a few at the same time. At one point there may have been more than a few but I wasn't really keeping track. I had decided just to let loose and enjoy myself. A few weeks later, I missed a period, but

I didn't notice at first. One morning at a brunch with a group of friends, at which I was nursing a glass of chilled white wine, a friend announced that she was four weeks pregnant with her second child. We all toasted. And just as I gulped down my wine it hit me that I hadn't had my period and it was two weeks overdue. I said I had to go and gave everyone a kiss on the cheek. I drove straight to the pharmacy and bought a pregnancy test. I went home and peed on it and looked in utter disbelief when the result was positive. I went back to the pharmacy and bought three more tests of different brands. After the fourth one came out positive, I bawled my eyes out in terror. I was pregnant! Holy shit! I called my mom, crying. She laughed at me. 'You've been wanting to get pregnant and now you're crying about it?' I was terrified and in a state of shock, but she calmed me down.

I had given up on getting pregnant. I had been told that I had fibroids in my fallopian tubes that were blocking the passage of the sperm and that every year after the age of 35 my chances of getting pregnant were reduced by around 15 per cent. Because of my 'advanced maternal age', as the doctors so kindly labeled women over 35, my chances of getting pregnant were not better than 5-10 per cent. The doctor had suggested I go out and find myself a nice chavista and try to make it happen. I had taken his advice and, well, it had worked! Someone's sperm had made it past the stubborn fibroids all the way to the eggs.

At this point in my story I can honestly and unequivocally state that this 'someone' was not Hugo Chávez. Three months after I gave birth, a CNN host asked me live during an interview if Chávez was the father of my baby. I'm not making that up. That kind of offensive misogynist crap only happens to women. Here I was, supposedly doing a serious interview on US-Venezuela relations, an interview that I had reluctantly accepted because I had just given birth, and that was the line of questioning. Was Chávez the father of my baby? No, Chávez was not the father. No, I'm not going to say who is. None of your beeswax.

My life was really changing fast. I had a baby. I had a new job. I had an apartment in Brooklyn and I still had my home in Caracas. I had chosen to be a single mother and to raise my son on my own. I wanted to be in charge of my own life and my new family. I was growing weary of the strongmen I had spent years observing and following, and never wanted to repeat the mistakes I had made in my past marriage and relationships. I was distrustful of my own judgment in men and wanted no interference in my personal life. I knew I was going to have to make a decision eventually about how my future would unfold, but before I could even begin to contemplate all of that, another life-changing event rocked my world. This time, it wasn't good.

Chávez falls ill

That life comes at us with monumental ups and downs simultaneously seems cruel. It's hard to celebrate the good when the bad hits you like an iceberg. Chávez had gone on a trip to Brazil and had then stopped in Cuba to meet with Fidel before coming home. It was June 2011 and nothing had seemed too abnormal. About a month earlier, Chávez had been limping around with a cane, claiming he had been injured while exercising and that it was only minor. But it was more than that. He had fallen to the ground while walking, screaming in pain and clutching the side of his leg. His doctors recommended a full examination, but he refused. He didn't want to undergo tests just as he was gearing up for one of the biggest moments of his political career: the launch of the newly created Community of Latin American and Caribbean States (CELAC), a long-cherished dream to bring together all 33 nations of the region in one sovereign organization, without the participation of the US and Canada. It was, he believed, time for Latin America and the Caribbean to join forces for collective progress and development without the influence of Washington. Canada always seemed to follow Washington's orders when it came to Latin America, so they were out too. Chávez had set the inaugural date for 5 July 2011 – Venezuela's Independence Day. It seemed to him a fitting occasion on which to launch an entity that he believed fulfilled the goal of Simón Bolívar, founding father of four South American nations. There was no way Chávez was going to forfeit that moment, so he postponed the medical exams and sucked in the pain. His health could wait another two months, or so he thought.

When he was in Cuba to finalize details for CELAC, now just one month away, Fidel noticed Chávez was in pain. Fidel knew what it was like to have intestinal discomfort, having suffered years of debilitating diverticulitis until finally over a foot of his own colon was removed in 2006. Chávez was squirming in his seat as they sat for their usual hours-long conversation. Fidel asked him what was going on. 'Nothing,' said Chávez. 'I'll deal with it later, after CELAC.' 'No,' Fidel responded firmly, 'you'll go see my doctors right now.' It was an order from the *Comandante en Jefe*. Chávez complied.

The exams showed a mass in his intestinal area that required immediate surgical intervention. His pelvic area had abscessed and the doctors went in to clean it out. Meanwhile, rumors started swirling in Venezuela when Chávez didn't return home the day after the trip to Havana, as he had promised. Finally, on 8 June, Nicolas Maduro announced on television that Chávez had undergone surgery for a pelvic abscess and was in recovery. No further information was given about the cause of the abscess or if his health was at risk, but the gossip mill went crazy. Cancer, claimed the opposition columnists. The government denied it. We all thought it impossible. He was totally healthy, how could he have cancer? But that's how the cancer demon works. One minute you're perfectly fine, the next your body is riddled with cancerous cells eating your insides. My father, the doctor, called me to express his sympathies. 'I know you don't want to hear this,' he said, 'but it's most likely a very advanced cancer that's metastasized. If something inside him abscessed, it's because it's infected and most likely spreading into his bloodstream.'

Chávez remained in Havana for several weeks. Venezuelan state television showed images of him in recovery, taking walks with his daughters and close aides. He conducted a few televised meetings from Cuba broadcast live on Venezuelan state media and appeared his usual self, with good humor and big smiles, focused on his policies and the progress of social programs in Venezuela. The CELAC inauguration was postponed until future notice. We all knew something was wrong, but no one who supported him wanted to believe he wasn't invincible. I thought about our trip to the 'Axis of Evil' the previous October. He had seemed fine, though he had been smoking an awful lot, more than I had seen him do in the past. Plus he had barely slept, and his food choices had been terrible – all that red meat, fried food and sugary black coffee. But cancer? Surely not.

A close friend of mine in the presidential guard, a colonel in the counterintelligence force, told me point blank that Chávez didn't have cancer. I stupidly believed him. He lied. The very next day Chávez went on television in a live broadcast from Cuba and told the world he had cancer. Once the abscess had been cleaned and the infection had healed, the subsequent exams had shown a large cancerous mass in his pelvic area. He would now be starting a combined treatment of radiation and chemotherapy, and would undergo surgery for removal of the tumor. Chávez later referred to the tumor as the 'size of a baseball'. He was optimistic about his recovery.

I cried as I watched his speech. He looked thin and frail, pale and trembling. His words were strong but his body was weak and sickly. He vowed to fight and never indicated that he could not, or that it was already too late. Most of the nation sobbed and prayed; some in the opposition rejoiced. Overall, there was a lot of praying. There were prayer sessions broadcast on television, held in communities, sponsored by the government. Venezuela is a very religious country, a very Catholic country, and it seemed as though everyone, including Chávez, believed Jesus would save him from the perils of cancer. I'm not religious so I kept my distance from the praying, though I shared the wishes for Chávez's prompt recovery.

While I was growing a new life in my uterus, Chávez was fighting for his own. Life comes at you and pinches hard to make sure you know you're not dreaming. I had to reconcile my own changes and evolving vision of my future with what was happening to Venezuela, and to Chávez. I already had one foot out the door, and now this whole cancer thing gave me a giant shove.

The government didn't want to release any information about Chávez's health. No official health record was made public during the entire duration of his illness – or ever, for that matter. Chávez was the only one who publicly discussed his health, often describing his treatments long after he had recovered, or talking about the pain he had felt at different times during the onset of the tumor and the course of treatment. There was no public information about medications he was taking, what his diagnosis was or even what kind of cancer he had. He would just say it wasn't 'organ specific' and that rumors about colon or prostate cancer were wrong. His illness was so unexpected and aggressive, that it seemed unreal. No chavista accepted the idea that he would die or be unable to remain president. There was no plan for 'after Chávez'.

A shocking revelation

Meanwhile, I had a double blow that seemed to seal my fate. My mother was still deep in a dedicated pursuit to find members of her father's Venezuelan and Spanish family. She decided to request the long form of her original birth certificate, in the hope that it would contain additional information that could aid her search. She went down to the Department of Records of the City of New York to request her document and was met by a reluctant clerk.

'I'm sorry, ma'am,' the clerk told my mother apologetically. 'I can't give you this birth certificate.'

What? My mom was confused. 'Of course you can, it's my own birth certificate!'

The clerk looked uncomfortable, shifting in her seat. 'I'm sorry ma'am,' she repeated.

'This is ridiculous,' my mom said, 'why can't you give it to me? I'm 68 years old!'

The clerk looked at her nervously. 'I'm not supposed to tell you this or I could lose my job, but the names you gave me don't match what's on your birth certificate.'

Now my mom was really confused. 'What the heck do you mean? Which names – mine? My mother? My father?'

The clerk again seemed really uneasy. 'It's the father, ma'am. The name doesn't match.'

She glanced around to make sure no one in her office was looking and she showed my mom her computer screen. It showed my mother's birth certificate, her date of birth and her mother's name, but the father's name on it was not Antonio Calderon. And her own last name was not listed as Calderon.

My mom looked at the short birth certificate that she had in her hand. It said her last name was Calderon. But the one on the screen had a different name. A name she had never seen before. Raeter, it said. Who the hell is Raeter? She looked at the document in her hand again and then she saw it. You had to really look hard, to focus on the name Calderon to see it. The document had been altered. Someone, her mother she assumed, had changed Raeter to Calderon on the copy of the birth certificate she had kept all these years. It didn't have a father's full name on it, just her mother's name and her name, and now she realized that it had been doctored. Antonio Calderon was not her biological father. So who was?

You can imagine that when she informed me of this discovery it was pretty mind-blowing. I had spent most of my adult life in Venezuela based on our family connections, on a grandfather I never knew but to whom I had felt tied in spirit and in passion for his homeland, which I had adopted. He was still the man who raised my mother during the first five years of her life and the person she considered to be her father. But the blood ties I had bonded with and believed in had turned out not to be real.

My mother eventually pieced together enough to figure out that her mother had been a pretty unconventional woman for her time. She had apparently had at least two affairs with married men and Antonio Calderon had been one of them. He was married to another woman and had a family with her when he fell in love with my grandmother. She also fell in love with Antonio and, when she became pregnant, he assumed it was his child and ran off with her.

His stridently Catholic, Spanish-Venezuelan family ostracized him for running out on his wife and child. They disowned him and his lover. They wanted nothing to do with his new family, which they considered illegitimate. Antonio and my grandmother went on to have another child, my mother's brother, before Antonio became sick with bone cancer from a skin melanoma and died. At some point in all this, my grandmother doctored my mom's birth certificate to change her last name to Calderon and then kept the secret until she died in her late forties.

Discovering all this after nearly 70 years was pretty astonishing.

For my mother, it was about relearning her own history and searching for her biological father and his family, which, as it turned out, were European Jewish, just like my father's side. For me, well, it meant that, in one sense, my Venezuelan adventure had been based on an illusion. Of course, to all intents and purposes that didn't matter: I had lived there for nearly 12 years; I had married and divorced a Venezuelan; I had raised a Venezuelan child; I had obtained Venezuelan nationality, and now I was carrying a child with a Venezuelan father. But, still, it was another sign that it was time to move on. The dream was unraveling.

Venezuela had become an inextricable part of my life and who I had become. But who was I really? I had no homeland. I was from everywhere and nowhere. Ever-evolving, ever-changing, ever-adapting. Once, when I was an adolescent, a kid asked me what I was. 'What are you?' he asked cruelly. I was overweight, so I dressed like a boy in big baggy clothes. I rode a skateboard. I wasn't feminine, I was uncomfortable in my body so I covered it up. I was a tomboy at a time when gender bending and different body sizes were not accepted. 'I'm just me,' I told him.

Chávez ponders the succession

With Chávez sick, Venezuela drifted towards a level of secrecy unprecedented for the Bolivarian Revolution. Chávez had been a master communicator, constantly sharing even the smallest detail with the public, televising his cabinet meetings and events. On his Sunday show, *Aló Presidente*, he spent hours mapping out his policies, projects and future plans. It was a level of transparency unequaled by any other government in the world and it was one of the aspects I most admired about him and the political process he had instituted in Venezuela. But everything went dark when he fell ill.

I was too preoccupied with figuring out my own living arrangements and deciding where I'd give birth and live with my baby to pay much attention to what was happening inside the government. I heard the rumors but didn't want to believe them. As Chávez grew sicker and his recovery seemed less likely, the plundering began. Even though he still remained at the helm of government, few decisions were made from the time he began his treatment until his death in early 2013. The infighting was brutal and the power struggles intensified.

A close friend, the ambassador of a Latin American country in Venezuela, later told me that, early on in his illness, Chávez asked him to come to the presidential palace. They were alone, with no aides or guards around. Chávez told him he probably wasn't going to survive the cancer. He asked for the ambassador's advice on who to name as his successor. He was contemplating a three-way share of power between Nicolas Maduro, Diosdado Cabello and Rafael Ramirez. The three of them represented the major power blocs within *chavismo*. Maduro embodied the grassroots, trade unionists and the political base of the party. Cabello was widely seen to control the military, or at least to command their respect; he was also considered to be the liaison with the business community and the political elites across the ideological spectrum. Ramirez, meanwhile, controlled the oil sector, nationally and internationally. The three of them seemed to be at odds. My ambassador friend gave Chávez the best advice he could, mainly that he had to choose just one person. The thought of three people having an equal role in running the government was a pipedream. It would have been a fight to the death.

Fidel Castro had always counseled Chávez that he couldn't be the mayor of Venezuela, that he had to delegate. He had to create a competent circle of trust that could effectively, and successfully, carry out his policies and implement his vision. If he tried to heed that advice, it never materialized. Chávez's grand vision of using Venezuela's natural and strategic resources to invest in domestic agricultural production, revive industry and diversify the national economy had not succeeded. The people he had trusted and charged with these responsibilities had failed him. Many projects had fallen by the wayside, riddled with corruption and incompetence. Industries that had been nationalized became dysfunctional, inefficient and underproducing. Many were plundered by a corrupt management and faced ruin. Whenever Chávez visited, extreme efforts would be taken to make everything look perfect and productive, and once he had gone everything would fall to pieces. Roads would be paved with cheap asphalt to make them look shiny and new for a presidential visit, only to crumble in the succeeding weeks. How was he to know this was happening if no one told him? If you couldn't trust those around you, then who could you trust?

Faced by his own mortality, Chávez had to make a decision. Despite a diagnosis that gave him less than two years to live, which was never revealed publicly, he believed his government would not survive without him. So, instead of accepting the bleak reality that his political movement and vision for his country would probably not succeed in the long term as he'd planned, he undertook a severely painful treatment process that would prop him up sufficiently to run for re-election as president in 2012. If he were to pass the baton to one of the chosen three, he did not believe that they would win the election. The opposition was surging now that Chávez's illness had been revealed, and the secrecy surrounding his diagnosis provided fodder for both the domestic and international media.

There were two different realities playing out in Venezuela after Chávez got sick. On the *chavista* side, there were calls for unity, prayer and a collective belief that Chávez would survive because he had to – he was their leader, he was stronger than cancer, and his job wasn't yet done. No other politician on the *chavista* side had the confidence of the majority of people. The opposition, meanwhile, saw this as their moment. Finally, there was a clear vulnerability they could exploit that would chip away at the unbending loyalty that had hitherto held sway. If people thought Chávez would die or would be too sick to run for the presidency, then they would be less likely to cast their vote for him. Chávez's cancer was used by the opposition as a metaphor for the Bolivarian Revolution, as though it were dying from within.

Notwithstanding this, Chávez won the election on 7 October 2012, with a solid majority of 55.1 per cent over opposition candidate Henrique Capriles Radonski. Even with terminal cancer, Chávez was politically invincible. Ironically, or tragically, even after his death Chávez remains the most popular politician in Venezuela. The opposition had offered no viable alternative that resonated with the people; its platform had been violent, hostile and angry. Chávez, on the other hand, had run a campaign pumped up on steroids and other medications that bloated up his body but gave him the energy he needed to appear strong and sufficiently healthy. He was often in so much pain during processions through crowds of thousands of supporters that he would be wincing through his smiles and waves, whispering to his aides to get him out of there so he could take his medication and rest.

I only knew bits and pieces of what was really going on behind the scenes. I had decided to return to New York once I was seven months pregnant and could no longer travel safely by air. I would give birth in Brooklyn, with the support of my parents, whom I knew I was lucky to have. I remained in touch with one of Chávez's daughters, who was with him during most of his treatments in Cuba. I sent pictures of my son when he was born and she sent Chávez's blessings.

Death of Hugo Chávez

I went back to Caracas for the presidential election, bringing my baby boy with me. When I saw Chávez in person for the first time since the previous year, I knew he was not doing well. He was swollen up like a balloon and could barely focus on anything for more than a few seconds because of the pain shooting through his body, which made him wince but which he tried to cover up with forced smiles. I voted for him and cheered him on, secretly wishing that he had not chosen to run but instead was living out his remaining days with his family, lounging on a hammock in his beloved homeland in the plains of Barinas. I knew he had chosen to sacrifice himself for the sustainability of his Bolivarian Revolution. He fully understood the choice he had made. He had given his life to ensure the movement would be consolidated and strong enough to continue without him. He would have no rest, no final days in peace. He forced his body to the maximum in order to win the election, and then he couldn't do any more.

In the days after his election, he fell gravely ill. It was as though he could finally let go and admit the pain, unleash the suffering. He went to Cuba for a bariatric treatment and more tumors were found. The cancer had overcome his body and he had accelerated his death by over-exertion. His organs were over-run with cancerous cells and malign infections. He still wanted to fight so that at least he would survive until January, when he would assume his new mandate, but he knew the odds were against him. The pain was crippling. He had two choices: to undergo more surgery to alleviate his situation as much as possible, or to let it go, which would probably mean death within a matter of days or weeks. He chose the surgery.

When I saw him on 8 December 2012, exactly two months after the election, on a televised broadcast with Simón Bolívar's sword in one hand, Nicolas Maduro on one side and Diosdado Cabello on the other, I knew it was over. He was going to die. He called for unity. He pleaded with his supporters to elect Maduro, then the Vice-President, if he didn't survive the surgery that he was to undergo within a matter of days. He seemed more honest and sincere than he had been about his health, humbled by the prospect of his mortality and the survival of his revolution. It was vital to maintain unity, he said, and it was essential to support Maduro. Maduro would carry on the Bolivarian Revolution; he was the chosen one.

Chávez left for Cuba the next day and didn't return until 18 February 2013. He was not conscious on his return and was kept in a military hospital until he was pronounced dead on 5 March 2013. Chávez had leiomyosarcoma in his bladder region, an extremely rare form of aggressive cancer in adults. The treatment for this type of cancer, often not detected until it is too late, was debilitating and life threatening.

The decision not to announce the type of cancer Chávez had was a political calculation, since his diagnosis was less than ideal. Had it come out publicly, it would have made his chances of winning re-election next to impossible. The deception was seen as being for the good of the people and the future of the revolution. But it was still deception. Did Venezuelans have the right to know Chávez's diagnosis before the election in 2012? Or would his political opponents, and Washington, have aggressively used it to their advantage, resulting in a devastating loss and a reversal of major social gains and regional alliances? Was Chávez just steadfast on remaining in power until death, hanging on with an iron fist until his last breath, or did he do it for the 'greater good' of his people and his country?

In the end, it didn't matter much. On 14 April 2013, Nicolas Maduro was elected as president by an extremely narrow margin, less than two per cent, and the country descended into the chaos, violence and instability from which it has yet to emerge. The opposition, and its international allies, believed that *chavismo* died with Chávez, that it was never a revolution, but rather a cult of personality, a dictatorial regime that only served itself. They were wrong – or so I thought.

Things fall apart

The opposition brought violence to the streets after Maduro's election, resulting in dozens of deaths. Its leaders called for regime change, a repeat scenario of 2002, when some of the same opposition politicians had briefly overthrown Chávez in a coup. This time, the opposition had no support from the military, and they failed. But the downward spiral into a permanent state of violent instability and political and economic chaos only worsened over the years that followed.

Chavismo initially rallied around Maduro so as to protect and defend Chávez's legacy. But the country grew ever more deeply divided. Maduro became more paranoid and secretive, tightening his inner circle. Erratic decisions were made, with catastrophic consequences for the nation's economy, food supply and basic services. The plundering from within continued. Billions of dollars were siphoned out of the country. Some fled with the money to live lucrative lifestyles abroad in Miami, Panama, Spain, the Dominican Republic, or some fiscal paradise of their choosing, while others stayed immersed in the government, continuing to profit from the rampant corruption.

I watched in horror as it all began to fall to pieces, wondering how it was possible that such a strong, vibrant democratic movement, which I had passionately believed in, was unable to survive without its inspirational leader. Maduro called for dialogue with the opposition a number of times but they either refused or sabotaged the process – they seemed to have no interest in negotiations and simply wanted the *chavistas* out. They wanted a negotiated regime change, and the Maduro government wanted to remain in power. There seemed to be no common ground and neither side was willing to budge. US agencies continued feeding the conflict, with millions of taxpayer dollars channeled to anti-government groups that were engaging in direct, violent attempts to overthrow Maduro. Private companies in Venezuela used their time-honored tactic of squeezing the government and making the economy scream by price gouging and hoarding of products, causing food shortages and mass anger against the government.

Corruption continued spreading and seemed unstoppable, like horrific flesh-eating bacteria devouring everything in sight. The corruption from within finally began eating away at the movement, rotting it from the inside out. Billions of dollars were embezzled out of the country during the year Chávez died. Many of Chávez's former cabinet members and most trusted intellectual advisors, such as Planning Minister Jorge Giordani and Education Minister Hector Navarro, publicly denounced the corruption and massive economic mismanagement taking place within Maduro's government. Those charged with leadership seemed to be the biggest offenders of all, yet anyone who dared to call them out on their betrayals was branded a traitor. There were many real traitors. Some fled the country with their plundered treasures, even becoming star witnesses in legal investigations against their comrades, others burrowed in deeper, becoming essential knobs of power in the government. If they fell, the whole thing crashed with them. Those from the left and former members of Chávez's government who decried the corruption were discredited, silenced, threatened and deemed treasonous. So the secrecy grew, the cover-ups widened and the idea of protecting and fighting for Chávez's legacy became ever harder to defend.

This is not to say that there were not millions of honest, hard-working people dedicated to maintaining and fighting for the revolution they had fought tooth and nail to build. These millions of Venezuelans committed to their homeland and to their fundamental rights and freedoms were the true legacy of Hugo Chávez and his Bolivarian Revolution. After Chávez's death, their struggle became compounded. They were no longer just defending themselves from a violent opposition, they were fighting against the very same people Chávez had entrusted with his power, with the survival and success of his policies. They were fighting against the very same corrupt system that, nearly 20 years earlier, Hugo Chávez had pledged to eradicate. It had come back in full force.

18

The slippery slope

So, what went wrong? Did we all deceive ourselves into believing we were doing something good, something extraordinary? Were we wrong? Was I wrong? I keep asking myself these questions as I continue to mourn the loss of Chávez and the dismantling of the Bolivarian Revolution. I know that some of you – probably many of you – reading this will think Chávez was a dictator who turned Venezuela into a corrupt narco-state. That's what you read in the papers and hear in the news, so it must be true.

I beg to differ. I was there, I knew him. I was there for his rise and there for his fall. Hugo Chávez was just a man with a dream. He believed in making his country stronger and better for his people. He believed in social justice, in equality, in fundamental freedoms. He loved and was loved. He had no hate in his heart that I ever saw, despite the widespread hatred against him. He was not a tyrant ruling with an iron fist. He was overwhelmingly elected by landslide majorities in multiple free and fair elections. He was even re-elected when he was dying of cancer – that's how popular he was in Venezuela. He abhorred corruption and abuse of power, and more often than not forgave and pardoned his adversaries, even when they attempted to overthrow him in a violent coup. Did he have authoritarian tendencies? Yes, but he was not an egoist, nor was he a narcissist as his detractors portrayed him. He had enormous empathy for others, and particularly for the poor and the marginalized. He never turned his back on someone in need, and this was not just a tactic to get a vote, it was something deeply rooted inside him that compelled him to help people. He tried to build his dream, which was a dream shared by millions, a dream centuries old. He made great strides during his time as president, with the help of millions of people, not just in Venezuela but around the world, though of course he also made many mistakes.

He propelled the creation of a system where people were valued over profits, where social justice was seen as the founding principle of government, where the economy was put at the service of people's needs and development. He promoted the concept of 'people's power' through grassroots, community-based governance, putting community councils in charge of local resources and development. His model was successful, if only for a short period. Yes, Venezuela had oil, lots of it, and there is no question that the oil wealth fueled the success of Chávez's social model. He aimed to make it sustainable, but died without achieving that. Too much was left unfinished and was ruined by his successors. Does that mean its failure was inevitable?

Chávez's habit of choosing loyalty over competence was a fatal mistake. So too was entrusting multiple responsibilities to a closed circle of confidants who were unprepared and unwilling to make hard choices. Regrettably, I've seen that same behavior in Donald Trump, who has surrounded himself with family members and loyal subordinates, giving them multiple responsibilities and duties for which they have no experience or knowledge. It's a standard authoritarian tactic – keeping a tight grip on power, refusing to appoint experienced, capable professionals and trust them to do important jobs. It stems from the paranoia that power addiction creates, and the narcissistic belief that no one else can do things better.

Those who remain in power for too long can develop these characteristics, even if they did not possess them before. And those who already had them, like Trump, are likely to become worse and dig their feet in deeper. America may be on the slippery slope to authoritarian rule, and the longer Trump remains in office, the harder it may be to remove him. He will distort and destroy the concept of the free press, crafting his own propaganda outlets, such as Fox News, to control the narrative. He will erode judicial independence by naming incompetent loyalists to federal courts and publicly discrediting judges and attorneys who challenge or criticize him. He will bend, mold and twist the law to serve his agenda, discarding and crushing any semblance of checks and balances. He will distract the public and his detractors through his petty daily quarrels while weakening the pillars of democracy. His scandalous and shockingly offensive behavior will mask his constant undermining of basic rights and freedoms, and the subtle expansion of his powers. He will strip the United States of America to its bare guts and try to rebuild it in his mold. He will fail, but only if enough people rise up to stop him.

No president should ever rule unchecked. No person should ever be given free rein to disregard the basic tenets of society, law and order, freedom and respect.

It is painful and hard to accept that a political model you believed in and fought for could be so rapidly distorted and demolished. Despite all the warning signs and the deteriorating social and economic situation, I continued to support Maduro throughout his first two years as president and believed that many of the difficulties the country was facing were due to the same external sabotage and aggressive tactics that the elite had waged against the Chávez government for years. The turning point for me came when I saw up close and personal what I considered to be severe corruption and criminal activity inside his government. And when I informed him of those activities, instead of initiating investigations against the people involved, he rewarded them. They were all promoted to powerful high-level positions where they were protected by Maduro himself. It was a brutal awakening.

I recalled the times when I had told Chávez of incidents of corruption within his government, even within his inner circle. Every time he'd responded with fury, never with reward. Even if in my opinion he did not go far enough, he always addressed the issue, ordering investigations of those involved. Sometimes those implicated were harshly punished, while at other times they were given a slap on the wrist. What I experienced with Maduro was the opposite. No investigations, no reprimands, only praise and more power. It was baffling to me, until I realized that he needed them. They were the loyal servants who enforced his decrees and persecuted his enemies and critics; he was prepared to overlook their crimes and plunders – even those who had committed murder. The whole thing reeked with the stench of deep-rooted corruption.

The way I discovered all of this was privileged and confidential;

going public with any details would violate my code of ethics and professional responsibility as an attorney. Nevertheless, I received threats, both tacit and direct, and was warned that if I broke my silence there would be consequences. To Maduro's credit, he did order the prosecution of dozens of former and current public officials accused of corruption – but only after he believed they had betrayed him or become critical of his policies and autocratic demeanor.

I refuse to believe that this is Chávez's legacy. Chávez made it his priority to provide high-quality, free healthcare to all Venezuelans. Recent reports from the United Nations and other credible sources show that Venezuelans are increasingly suffering and even dying from lack of access to essential medicines and health supplies. Public hospitals are depleted and in ruin, while Maduro kisses gold bars on television and pledges a mythical 'economic prosperity' to those who continue to vote for and support him. Chávez vowed to rescue homeless children from begging in the streets, an all-too-common sight when he was first elected in 1998. He achieved that goal, providing homes, food and widespread economic support for families. Under the Maduro government, children have returned to the streets in droves, begging passers-by for spare change and digging through garbage for food. I imagine Hugo Chávez would be turning in his grave if he could see what Venezuela has become on the watch of his former lieutenant.

Despite his enormous unpopularity and the severe crisis impacting Venezuela, a desperate populace reelected Maduro to a new six-year term during a snap election called by his government in May 2018. He made false promises of millions in 'cash bonuses' to those who'd vote for him, which never materialized after the election, and to those who considered not voting, subtle threats were made insinuating they'd lose their state benefits, which included subsidized food and housing. The opposition boycotted the election, which all but assured Maduro's victory, and the other candidates that chose to run against him ended up calling the process a 'sham' due to alleged widespread irregularities, abuse of state power, intimidation and fraud; they rejected the results. A hardcore base of support stood by Maduro, celebrating his re-election as a triumph over foreign aggression and a blow to the treasonous opposition that had called for international sanctions and intervention to force regime change. Maduro may not have been popular, but he still had control over the world's largest oil reserves. Without a doubt, there were many nations who would still do business with him.

In the end, people are just people. Presidents are ordinary men and women trying to do what they believe are extraordinary things for their countries, whether we agree with them or not. They are humans replete with flaws and vulnerabilities, but many also have great courage and determination, compassion and foresight.

Some are more genuine than others. As this book has shown, I have known many. Over the years before and after Chávez's death, I became close to Rafael Correa in Ecuador and Evo Morales in Bolivia. I spent time with José Pepe Mujica in Uruguay and with Fidel and Raúl Castro in Cuba. I saw them as people pursuing a dream; people who dedicated themselves to making their countries better. They all made mistakes, just as Chávez did. Some of them let power go to their heads, while others rejected that road. Some never fully achieved their potential to change not just their countries, but inspire others around the world. Some knew when it was time to tidy up and take a bow. Others kept waiting for the right moment to hand over the reins of power to another who would follow in their footsteps and carry on their legacy. The longer one remains in power, the harder it is to let go. As I saw over and over again, power is a dangerously corrupting force, and an addiction.

Pepe Mujica was the only president I was privileged to know who had no ambition or thirst for power or its exploits. He chose to remain in his humble one-room, rural home throughout his presidency, continuing to farm vegetables on his modest plot of land. He eschewed the wealth and material privileges his office afforded him, often drove his own car to the presidential palace ' and flew economy on commercial airliners when it was necessary to travel. When his term was up, he relinquished power without a second thought. His only objective was to better the lives of his fellow citizens, not to enrich his own with material wealth or benefits. During a visit to his small cottage on the outskirts of Montevideo, where he had lived for years with his wife Lucia

Topolansky, a senator who later became vice-president, Mujica told me that his plan after his presidency was to adopt Syrian refugee children and build a school for them nearby. Pepe had never had children of his own. He was a former leftist activist who had spent nearly 13 years in prison during the dictatorship in Uruguay, after being shot multiple times in his stomach. His wife had also been imprisoned for 13 years and tortured. They knew all too well how dangerous power could become if left unchecked. Pepe once confessed to me that there was no university that taught you how to be president, adding: 'It was all learning on the job, and some are quicker learners than others.'

As for Chávez, I believed him to be genuine, for all his human flaws. He gave his life for his country and for his fellow citizens. He tried his best to improve the lives of ordinary Venezuelans, to make them feel important, cared for and involved. I think he succeeded during his time as president in transforming Venezuela into a more inclusive, politicized, vibrant society, though so much of that has unraveled under the government of his successor. I believe his most important legacy, the one that will never be destroyed despite all the disarray affecting Venezuela since his death, was his fostering of democratic, grassroots governance and the empowerment of community-based councils. Participate in society on a local and global level and fight for your principles, ideals and dreams, he said. Be humble and self-critical; don't be afraid to pause, reflect and learn from your mistakes. Recycle, recreate and rebuild on your successes. There are others who will join you.

As for me, this has been quite a ride so far. I have traveled the world with presidents, met some of the most controversial, vilified and remarkable leaders in modern history, spoken on stages at major international events with Fidel Castro, Hugo Chávez and Vladimir Putin. I have flown in military planes, helicopters, luxury jets and presidential aircraft, jogged the streets of Moscow, Paris, New York, San Francisco, Los Angeles, Caracas, Buenos Aires, La Paz, Quito, Havana, Vienna, Berlin, London, Rome, Naples, Lyon, Minsk and Milan. I have dined with Oscar-winning actors and partied with Grammy-winning artists. I have been on television, in film, and on the covers of magazines and newspapers.

I have confronted and challenged the CIA, the Pentagon and the

State Department and have been wooed by intelligence agencies from several nations, some of them quite unsavory – though I can assure you I gave in to none of them. I have been loved and hated by millions; spat at, threatened, kissed, groped and embraced by strangers.

Being behind the scenes of some of the most influential moments in recent history and getting to know some of the world's most powerful and misunderstood men has been an unbelievable, unexpected privilege. I have had incredible experiences that have inspired and transformed my life. But, without question, the most beautiful, extraordinary adventure I've ever had has been becoming a mother to a bright, marvelous boy who is full of wonder and joy. Being a mom trumps everything else I've done up to this point.

Motherhood has made me more understanding and patient with humanity. Becoming a mother has taught me the unbelievable, potent value of pure, unconditional love for others. This is not to say that I am no longer passionate about social justice and the need to change many aspects of our system. But I think I have become more tolerant of my detractors and those I disagree with – though some will surely scoff at this assertion. I have come to understand that a human-driven revolution is not revolution if it's not constantly evolving, reflecting, adapting, listening and pausing to breathe. We must be mindful of the moment and visionaries of the future to be moms, and also to be participatory citizens. I've learned to tolerate a lot of crap – literally – along with frequent temper tantrums, because they are necessary to growth, survival and healthy development. The rewards for putting up with crap can be priceless and pretty darned amazing.

My son came home crying from preschool one day. He said his teacher had told him he had to choose what he wanted to be when he grows up. He said he wants to be everything, but she told him he couldn't: he had to choose just one thing. He was five. I told him he could be everything and anything he ever wants to be. He can be and do as many things as he wants. Don't let anyone tell you different, I assured him. Never conform just for the comfort of others who are afraid of difference or complexities.

I thought about all the things I'd ever been called, or told I couldn't do. I thought of how I stepped into the realm of forbidden bogeymen and gained a glimpse of their humanity. I saw the bad stuff too. But I chose not to be forced into believing the one-dimensional vilification and to go beyond the scaremongering. Because of the risks I've taken, the company I've kept and the decisions I've made, some may forever see me as a tyrant-lover, or a 21st-century Mata Hari. Others will always put me on a pedestal as *La Novia de Venezuela* (The Girlfriend of Venezuela). I know that some people will never take me seriously. They will only see me as a useful idiot co-opted by anti-American movements to do their bidding. Or just as one of Chávez's girlfriends, and maybe Fidel's too.

The experiences I've had have enriched my life, given me a broader, more nuanced perspective. I've learned to look past the headlines to seek the truth. There is always more than one side to a story. My unique experiences have also taught me the value of our flawed democracy and system of justice here in the United States. Having lived in a lawless, corrupt society, where people feel helpless and vulnerable and have no faith in their public institutions, I have learned to cherish, protect, yet also work to better our bruised system. We should never allow ourselves to go down the path to an authoritarian state, led by charismatic, demagogic men making big promises that are unattainable, while accumulating ever greater power for themselves.

I will continue to fight for social justice and against abuse of power in all its forms, carrying with me the harsh, but also inspirational, lessons I learned in Venezuela. No system is perfect, no leader is without flaws. It is the people who must hold them to account through active, conscientious participation and oversight, always keeping a watchful eye against the dangers and temptations of pervasive corruption and power addiction. And I continue to believe that external interference in any nation's affairs can be a destructive force and detrimental to the sovereign will of the people. Support and solidarity can be helpful, but interventionism and meddling can lead to destabilization and war.

I have enjoyed confidence of so-called tyrants, and I don't regret it. My skin has grown thick, my eyes have seen what few have been privy to, and I have gained a greater understanding of international politics and the intricacies of socio-economic power. Others may not like the choices I have made or the company I have kept. They may question my motives and my reasoning. But, if there is one thing I have learned through this journey, it's that I will never define myself or live my life for the comfort and convenience of others.

Index

Acknowledgements

Everything I am, everything I've accomplished and everything I have I owe to my Mom and Dad, who have supported me on my unconventional life path, despite how incredibly difficult it has been for them as parents and the immense anxiety I surely caused them every step of the way. One thing I've learned on this crazy journey is to hold those dearest to you close and fill them with love. You never know what tomorrow will bring and you never want to regret not loving or thanking someone enough. So I thank my amazing parents for standing by me, unwaveringly, and cheering me on as I forge ahead. And I'm grateful for the love from my brother, who has provided advice, guidance and support to his little rebellious sister. I'm glad we're on the same side.

My initial reader and time-trusted friend Sarah was pivotal in pushing me to keep writing and convincing me that yes, I have a story to tell and a plume with which to write it. I will be forever grateful to her for convincing me to keep writing. My pen is mightier than the swords pointed towards me. Thankfully, I also have a community of friends around the world who buffer the blades of my adversaries and haters and provide comforting refuge from the madness in our lives. To them all my unconditional love and loyalty.

My gratitude to my editor, Chris Brazier, and publisher, New Internationalist, for bringing the book to fruition and taking the risk on a controversial subject that few were brave enough to embrace.

Most of all, I am grateful for my son Zachary, who is my North Star, my guiding force and my inspiration to fight for a better, more compassionate and just world. I tell my truths for him, so that he knows where he came from, and that he too has the fire in his belly and the passion in his heart to fight for his dreams. Be brave enough to live creatively and unconventionally.

The Memory We Could Be

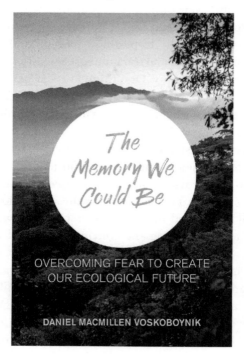

The Memory We Could Be illustrates in powerful, human terms the world we could lose and the world we can still win. It evokes an ecological future in which competition must make way for co-operation and connection.

In this book you will peer into the black box of the past and journey through the destruction of human history. If we can understand how we got here and accept our current predicament then we may still be able to act in ways that will allow us to be honoured by future generations.

Daniel Macmillen Voskoboynik avoids the sterile, technical language that so often surrounds climate change and seeks instead to inspire, bringing a wealth of different voices into the conversation to help us confront our fears.

Price: UK £9.99
ISBN 978-1-78026-440-0

Bordered Lives

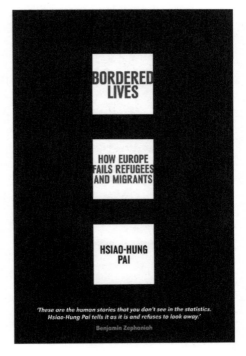

What is it like to flee from persecution or poverty, risking your life to cross the sea in an unsafe boat, only to find yourself trapped in Europe's asylum system?

In *Bordered Lives*, **Hsiao-Hung Pai** spends time with migrants and asylum-seekers who have been rescued at sea and absorbed into dismal reception camps. She follows the journey of the individuals she comes to know best as they travel north through Italy and into Germany and France, encountering privatized reception facilities, incomprehensible bureaucracy and the hostility of far-right groups.

Ultimately she shows that the 'refugee crisis' of the headlines is rather a crisis in Europe's response.

Price: UK £9.99, US $16.95
ISBN 978-1-78026-438-7

The Equality Effect

THE
EQUALITY
EFFECT
Improving life for everyone

DANNY DORLING

Illustrations by
Ella Furness

Foreword by
Owen Jones

When world leaders of all persuasions make such stark, unambiguous statements, you would be forgiven for thinking we live in a world in which greater equality is being given the highest priority. Unfortunately the rhetoric and the reality often do not match up.

The Equality Effect delivers the overwhelming evidence behind these pronouncements, including groundbreaking new research on the correlation between equality and environmental progress.

Backed by statistics throughout and with a sprinkling of witty illustrations, **Danny Dorling** demonstrates where greater equality is currently to be found, and how we can set the equality effect in motion everywhere.

Price: UK £9.99, US $16.95
ISBN 978-1-78026-390-8